WITHDRAWN

footsteps IN THE FOG

Alfred Hitchcock's San Francisco

Jeff Kraft and Aaron Leventhal

Foreword by Patricia Hitchcock O'Connell

S A N T A
M O N I C A
P R E S S

Published by:
Santa Monica Press LLC
P.O. Box 1076
Santa Monica, CA 90406-1076
1-800-784-9553
www.santamonicapress.com
books@santamonicapress.com

Printed in the United States

Santa Monica Press books are available at special quantity discounts when purchased in bulk by cor-
porations, organizations, or groups. Please call our Special Sales department at 1-800-784-9553.

ISBN 1-891661-27-2

Library of Congress Cataloging-in-Publication Data

Kraft, Jeff, 1969-
    Footsteps in the fog : Alfred Hitchcock's San Francisco / by Jeff
Kraft and Aaron Leventhal; foreword by Patricia Hitchcock O'Connell.
        p. cm.
    Includes bibliographical references.
    ISBN 1-891661-27-2
    1. Hitchcock, Alfred, 1899—Criticism and interpretation. 2. San Francisco (Calif.)—In motion pictures. I. Leventhal, Aaron,
1967- II. Title.

    PN1998.3.H58 K73 2002
    791.43'0233'092—dc21
                                        2002009149

Book and cover design by *Ohm on the Range Design*, Los Angeles
Please visit www.footstepsinthefog.com
Send comments to: feedback@footstepsinthefog.com

Contents

We dedicate this book to Aaron's son Ethan, born April 2001, and to the memory of Jeff's father Fred Kraft, who passed away during the making of this book.

Without the help and support of many generous, knowledgeable, and talented people, this project would be nothing more than another computer file. We would like to thank everyone who participated in this effort.

Our publisher Jeffrey Goldman, of Santa Monica Press, helped us conceptualize and focus the framework behind the book, edit the text, and support and encourage us with his keen sense of humor. We are particularly grateful to Patricia Hitchcock O'Connell for writing the foreword. We would also like to thank Patricia's daughter, Tere O'Connell Carrubba, for providing valuable personal insights, and letting us use personal family photographs. Ken Niles provided a masterful design and layout, which transformed our choppy text documents and piles of photos into an elegant book. Thanks also to the attorneys Leland Faust and Steve Kravitz at Taylor and Faust, who represent the Hitchcock Trust. Their support of this project was invaluable in getting it off the ground.

Maybe more than anyone, our spouses Laura Ackerman and Cheryl McDonald were key to keeping us on track. Laura contributed photographs, designed the initial version of the maps, read draft after draft, spent countless hours formatting digital images, and provided ongoing support and advice during the writing of the book. Cheryl gave legal advice during contract negotiations with our publisher, read drafts of the book, joined us on research and location scouting trips, and provided ongoing support and encouragement.

We would also like to mention a number of other family members and friends. Karen Ackerman provided valuable legal advice in setting up Kraft-Leventhal Productions, Inc. Peggy Kraft offered tremendous support and encouragement during the writing of this book. Our firm and sometimes brutally honest editors included David Jouris, Ann McDermott, David Goldstein, Nani Coloretti, Michael Cunningham, Shawn Blosser, Karen Ackerman, and Nina Goldman. Mimi Seitz shared invaluable information about San Francisco during the fifties and sixties. Matt Newman and Richard Robbins helped with Bay Area location research. Jeff Slattery and Brooke Oliver provided us with legal advice during our contract negotiations with our publisher. And thanks, too, to Jacqueline Leventhal for providing baby-sitting services.

A number of staff members at various libraries helped us with our research of facts, places, and photographs. We wish to thank Barbara Hall, Robert Cushman, and Faye Thompson at the Margaret Herrick Library at the Academy of Motion Picture Arts and Sciences. The Herrick Library's collections of studio records, documents, and stills were the single most important source for this book. Patricia Akre and Selby Collins at the San Francisco History Center at the San Francisco Public Library provided assistance with historical photos of San Francisco. Roxane Wilson, Audrey Herman, and Anthony Hoskins helped us find a treasure trove of information and historical photographs at the Sonoma County Public Library. Paul Stubbs and Rita Bottoms at the Special Collections

Library at the University of California at Santa Cruz provided valuable photographs and information about the Hitchcock retreat at Scotts Valley. Susan Snyder at the Bancroft Library at the University of California at Berkeley was highly knowledgeable about the library's extensive Bay Area photography collection. Anne McMahon at the Santa Clara University Archives found a copy of Hitchcock's commencement speech. Gary Fong at the *San Francisco Chronicle* photography archives and Thomas Gilbert at TimePix were both helpful. Denise Sallee at the Harrison Memorial Library at Carmel and Rachel McKay at the Museum of Art and History at Santa Cruz both provided useful photographs and research assistance.

Additionally, we would like to thank Thomas P. Wolfe, Chief Concierge at the Fairmont Hotel, and Michelle Heston, Director of Public Relations at the Mark Hopkins, who helped us scout and photograph Nob Hill. David Ruiz of Pacific Air Services, Priscilla Moon, Simone Wilson, Peter Flannery of Bryan's Meats, Robert D. Haines Jr. of the Argonaut Book Shop, Jeffrey Burns from the Archdiocese of San Francisco, Steven Pettinga of the *Saturday Evening Post*, Chris Wedel of The Tides Wharf Restaurant, Georgia Chronopoulos at Covello & Covello, and Marci Rovetti of Podesta Baldocchi offered valuable photographs. Ann Gamba gave a wealth of information about the Hitchcock retreat in Scotts Valley.

There were a number of authors of excellent books and articles about Alfred Hitchcock that we relied heavily on for this book. For the book as a whole, the writings of Francois Truffaut, Donald Spoto, Robert A. Harris, and Michael Lasky provided invaluable reference materials and information. For the *Vertigo* chapter, Dan Auiler's book on the making of *Vertigo* was extremely useful. For the chapter on *The Birds*, Kyle B. Counts and Camille Paglia were outstanding sources. For information about 20th century Sonoma County history, Gaye LeBaron was incredibly generous with her vast knowledge. Stephen Rebello's book on the making of *Psycho* was also very useful.

Park docent Kurt Loesch was the most knowledgeable source we found about the filming of *Rebecca* at Point Lobos and directed us to the production photos he obtained for the Carmel Library. We would also like to thank the Bianchi Family of Valley Ford, and Donna Freeman, and Wes and Hazel Mitchell of Bodega Bay for information about the filming of *The Birds*. Mary Leah Taylor and Rick Williams, owners of the Potter School House, provided us information and historical photographs.

From the studios, we would like to thank Cindy Chang at Universal, Marlene Eastman at Warner Brothers, and Margaret Adamic at Disney. We would like to thank Daniel Selznick and Selznick Properties, Ltd., for allowing us to publish off-camera photos from *Rebecca*. Robert Zerkowitz from the Wine Institute provided photos of Cresta Blanca.

Finally, we would like to thank everyone who reads our work, particularly for indulging our obsession with facts and details about the history of San Francisco and the indelible footsteps Hitchcock left on our streets.

— JEFF KRAFT AND AARON LEVENTHAL, OCTOBER 2002

Foreword

Over the course of his life, my father Alfred Hitchcock fell more and more in love with the San Francisco Bay Area. Although he did make several films in Northern California, it was also the place where he could go and relax and be himself.

Wanting to escape Hollywood, my father and mother Alma looked for a weekend home. We had always had a country home in England away from London. Exploring Northern California in 1940, my parents fell in love with Scotts Valley. It was a peaceful hilly area between Santa Cruz and the southern end of the San Francisco peninsula. They found a house with a spectacular view of Monterey Bay, and decided that it was an ideal equivalent to their English country home, Shamley Green. They did not actually move there until 1942 when *Shadow of a Doubt* brought my father north for filming.

When my parents bought the house they also acquired a vineyard. The grapes were sold and the wine marketed as Cresta Blanca. However, we did keep some of the grapes and our caretaker Joe Cheisa would make our own wine. It was delicious! My parents enjoyed this so much. Eventually my parents would stay in Los Angeles during the week and retreat to Scotts Valley on weekends. As I grew older and had a family of my own, my parents loved bringing their granddaughters there. We spent many family vacations up on the hill, and my father enjoyed bringing friends from Los Angeles there as well. Among the many guests were Princess Grace of Monaco and her family, and Ingrid Bergman.

During the filming of *Shadow of a Doubt*, my father asked me to help coach Edna May Wonacott to help her prepare for her role as Ann Newton. It was a great experience being on the set all the time. My father enjoyed Santa Rosa very much because he loved bringing menace to a small town and he was able to use a lot of the local people to work on this film. During some off time while shooting, the crew would have gin rummy tournaments. My father had never played before, so they taught him. Amazingly enough he won the competition!

Hitchcock, his wife Alma, and daughter Patricia (standing) on the Psycho set, 1960

My father found San Francisco a very cosmopolitan city, similar to Paris, France. He enjoyed the atmosphere, food, and weather. One of his favorite restaurants was Jack's. He usually lunched there with my mother and Sam Taylor, a local attorney and a very close friend. He almost always ate the rex sole, which he loved. Of course he also loved to go to Ernie's for dinner. He was great friends with the owners, Roland and Victor Gotti. My father, being an incredible wine connoisseur, would keep several cases of his favorite wines in their cellar so when he dined there he would be able to have them. He also loved sharing wines with the Gottis, and on numerous occasions would have cases delivered to them. The Gottis and Ernie's continued to be great family friends for many years until its closing.

While filming *The Birds* in Bodega Bay, my mother and father would take advantage of shopping in San Francisco. Their favorite places to go were Dunhill's (my father loved to go cigar shopping there) and Gump's. My mother also loved to go to Elizabeth Arden's.

My father passed away in April of 1980 and my mother in July of 1982. I know that some of their most happy times were spent in the San Francisco Bay Area. *Footsteps in the Fog* pays great homage to my father's life and work in Northern California. And it brings me much happiness to recall such wonderful memories as my mother gardening and my father reading and relaxing while enjoying the beautiful surroundings of Monterey Bay.

— PATRICIA HITCHCOCK O'CONNELL, OCTOBER 2002

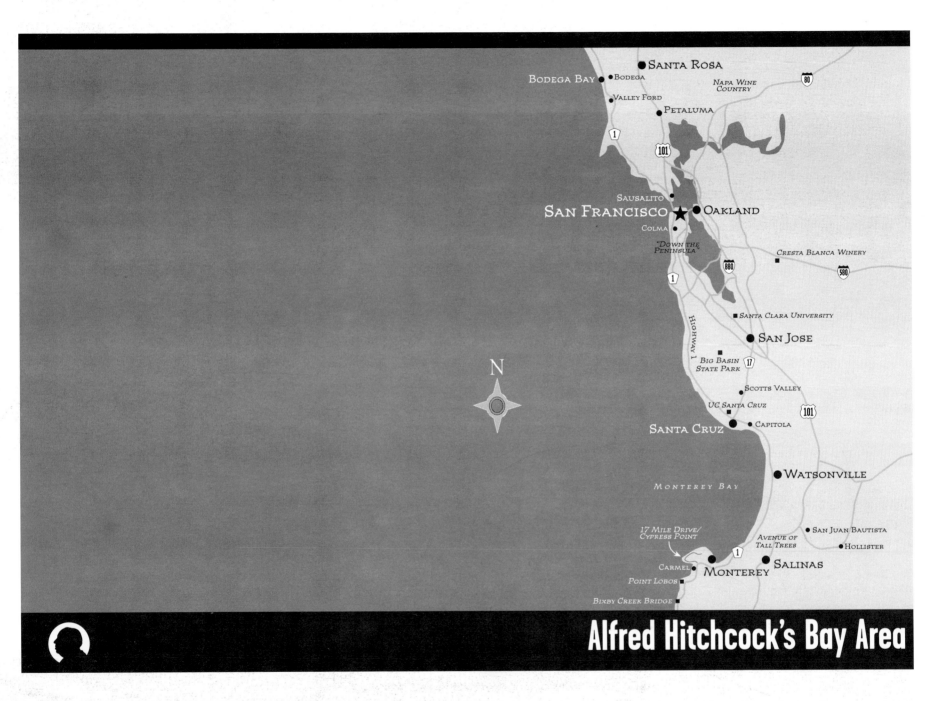

SANTA ROSA

BODEGA BAY • BODEGA

Napa Wine
Country

80

VALLEY FORD

• PETALUMA

1

101

SAUSALITO

SAN FRANCISCO ★ • OAKLAND

COLMA

"Down the
Peninsula"

Cresta Blanca Winery

880

580

1

■ Santa Clara University

Highway 1

SAN JOSE

Big Basin
State Park

17

Scotts Valley

UC Santa Cruz

101

N

SANTA CRUZ • Capitola

WATSONVILLE

Monterey Bay

17 Mile Drive/
Cypress Point

Avenue of
Tall Trees

• San Juan Bautista

• Hollister

1

Carmel

MONTEREY

Point Lobos

SALINAS

Bixby Creek Bridge

Alfred Hitchcock's Bay Area

Introduction

Alfred Hitchcock's San Francisco

"San Francisco would be a good location for a murder mystery."

—Alfred Hitchcock

Alfred Hitchcock's connection to the San Francisco Bay Area can be traced to the filming of *Rebecca*, his first American picture, in 1939 (released in 1940). Hitchcock made his first 23 films while in England, the country where he was born. Due to the severe downturn in the British movie industry in the 1930s, Hitchcock decided to leave England and continue his movie career in Hollywood.

While filming *Rebecca*, which stars Laurence Olivier and Joan Fontaine, Hitchcock became friends with Fontaine's mother and stepfather who lived in Saratoga, 40 miles south of San Francisco. *Rebecca* itself uses background footage of coastal scenes from Monterey County. By that time, Hitchcock and his wife Alma had fallen in love with the area and

decided to search for a property to buy. The Fontaines recommended the Vine Hill area, near Scotts Valley. The Fontaines knew the area well, since Joan Fontaine had attended high school in nearby Los Gatos.

In 1940, while filming *Foreign Correspondent,* Hitchcock discreetly purchased a ranch near Scotts Valley. A wine connoisseur, Hitchcock admired Northern California for its grape-growing climate, and he also purchased a vineyard adjacent to his ranch.

Hitchcock biographer Donald Spoto quotes Hume Cronyn on Hitchcock's fondness for the wine country:

> "Hitch asked me if I had ever been in Northern California. I said no, and he told me what a marvelous country it is, with miles and miles of vineyards. 'When the day's work is done, we go out to the vineyards and squeeze the grapes through our hair,' he said. I suggested that this sounded more like a part for him than for me. All I could see was Hitchcock as Bacchus."

The Scotts Valley ranch became a weekend escape from the pressures of Hollywood over the next three decades, and became the catalyst that led to Hitchcock's filmmaking in—and personal connections to—the San Francisco Bay Area. He blended both his work and personal life, with his ranch as the jumping-off point: He entertained Hollywood stars, researched nearby locations for his films, and frequented San Francisco's fine restaurants and culture.

HITCHCOCK AT HOME ON HIS SCOTTS VALLEY RANCH, DATE UNKNOWN

HITCHCOCK WITH PRODUCER JACK SKIRBALL IN COURTHOUSE SQUARE IN SANTA ROSA
DURING THE FILMING OF *SHADOW OF A DOUBT*, 1942

Starting with *Shadow of a Doubt* (released in 1943), some of Hitchcock's most admired films were set principally in the Bay Area. His intimate familiarity with the region allowed him to blend his stories with the area's unique geography. The "all-American" Santa Rosa is a cozy setting for the dark *Shadow of a Doubt*. Big Basin Park, the Avenue of Tall Trees, San Juan Bautista, Cypress Point, and, of course, the streets of San Francisco are central characters in *Vertigo* (1958). *The Birds* (1963) is set in the quaint towns of Bodega Bay and Bodega, with a movie reference to a real-life bird attack near Santa Cruz. Some of his other movies, including *Rebecca* (1940), *Suspicion* (1941), *Psycho* (1960), *Marnie* (1964), *Topaz* (1969), and *Family Plot* (1976), also include a scene or sequence of scenes filmed in or inspired by the San Francisco Bay Area.

Hitchcock, with the assistance of a talented team of collaborators (such as art directors and set designers Robert Boyle, Henry Blumstead, Joseph Hurley, and Robert Clatworthy), used four primary filmmaking techniques to convey the settings of these movies. First, the director filmed live-action footage with the principal actors on location. Hitchcock was a master of composing visually dramatic shots, tying the geographic characteristics of the location to the setting and plot. Second, he meticulously re-created interiors and exteriors on studio sets, exhaustively researching the subtlest details of actual locations to add authenticity. Third, Hitchcock took background footage on location, sometimes sending out a second unit led by the assistant director. He frequently used the resulting film as rear projection footage in combination with live actors on studio sound stages, known as "process shots." Finally, he often modified the images he filmed with special effects, such as matte paintings, thus adding scenery or architecture to enhance the film's settings.

For purposes of this book, we use a broad definition of "the San Francisco Bay Area," including other parts of Northern—and sometimes even the Central Coast of—California. If a location is a day trip away from San Francisco, it is eligible for inclusion.

The pages of this book explore Hitchcock's passion for the San Francisco Bay Area, and the meticulous use of its sites and locations in the scenes of his movies. We follow in Hitchcock's footsteps, playing detective to unravel the mysteries of the San Francisco Bay Area locations featured in his films. We research the permits he filed, the notes he took, studio records of his filmmaking, and any other evidence he left, such as which doorways he chose to shoot, and why he selected one apartment building over another. We go scene-by-scene through his Bay Area movies.

In following Hitchcock's footsteps, at times we are walking a well-marked path. This book gratefully includes information discovered by authors Dan Auiler, Gaye LeBaron, Camille Paglia, Donald Spoto, François Truffaut, Kyle Counts, and others. However, in many instances, we uncover footsteps other Hitchcock authors have not identified, which often have been obscured by the passage of time.

HITCHCOCK WITH JAMES STEWART AT MISSION DOLORES DURING THE FILMING OF VERTIGO, 1957

We examine buildings and locations pictured in Hitchcock's films and compare these on-screen images to historical and contemporary photos of the same buildings and locations. Additionally, we show archival photos of Hitchcock on location, behind the scenes of his movies, to round out the images of Hitchcock's San Francisco Bay Area. We also include maps to place the buildings and locations in their geographic context.

We then combine the pieces, placing the images and descriptions with insights into why Hitchcock selected the locations he chose to use.

HITCHCOCK WITH HERB CAEN AT JACK'S RESTAURANT, 1951

To complete the story, we explore Hitchcock's personal experiences in the area he came to call a second home: Dining at the popular Ernie's, socializing with the venerable San Francisco columnist Herb Caen, living in Scotts Valley, and enjoying the Bay Area's culture, food, and lifestyle.

What we ultimately discover is that Hitchcock's footsteps make an indelible mark on the region, and in turn the region leaves a dramatic mark on his films. His movies offer insightful glimpses into the geography, lifestyle, history, and glorious mystery of the San Francisco Bay Area, spanning four decades. Hitchcock left a gift for residents and visitors to the Bay Area: an enduring image of not only drama and suspense, but also a view of Northern California from the eyes of a true fan of the area.

HITCHCOCK DIRECTING ROD TAYLOR AND SUZANNE PLESHETTE ON THE SET OF THE BIRDS, 1962

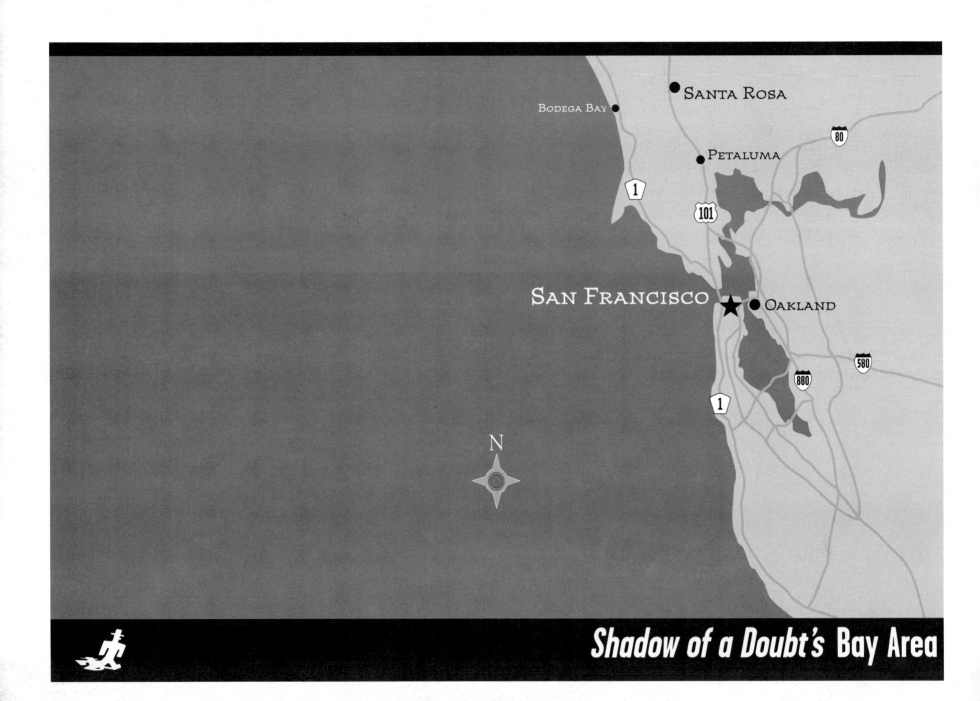

BODEGA BAY

SANTA ROSA

PETALUMA

80

1

101

SAN FRANCISCO

OAKLAND

580

880

1

N

Shadow of a Doubt's Bay Area

Shadow of a Doubt

Darkness Descends on Small-Town Santa Rosa

"I'll always think of this lovely town. It's a place of hospitality, kindness, and homes. Homes."

—UNCLE CHARLIE, SHADOW OF A DOUBT

Setting the Stage

Many film critics consider *Shadow of a Doubt* (released in 1943) a true American classic, as well as one of Hitchcock's most personal films.

Shadow of a Doubt is about a "typical" American family that is visited by Uncle Charlie Oakley, played by Joseph Cotten, a fugitive living on the East Coast who is looking to hide from the law and start a new life in the sleepy town of Santa Rosa. His niece and namesake, "Young Charlie," played by Teresa Wright, slowly discovers the truth about her uncle, who is actually the "Merry Widow" murderer.

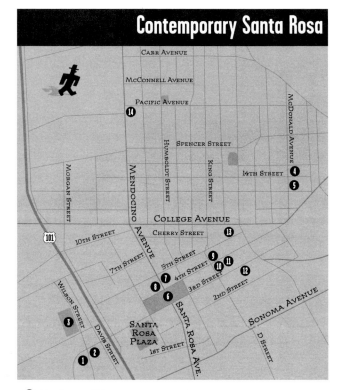

Contemporary Santa Rosa

After considering many small towns in California, Hitchcock chose Santa Rosa, 45 miles north of San Francisco, as the setting for *Shadow of a Doubt*. Santa Rosa held great allure for Hitchcock because it represented the quaint goodness often associated with small towns. Santa Rosa would act as the perfect counterpoint to the dark, twisted plot he would unleash.

It is notable that Hitchcock chose playwright Thornton Wilder to write the screenplay. Wilder was well known for writing the quintessential play about small-town America, *Our Town*, set in the fictitious Grover's Corners. He was a perfect choice for capturing the mores and lifestyle Hitchcock wanted to portray.

Hitchcock faced a number of personal challenges during the writing and filming of *Shadow of a Doubt*. His mother passed away while he was working on the project. Also, he clearly had a growing unease and guilt over the fact that he was living in the United States while World War II raged in Europe.

These issues lead to the sinister feeling of the movie, as well as a number of authentic touches that reflect Hitchcock's—and the world's—turmoil. Soldiers walk the streets and patronize bars and restaurants in numerous scenes. War bond posters are visible in a number of establishments, including the bank where Young Charlie's father Joe Newton, played by Henry Travers, works.

The filming too was impacted by the war. Blackouts ordered during outdoor nighttime filming caused a number of delays. Also, the U.S. government restricted the total set construction budget to $3,000. Ironically, the small set budget gave the film a more realistic feeling. Much of the action takes place in actual public spaces, with all of the street signs, foot traffic, parked cars, and other facets of Santa Rosa life present in full detail.

The movie serves as a window onto Santa Rosa of the 1940s. Many locals are extras in the film, and the movie uses local businesses and architecture as the backdrop for numerous scenes.

❶ The Courtyard Marriott
❷ Former site of the Grace Brothers Brewing Company
❸ Railroad Square *(See map on page 42 for detail)*
❹ 904 McDonald Avenue ("Newton" house)
❺ Geary house
❻ Old Courthouse Square *(See maps on pages 28 and 30 for detail)*
❼ The Rosenberg Building
❽ Exchange Bank on the former site of the Postal Union
❾ Arrigoni Deli on the former site of the Arrigoni Market
❿ Barnes & Noble bookstore in the Rosenberg's Department Store building
⓫ Former site of the Tower Theater
⓬ Sonoma County Library on the former site of the Santa Rosa Public Library
⓭ A parking lot on the former site of the Methodist Episcopal Church South
⓮ College Grocery

Filming "On Location" in Santa Rosa

When *Shadow of a Doubt* was released, Santa Rosa had a population of just 13,000 people. Today, Santa Rosa has swelled to 130,000 people. During the interval, much of the downtown has been rebuilt, but the town still retains its all-American charm, as well as a number of key sites from *Shadow of a Doubt*.

MOVIE PREMIERE AT THE CALIFORNIA THEATRE, 1937

The Santa Rosa of the 1940s had a small town atmosphere. As actress Teresa Wright said in Donald Spoto's *Dark Side of Genius*:

"We were the first film company to work in Santa Rosa, and everyone there got involved in one way or another. Edna May Wonacott, who played the younger sister, was the daughter of a Santa Rosa grocer, and the local policeman carefully coached the actor policeman. Everyone was wonderful to us, even when our nighttime shooting interrupted their quiet routine."

Filming on location in Santa Rosa was a trend-setting idea. After the early days of silent movies, most directors chose not to film "on location" outside of Hollywood studios. Hitchcock's choice was partially one of necessity, and partially a product of his vision for the setting. According to Gaye LeBaron, a local historian and columnist for Santa Rosa's *Press Democrat* newspaper:

"'Shadow' is Santa Rosa's crown jewel. It started the flood of movie-makers coming this way... Hitchcock was the first director in 'modern' movie history to take his show on the road. When the War Production Office slapped a ceiling on the amount of money that could be spent to make a movie during World War II, Hitchcock decided not to build a town, but to find a town to build his film around."

Making a movie on location was so novel during the 1940s that *Life* magazine sent a team of photographers to record the filming. The *Press Democrat* ran almost daily updates on the progress of the filming (even today, it runs nostalgia stories about Hitchcock).

Appropriately, *Shadow of a Doubt* made its West Coast premier at Santa Rosa's California Theatre, located at 435 B Street, on February 6, 1943. Like the small town that was once Santa Rosa, the California Theater no longer exists.

Uncle Charlie Comes to Santa Rosa

The film opens with a brief shot of couples dancing in a formal ballroom to what we will later learn is the "Merry Widow Waltz." The scene then cuts quickly to a long panoramic view of the dirty decaying cityscape of Newark, New Jersey. The shot shows the Pulaski Skyway, a large bridge over the Hackensack River linking Newark with Jersey City.

In a working-class neighborhood, through the window of a brownstone, Charles Oakley — or "Uncle Charlie" — is introduced lounging on his bed. After a tip from his landlady, he eludes two men amid the squalor of the neighborhood. Uncle Charlie escapes to a seedy pool hall, where he uses a pay phone to send a telegram to his family in Santa Rosa, telling them he is coming for a "visit."

The East Coast prelude to the main story is important only as it provides a hint to the audience about Uncle Charlie's sinister secret and seedy bachelor lifestyle. It sets up a perfect contrast between the moral and physical decay of American big cities compared to the virtues of small towns like Santa Rosa.

Next, the setting of *Shadow of a Doubt* changes to sunny Santa Rosa, California, where the rest of the film takes place. When Uncle Charlie sends the telegram to the Newtons, he tells the operator to send it to "Santa Rosa…Santa Rosa, California," and the film cuts to a wide aerial shot of Santa Rosa. As the city comes into view, a light, airy music begins playing in the background. The view is of downtown buildings in the distance with a church in the middle-left side of the shot and a residential neighborhood in the foreground.

OPENING AERIAL SHOT OF SANTA ROSA

STORYBOARD SKETCH OF A SHOT OF SANTA ROSA
FROM A HILL ABOVE THE CITY

The buildings of Courthouse Square—the large rectangular Rosenberg Building, the Bank of America Building with its clocktower, and the Sonoma County Courthouse (all near Fourth Street and Mendocino Avenue)—are shown prominently in the middle-right portion of the shot. A church (probably located on Seventh or Eighth Street near Mendocino Avenue) is shown in the middle-left portion of the shot. These buildings are framed by mountains in the background and houses and a residential street in the foreground.

The arrangement of the buildings (particularly the Rosenberg and clocktower buildings relative to the courthouse), provides a clue about where the shot was taken from. The Rosenberg Building, a long rectangular-shaped structure, is shown from an angle, with both the long western (along Mendocino Avenue) and shorter southern (along Fourth Street) sides visible. Based on this angle, the shot had to be taken from southwest of downtown, looking toward the northeast from a nearby residential neighborhood.

According to studio correspondence, the production team wanted to take this shot of Santa Rosa from a hill above the city. This is corroborated by a storyboard sketch showing the shot being taken from a hill looking down on Santa Rosa. There are no hills in the city that would have provided the appropriate directional view. Thus, the shot must have been taken from a tall man-made structure nearby, but southwest of, downtown.

In the 1940s, only three structures west of Courthouse Square stood tall enough to film such a view. One was the four-story Hotel La Rose. A second was a water tower at Fourth and Wilson Streets. Both of these sites, however, are too far to the north to provide the appropriate angle.

The final candidate is the Grace Brothers Brewing Company building located at Second and Wilson Streets. The brewery, a five-story Santa Rosa landmark, would have been tall enough to offer an overview of Courthouse Square. The brewery closed its doors in 1966 after more than 80 years of business. The site is being redeveloped into a hotel today and sits one block east of the Courtyard by Marriott Hotel on Railroad Street.

THE GRACE BROTHERS BREWING COMPANY AT SECOND AND WILSON STREETS, 1941

The contemporary photo on this page, looking northeast toward Courthouse Square, was taken from the Courtyard by Marriott Hotel, and it shows the Rosenberg and clocktower buildings with almost the exact same angle as the opening shot of Santa Rosa in the movie. While the mountains are not exactly aligned, the Grace Brothers Brewery tower was one block east and on the northern side of its lot on Third Street. This provides strong evidence that the shot in the movie was taken from the Grace Brothers Brewery.

Given the movie shot was taken from the Grace Brothers' building, the residential street in the bottom of the shot is a view of Third Street looking east from Wilson Street, which had old wooden houses when the movie was filmed. Today, the street has commercial buildings, with the freeway cutting through, as shown in the contemporary view.

CONTEMPORARY VIEW LOOKING NORTHEAST TOWARD COURTHOUSE SQUARE FROM THE COURTYARD BY MARRIOTT AT 175 RAILROAD STREET

VIEW OF THIRD STREET WITH WOODEN HOUSES FROM THE GRACE BROTHERS BREWING COMPANY, 1941

Next, the view zooms to Courthouse Square, in the heart of downtown Santa Rosa. A friendly local policeman is shown directing traffic.

This square is shown many times in *Shadow of a Doubt*, from almost every conceivable view and angle. Fourth Street near Mendocino Avenue was blocked off for three straight days during filming, due to its intense use. Hitchcock changes the perspective from—and time of day during—which he films this area, and thus keeps it visually fresh and appealing. At the same time, he uses recurring motifs such as the policeman and the clocktower.

COURTHOUSE SQUARE, LOOKING SOUTHWEST FROM MENDOCINO AVENUE

These opening scenes help set up Santa Rosa as a pleasant and quiet small town, unprepared for the sinister Uncle Charlie.

COURTHOUSE SQUARE AS IT APPEARS IN THE FILM

Courthouse Square

As noted above, Courthouse Square is shown extensively in *Shadow of a Doubt*. In numerous scenes, characters walk the streets, and go in and out of buildings in or around the square.

When *Shadow of a Doubt* was filmed in 1942, Courthouse Square was bordered by Third and Fourth Streets to the north and south, and Exchange and Hinton Avenues on the east and west. Mendocino and Santa Rosa Avenues also dead-ended on the north and south sides of the square, respectively.

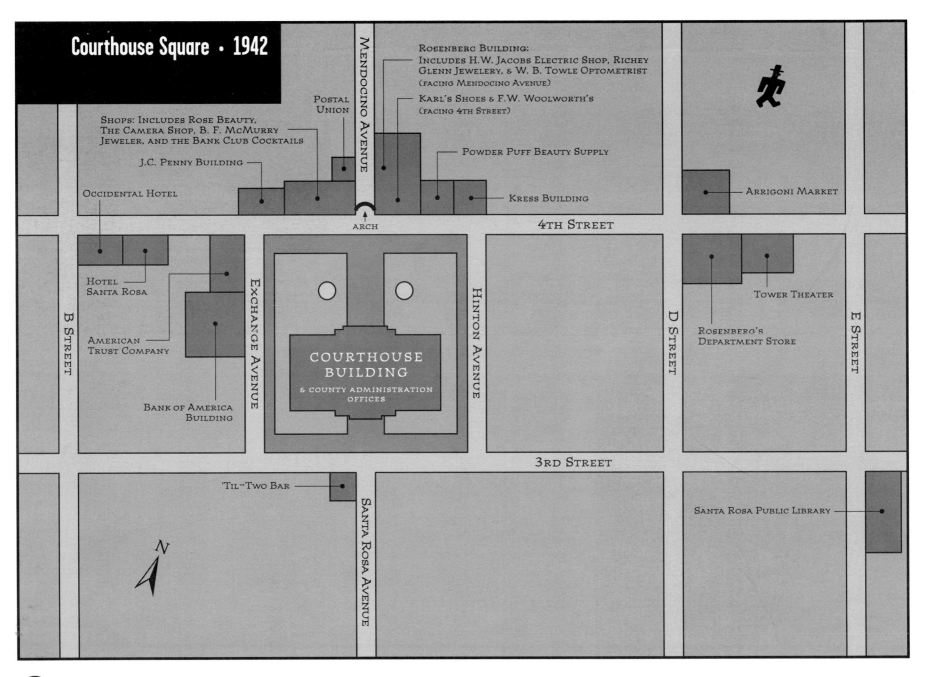

Courthouse Square · 1942

ROSENBERG BUILDING:
INCLUDES H.W. JACOBS ELECTRIC SHOP, RICHEY
GLENN JEWELERY, & W. B. TOWLE OPTOMETRIST
(FACING MENDOCINO AVENUE)

KARL'S SHOES & F.W. WOOLWORTH'S
(FACING 4TH STREET)

POSTAL
UNION

SHOPS: INCLUDES ROSE BEAUTY,
THE CAMERA SHOP, B. F. McMURRY
JEWELER, AND THE BANK CLUB COCKTAILS

POWDER PUFF BEAUTY SUPPLY

J.C. PENNY BUILDING

ARRIGONI MARKET

OCCIDENTAL HOTEL

KRESS BUILDING

MENDOCINO AVENUE

ARCH

4TH STREET

HOTEL
SANTA ROSA

EXCHANGE AVENUE

COURTHOUSE
BUILDING
& COUNTY ADMINISTRATION
OFFICES

HINTON AVENUE

TOWER THEATER

ROSENBERG'S
DEPARTMENT STORE

AMERICAN
TRUST COMPANY

B STREET

D STREET

E STREET

BANK OF AMERICA
BUILDING

3RD STREET

'TIL-TWO BAR

SANTA ROSA AVENUE

SANTA ROSA PUBLIC LIBRARY

N

LOOKING WEST ON FOURTH STREET TOWARD MENDOCINO AVENUE, THE EMPIRE BUILDING, AND AMERICAN TRUST COMPANY, 1935

SONOMA COUNTY COURTHOUSE, BANK OF ITALY (LATER BANK OF AMERICA)
AND AMERICAN TRUST COMPANY, 1925

A POLICE OFFICER DIRECTS TRAFFIC WITH BANK OF AMERICA IN THE
BACKGROUND OF THE SHOT

Most of the buildings that encircle the square are shown in the movie. The Courthouse, with county administrative offices attached on either side, sat at the center of the square facing north, opposite Mendocino Avenue.

The Bank of America building—with its distinctive clock tower—is clearly visible over the policeman's shoulder in the opening scene. At the time of filming, this building was on Exchange Avenue between Third and Fourth Streets.

To the right of the Bank of America building, the American Trust Company is visible briefly. It is a one-story bank with neoclassical columns. This bank is where Joe Newton works, and where the interior bank scenes take place.

In the opening shot of Courthouse Square with the policeman directing traffic, the letters "SA" are visible in the upper right-hand corner of the shot. These letters were on a double-sided arch that hung like a banner over Mendocino Avenue near the corner of Fourth Street. Looking north down Mendocino Avenue it says "Redwood Highway." Looking south towards the courthouse, the arch reads "Santa Rosa."

Old Courthouse Square, as it is known today, has changed dramatically since the 1940s, and is virtually unrecognizable. The first transformation started in 1969, when the Rogers Creek Fault earthquake damaged a number of the key buildings and streets.

IN THE FILM, THE LETTERS "SA" FROM THE SANTA ROSA/REDWOOD HIGHWAY ARCH (AT THE INTERSECTION OF MENDOCINO AVENUE AND FOURTH STREET) ARE VISIBLE

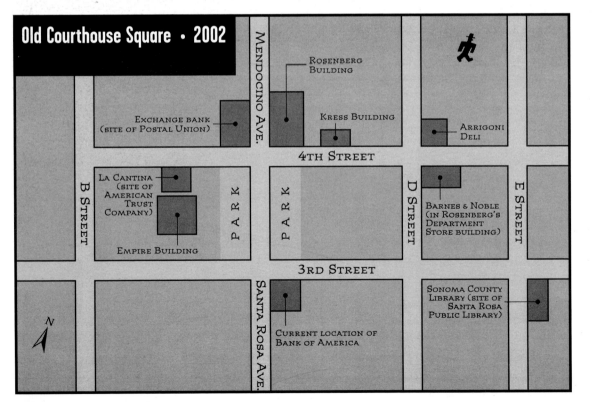

Old Courthouse Square · 2002

ROSENBERG BUILDING

EXCHANGE BANK (SITE OF POSTAL UNION)

KRESS BUILDING

ARRIGONI DELI

MENDOCINO AVE.

4TH STREET

LA CANTINA (SITE OF AMERICAN TRUST COMPANY)

EMPIRE BUILDING

B STREET

PARK

PARK

BARNES & NOBLE (IN ROSENBERG'S DEPARTMENT STORE BUILDING)

D STREET

E STREET

3RD STREET

SANTA ROSA AVE.

CURRENT LOCATION OF BANK OF AMERICA

SONOMA COUNTY LIBRARY (SITE OF SANTA ROSA PUBLIC LIBRARY)

N

CONTEMPORARY VIEW LOOKING SOUTHWEST FROM THE INTERSECTION OF MENDOCINO AND FOURTH STREETS. NOTICE THE CANOPY FROM THE ROSENBERG BUILDING IN THE UPPER LEFT CORNER. ALSO NOTE THAT THE SONOMA COUNTY COURTHOUSE NO LONGER EXISTS.

THE COURTHOUSE AND SANTA ROSA/REDWOOD HIGHWAY ARCH, LOOKING SOUTH DOWN MENDOCINO AVENUE FROM ROSS STREET, 1941

The Courthouse and county offices seen in the movie no longer exist. They were dynamited and moved out of the downtown area after being damaged in the 1969 earthquake. Mendocino and Santa Rosa Avenues were then extended into the middle of the square and joined, cutting the square in two. Finally, Hinton and Exchange Avenues were removed. Many other historic buildings along Fourth Street between the square and the freeway were cleared for redevelopment.

CONTEMPORARY VIEW OF THE FORMER BANK OF AMERICA BUILDING

The Bank of America building with the clocktower is today called the "Empire Building," and no longer houses a bank. It also has the new address of 37 Old Courthouse Square, since its former street, Exchange Avenue, was removed. The name "Empire Building" comes from Empire College which was located in the building in the sixties and whose name is engraved above the front entrance. Today, the building is home to a law firm and the Sonoma County Bar Association.

In the mid-1950s, Bank of America moved out of the clocktower building, and into a newer building across the square on the corner of Third Street and Santa Rosa Avenue. Bank of America was founded in San Francisco by A.P. Giannini in 1904, and was originally called the Bank of Italy. Some older photos of the clocktower building show the old Bank of Italy signs.

On a sad note, the Santa Rosa/Redwood Highway arch, a notable landmark in Santa Rosa for the first half of the twentieth century, no longer exists.

CONTEMPORARY VIEW LOOKING NORTH DOWN MENDOCINO AVENUE FROM COURTHOUSE SQUARE, WITH THE EXCHANGE BANK BUILDING ON THE LEFT AND ROSENBERG BUILDING ON THE RIGHT. NOTE THE DISAPPEARANCE OF THE SANTA ROSA/REDWOOD HIGHWAY ARCH THAT ONCE STRETCHED OVER THIS INTERSECTION.

THE NEWTON HOUSE AS IT APPEARS IN THE FILM

CONTEMPORARY VIEW OF 904 McDONALD AVENUE

The Newton House

Following the overviews of downtown Santa Rosa, the camera zooms into a lovely tree-lined street, and settles on a second-story window of a white wood house. The introduction of Santa Rosa parallels the opening of the film: an initial panoramic shot, followed by a series of zooms, and finally a bedroom window. This house, where the Newton family lives, contrasts sharply with the dark, blighted Newark neighborhood of the film's opening sequence.

The house used by Hitchcock for the Newton residence is at 904 McDonald Avenue. Located in an elegant old Santa Rosa neighborhood, the house looks as it did in *Shadow of a Doubt*. The second story wrought iron railing, large yard, and detached garage on 14th Street (where Uncle Charlie tries to kill Young Charlie with car exhaust fumes) are still there today. (Note: This house is a private residence. Please do not disturb the occupants.)

In an interview with French director and film critic François Truffaut, Hitchcock explained how he chose the house:

> "Before the writing, [screenwriter Thornton] Wilder and I went to great pains to be realistic about the town, the people, and the décor. We chose a town and we went there to search for the right house. We found one, but Wilder felt that it was too big for a bank clerk. Upon investigation it turned out that the man who lived there was in the same financial bracket as our character, so Wilder agreed to use it. But when we came back, two weeks prior to the shooting, the owner was so pleased that his house was going to be in a picture that he had it completely repainted. So we had to go in and get his permission to paint it dirty again. And when we were through, naturally, we had it done all over again with bright, new colors."

In addition to the paint touches, the crew also added some ivy to the outside of the house for the filming.

The house depicted in the movie has a number of differences from the real McDonald Avenue house. The external stairway leading from the second story of the house to the backyard never actually existed. This stairway was added by Hitchcock to advance the plot. The stairway functions as a way for both Young Charlie and Uncle Charlie to enter and exit the house secretly, without passing through the main part of the house, and is the setting for a murder attempt later in the film. In reality, the scenes on the back stairs were filmed on a Hollywood sound stage. The crew was able to circumvent the War Production Board limits on set construction costs by building the back stair set with used lumber.

THE REAR STAIRCASE OF THE "NEWTON" HOUSE

CONTEMPORARY VIEW OF THE BACK OF 904 McDONALD AVENUE.
NOTE THE ABSENCE OF A REAR STAIRCASE.

Hitchcock originally wanted to film in the interior of the actual house. However, it was not big enough to allow for film equipment inside, and thus these scenes were done on a set in Los Angeles as well.

Hitchcock captured time and place by using the setting to further elements of the plot. The interior of the home faithfully represents the stolid middle-class values of the 1940s. Unlike the ostentatious hotels of the "wicked" big cities contemptuously described by Uncle Charlie in the film, the Newton house was comfortable, durable, practical, exceedingly tidy, and well organized despite the presence of two young children.

Later in the movie, in a comic interlude, Joe Newton and next-door neighbor Herbie Hawkins (Hume Cronyn) retreat to the house's porch to discuss their chief hobby—planning and solving murder mysteries. This scene is notable because it was filmed on the actual porch of 904 McDonald Avenue.

THE LIVING ROOM STUDIO SET AS IT APPEARS IN THE FILM

THE KITCHEN STUDIO SET AS IT APPEARS IN THE FILM

THE FRONT PORCH OF THE "NEWTON" HOUSE

CONTEMPORARY VIEW OF THE FRONT PORCH OF 904 McDONALD AVENUE

As an interesting side note, Wes Craven filmed the house located at 824 McDonald Avenue, just down the street from the Newton house, for the horror film *Scream*. Although Hitchcock did not film at this house, he spent time socializing with the owner, Judge Don Geary. According to Santa Rosa's *Press Democrat*, Hitchcock and the judge became friends and would sit on the front porch drinking evening highballs. From this vantage point, Hitchcock reputedly kept an eye on the expensive studio-owned filmmaking equipment being stored down the block at the Newton house.

After the shots of the outside of the Newton house, the camera zooms into the bedroom of Young Charlie Newton, who is lying on her bed. The phone rings, and it is answered by the comically precious Ann Newton (played by Edna May Wonacott), Young Charlie's little sister.

Young Charlie goes to the Postal Union to send a telegram to her uncle, urging him to visit. She learns that Uncle Charlie has already sent a telegram to the Newtons announcing his impending visit. The two Charlies have an almost telepathic connection.

Young Charlie's errand gives us another view of downtown Santa Rosa. The Postal Union scene was filmed at the Santa Rosa Postal, Telegraph and Cable Office. At the time of filming, this office was located at 311 Mendocino Avenue, between Fourth and Fifth Streets, near Courthouse Square.

Following the 1969 earthquake, this office was removed. Today, the large Exchange Bank building, built after Courthouse Square was renovated, occupies the space where the old Postal, Telegraph and Cable Office once stood.

While Young Charlie is talking to the telegraph clerk, there are several signs partially visible through the storefront window. These include the H.W. Jacobs Electric Shop at 312 Mendocino Avenue, Richey Glenn Jewelry at 310, and W.B. Towle Optometrist at 308—all actual businesses at the time. None of these businesses exist today.

YOUNG CHARLIE AT THE POSTAL UNION AND TELEGRAPH OFFICE WITH A BACKGROUND VIEW OF THE STOREFRONTS ON MENDOCINO AVENUE.

Edna May Wonacott

TO ADD AUTHENTIC LOCAL COLOR TO THE FILM, Hitchcock wanted to cast a local girl in the role of Ann Newton. He envisioned someone with freckles, pigtails, and glasses. He ended up choosing Edna May Wonacott, the 10-year-old daughter of the owner of the College Grocery at 1220 Mendocino Avenue. Hitchcock reportedly chose her for the role because her father's grocery store reminded him of his family's store in England.

Edna May signed a seven-year movie contract that permitted her to make two movies a year during the summer when she was not in school. She went on to play a few other minor movie parts.

During the location filming, the crew and some of the cast stayed in the Occidental Hotel, located at Fourth and B Streets, which served as the headquarters for the crew in Santa Rosa. At the hotel, members of the crew met Vivian Sorensen Keegan, a Santa Rosa girl, whose father worked there. Vivian ended up serving as Teresa Wright's double in the scene where Young Charlie rushes to the library and is nearly hit by a car. The hotel was torn down many years ago during redevelopment efforts.

HITCHCOCK ON THE SET WITH EDNA MAY WONACOTT

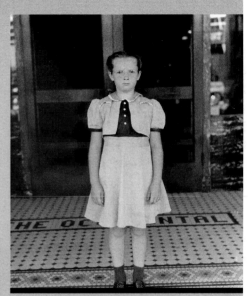

EDNA MAY'S CASTING PHOTO

OCCIDENTAL HOTEL, 1935

Looking north down Mendocino Avenue from Fourth Street with the Postal Union and Telegraph Office on the left side, and local business signs on the right

Contemporary view looking north down Mendocino Avenue with the Exchange Bank on the left and the Rosenberg Building on the right

Also, when Young Charlie exits the telegraph office and turns north on Mendocino Avenue, there is a view of the Courthouse and a number of businesses: Rose Beauty in the Dougherty Shea Building, the Camera Shop and B.F. McMurry Jeweler at 317 Mendocino Avenue, and the Bank Club Cocktails at 319.

YOUNG CHARLIE WITH VIEW SOUTH DOWN MENDOCINO AVENUE, WITH
THE COURTHOUSE AND STOREFRONTS IN THE BACKGROUND

CONTEMPORARY VIEW LOOKING SOUTH TOWARD COURTHOUSE SQUARE
ON MENDOCINO AVENUE FROM ROSS STREET

The Rosenberg Building occupies almost the entire east side of the 300 block of Mendocino Avenue, and once housed all of the shops visible through the post office window behind Young Charlie. The massive building also has storefronts on the 600 block of Fourth Street. The building was constructed soon after the 1906 earthquake, and while it is virtually unchanged today, none of the businesses shown in *Shadow of a Doubt* still exist. Instead, the ground floor of the Rosenberg Building has new retail stores, and the upper floors are residential apartments.

LOOKING SOUTH DOWN MENDOCINO AVENUE FROM FOURTH TO ROSS STREETS, 1955

Uncle Charlie's Arrival at Railroad Square

The scene fades into a train belching black smoke, an ominous portent of trouble approaching. A train arrives from the south, with Uncle Charlie on board, at Santa Rosa's Railroad Square.

UNCLE CHARLIE'S TRAIN ARRIVING AT RAILROAD SQUARE

CONTEMPORARY VIEW OF THE RAILROAD DEPOT, LOOKING SOUTH TOWARDS SAN FRANCISCO

As the train pulls into the Railroad Depot, the Newtons drive into Railroad Square from the east on Fifth Street. As they arrive, park, and get out of their car, the Hotel La Rose and other buildings are visible in the background.

The Hotel La Rose is the architectural gem of the Railroad Square Historic District. This three-story stone building was built by the same Italian stone masons who built the Railroad Depot. The hotel, located on the corner of Wilson and Fifth Streets, was built in 1907. During Prohibition, local legend holds that the Santa Rosa sheriff was tarred and feathered for trying to close the hotel's two bars. The bars in the hotel never stopped serving Sonoma County red wine to the clientele. When federal authorities closed one bar down, the hotel would open the other. Recently remodeled, the Hotel La Rose today remains a working hotel and restaurant.

THE NEWTONS' CAR PASSING THE HOTEL LA ROSE ON THE SOUTHEAST CORNER OF FIFTH AND WILSON STREETS

CONTEMPORARY VIEW OF THE HOTEL LA ROSE

THE TWO CHARLIES HUGGING WITH THE LEE BROTHERS BUILDING IN THE BACKGROUND

CONTEMPORARY VIEW OF THE LEE BROTHERS BUILDING

In addition to the Hotel La Rose, a long, narrow building is visible in the left side of the frame as the Newtons drive into Railroad Square. This building is the Railroad Express Agency Building (not pictured) located at 11 Fifth Street. It was built in 1915 and was home to railroad administration functions. Today, the building houses a café.

Once the train arrives and the Newtons greet Uncle Charlie, the film offers a tour of some of the other buildings around Railroad Square. As the two Charlies hug, there is a background view of the columns and cornice of a one-story building to the right of a group of trees.

This is the Lee Brothers Building, at 100 Fourth Street. The building, constructed in 1906, has five distinctive columns and other architectural details such as the rooftop cornice visible in the movie. Today, the building looks just as it did during the filming of Shadow of a Doubt.

The Newtons and Uncle Charlie walk back to the car. There is a partial view of a stone building behind Uncle Charlie and the train depot. This building is the Western Hotel, at 10 Fourth Street. The hotel was built in 1903 of locally quarried stone, and restored following the 1906 earthquake. By the 1940s, the hotel was quite popular, and was frequented by tourists and businessmen. The facade was restored in 1980, and today the building looks the same as it did in the 1940s. The building is no longer a hotel but instead houses shops and offices.

THE WESTERN HOTEL, VISIBLE BEHIND UNCLE CHARLIE

CONTEMPORARY VIEW OF THE WESTERN HOTEL BUILDING

The Railroad Depot at Railroad Square

RAILROAD SQUARE WAS THE MAIN COMMERCIAL DISTRICT in western Santa Rosa from the early 1900s through World War II. When *Shadow of a Doubt* was filmed, the square was a charming, highly functional hub with all the amenities and services needed for tourists and business travelers. The square included numerous hotels, restaurants, and commercial services.

Hitchcock uses the historic buildings in the square to great effect. The square serves both as a scenic backdrop and as a way to convey the excitement generated by the arrival of visitors into the small town of Santa Rosa.

The Northwestern Pacific Railroad Depot is at the heart of the square and is featured prominently in the movie. The depot was built around 1904 of locally quarried basalt and is listed on the National Register of Historic Places. The building is located between the ends of Fourth and Fifth Streets (near Wilson Street), across the freeway from downtown, and is now home to the Greater Santa Rosa Convention and Visitors Bureau.

Passenger service ended in 1958. During the 1960s and 1970s, the area became run down and seedy flophouses appeared. In the mid-1980s, Railroad Square's charming stone buildings were restored and today house antique stores, cafés and restaurants.

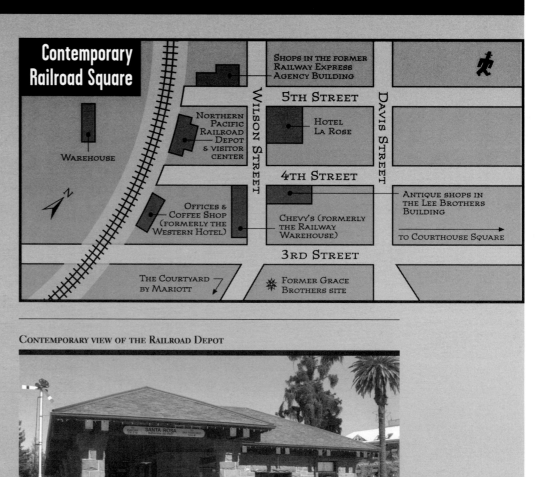

Contemporary Railroad Square

WAREHOUSE

NORTHERN PACIFIC RAILROAD DEPOT & VISITOR CENTER

OFFICES & COFFEE SHOP (FORMERLY THE WESTERN HOTEL)

SHOPS IN THE FORMER RAILWAY EXPRESS AGENCY BUILDING

WILSON STREET

DAVIS STREET

5TH STREET

HOTEL LA ROSE

4TH STREET

ANTIQUE SHOPS IN THE LEE BROTHERS BUILDING

CHEVY'S (FORMERLY THE RAILWAY WAREHOUSE)

TO COURTHOUSE SQUARE

3RD STREET

THE COURTYARD BY MARIOTT

FORMER GRACE BROTHERS SITE

CONTEMPORARY VIEW OF THE RAILROAD DEPOT

The Railroad Depot at Railroad Square

HITCHCOCK WITH
JOSEPH COTTEN,
TERESA WRIGHT,
HENRY TRAVERS, AND
CREW IN FRONT OF
THE DEPOT IN
RAILROAD SQUARE

Walking the Downtown

The day following Uncle Charlie's arrival, a doting Emma Newton (Patricia Collinge) brings Uncle Charlie breakfast in bed. Afterwards, both Uncle Charlie and Young Charlie walk through downtown Santa Rosa, on their way to the bank. There is a close-up shot of the two Charlies on the street as they encounter two of Young Charlie's girlfriends.

This shot was taken at the northeast corner of Mendocino Avenue and Fourth Street. The striped awning of Karl's Shoe Store and F. W. Woolworth Co. at 603 Fourth Street in the Rosenberg Building is visible in the background.

VIEW OF THE ROSENBERG AND KRESS BUILDINGS ON FOURTH STREET LOOKING EAST FROM MENDOCINO AVENUE, 1953

YOUNG CHARLIE AND UNCLE CHARLIE WALK UNDER THE STRIPED CANOPY OF THE ROSENBERG BUILDING, LOOKING EAST ON FOURTH STREET

CONTEMPORARY VIEW OF THE ROSENBERG BUILDING CANOPY AT THE CORNER OF FOURTH STREET AND MENDOCINO AVENUE.

UNCLE CHARLIE AND YOUNG CHARLIE'S FRIENDS UNDER THE STRIPED AWNING OF THE ROSENBERG BUILDING, WITH VIEWS OF SHOP SIGNS IN THE BACKGROUND

CONTEMPORARY VIEW OF THE ROSENBERG AND KRESS BUILDINGS ON FOURTH STREET LOOKING EAST FROM MENDOCINO AVENUE

Young Charlie introduces her uncle to her friends. During the shot, the camera pans down the street further east while the two Charlies wait at the light to cross the street.

LOOKING WEST ON FOURTH STREET, WITH THE KRESS AND ROSENBERG BUILDINGS IN THE BACKGROUND, 1953

Two more shops are visible in this part of the scene. One is the S.H. Kress and Company Department Store, at 613 Fourth Street. The movie only shows a sign that reads "ess," the last three letters of "Kress." A sign for "Powder Puff Beauty Shop," at 606 Fourth Street, is also shown. It is just visible in the upper right-hand corner of the screen, as the two Charlies pause at the intersection. Neither of these businesses exist today. However, the Kress name remains emblazoned on the building in the same location.

CONTEMPORARY VIEW OF THE KRESS BUILDING

After the light turns, the two Charlies cross Mendocino Avenue. A policeman is direct-ing traffic, as two military men walk by among the crowd. Santa Rosa reportedly had as many as 7,000 military troops stationed there in 1942, a large number for a town of 13,000 civilians. Thus, it is a realistic touch to add military personnel to the movie scenes taken in public places in Santa Rosa.

Next, the Charlies turn onto Exchange Avenue, and the J.C. Penney Company building, at 537 Fourth Street, is shown briefly in the background. The J.C. Penney Company stayed in that building for many years until a new building was constructed in the 1960s. Today, the current location is used for retail and commercial space.

YOUNG CHARLIE AND UNCLE CHARLIE WALKING DOWN EXCHANGE AVENUE WITH THE J.C. PENNEY SIGN . . .

THE J.C. PENNEY SIGN IS PARTIALLY VISIBLE IN THE MIDDLE-LEFT PORTION OF THIS PHOTO OF FOURTH STREET AND MENDOCINO AVENUE, TAKEN FROM EXCHANGE AVENUE, 1941

. . . AND THEN THE GRACE BROTHERS SIGN SHOWN IN THE BACKGROUND

WIDE-ANGLE VIEW OF COURTHOUSE SQUARE LOOKING EAST DOWN FOURTH STREET, 1941

As the camera angle changes directions and widens, the scenic Courthouse Square is shown once again. There is a view east down Fourth Street at the corner of Exchange Avenue. The Courthouse Building, the large sign for the Grace Brothers Brewing Company, the police dispatch radio tower, and the sign on Rosenberg's Department Store are all visible in the background.

As Uncle Charlie and Young Charlie pass the Courthouse, they take a right turn and approach a columned bank entrance at Exchange Avenue and Fourth Street. This is the bank where Joe Newton works.

In the bank, Uncle Charlie loudly and boorishly jokes with Joe Newton about embezzling money from the bank. A war bonds poster is visible above Joe's head. Uncle Charlie then deposits $40,000 in cash, an enormous sum of money in 1942, and manages to attract flirtatious attention from Widow Potter, a friend of the bank president's wife.

The brief exterior and lengthy interior bank scenes were filmed at the American Trust Company on the western corner of Fourth Street and Exchange Avenue (now roughly Mendocino Avenue and Fourth Street at Courthouse Square). The filming in the bank took almost an entire day and bank employees going about their normal business served as extras, including bank manager Harold Bostock.

LOOKING WEST ON FOURTH STREET TOWARD MENDOCINO AVENUE, 1935. NOTE THE EMPIRE BUILDING AND AMERICAN TRUST COMPANY.

The building shown in the movie was taken down in 1950 and rebuilt, in an attempt to provide a more modern home for the bank. The new building was then demolished in the late 1960s during the post-earthquake reconstruction of Courthouse Square. Today a Mexican restaurant, La Cantina, sits on the site where the bank was located, next to the Empire Building.

CLOSE-UP OF COLUMNS OF AMERICAN TRUST COMPANY AS YOUNG CHARLIE AND UNCLE CHARLIE ENTER THE BANK

LEFT TO RIGHT: THORNTON WILDER, BANK MANAGER HAROLD BOSTOCK, SECRETARY OF SANTA ROSA CHAMBER OF COMMERCE CHARLES DUNWOODY, AND ALFRED HITCHCOCK INSIDE THE AMERICAN TRUST COMPANY

JOE NEWTON'S TELLER WINDOW

Detective Graham Moves In

The next scene introduces Detectives Jack Graham (MacDonald Carey) and Fred Saunders (Wallace Ford), who are investigating Uncle Charlie. After photographing the house under the ruse of "documenting a typical American family," Graham asks if Young Charlie will show him around town and have dinner with him that evening.

The movie cuts to Graham and Young Charlie eating dinner at Gunner's Grill, a casual storefront diner. The sign out front says, "Short Orders—Steaks—Chops—Open All Night." The restaurant continues the World War II theme with both its name, an allusion to an artillery man, and the interior, which features servicemen eating dinner at the counter and military recruiting posters on the walls.

RIGHT TO LEFT: DETECTIVE GRAHAM, YOUNG CHARLIE, KATHERINE AND HER FRIEND IN FRONT OF THE TICKET BOOTH AT THE TOWER THEATER

In reality, there was no Gunner's Grill in Santa Rosa. The scene was filmed on a recycled studio set originally used in another film.

After leaving the restaurant, Graham and Young Charlie soon bump into Young Charlie's friends Katherine and Shirley, in front of a movie theater's ticket booth. The scene was filmed in front of the Tower Theater, located at 730 Fourth Street near Rosenberg's Department Store. The theater was constructed in the late 1930s in the dramatic Art Nouveau style. Today, the building no longer exists.

TOWER THEATER, 1939

Rosenberg's Department Store

ROSENBERG'S DEPARTMENT STORE, 1943

ROSENBERG'S DEPARTMENT STORE WAS LOCATED AT 700 FOURTH STREET, NEXT TO THE Tower Theater, and a few blocks from Courthouse Square. The store is different from the Rosenberg Building, located at the corner of Mendocino Avenue and Fourth Street in Courthouse Square. The department store—particularly the tall thin sign that juts above the building and is visible from Courthouse Square looking east on Fourth Street—is shown briefly in the movie.

Like the Tower Theater, the building was built in the 1930s in the Art Nouveau style. Unlike the Tower Theater, however, it still stands today. It was converted into a Barnes & Noble bookstore, but retains the original exterior.

Years after *Shadow of a Doubt*, Alfred Hitchcock reportedly visited Rosenberg's Department Store once again, during the filming of *The Birds* in 1962. According to local lore he bought a nightgown for Tippi Hedren to use in the film because he knew the exact look he wanted.

TOWER THEATER AND ROSENBERG'S DEPARTMENT STORE ON FOURTH STREET, LOOKING WEST FROM E STREET, 1939

CONTEMPORARY VIEW OF BARNES & NOBLE BOOKSTORE IN THE ROSENBERG'S DEPARTMENT STORE BUILDING

After the scene in front of the theater, the tone of the film changes dramatically as Young Charlie figures out that Detective Graham is investigating Uncle Charlie as a murder suspect. Young Charlie and Detective Graham are talking in Courthouse Square. Behind them, the Bank of America building looms in the background. Another camera angle looks north down Mendocino Avenue and shows the blurry letters "Redwood Highway" on the arch behind Detective Graham.

VIEW OF THE "REDWOOD HIGHWAY" SIGN SPANNING MENDOCINO AVENUE AT FOURTH STREET, 1949

YOUNG CHARLIE AND DETECTIVE GRAHAM IN FRONT OF BANK OF AMERICA

"REDWOOD HIGHWAY" SIGN VISIBLE TO THE LEFT OF DETECTIVE GRAHAM'S HAT

Filming Santa Rosa at Night

THE NIGHTTIME SCENES OF YOUNG CHARLIE WALKING ON SANTA ROSA'S STREETS HAVE an interesting historical context. These scenes include Young Charlie walking with and being dropped off by Detective Graham at home after their date, walking to the library, and running from the Newton house after dinner.

Many of these scenes were shot between midnight and 4 A.M. on August 18, 1942. The film crew had to race to complete their night shooting by midnight on August 19, since a "dim-out order" was going into effect. This order was meant to protect Bay Area towns from the possibility of enemy bombing. The huge studio lights necessary for exterior night scenes were tremendously bright and could have made the town a visible target.

According to Hitchcock, quoted in the August 17, 1942 *Press Democrat*:

> "We have the permission of the Army to shoot until midnight tomorrow and we are going to try to finish our outdoor night shots by that time."

The local newspaper ran headlines such as "Movie Cast Still Working as Dawn Nears" and "Movie Makers in Effort to Beat Deadline on Dim-out."

According to an editorial in The *San Francisco Call-Bulletin* from August 18, 1942, the dim-outs were taken very seriously:

> "Public compliance with the dim-out regulations has been good, but not good enough—according to official reports.... There is no excuse for deliberate violation, and those who persist in it will be proper subjects for disciplinary action."

The night street scenes include at least one continuous block-long shot. Because this sequence was filmed at night with the dolly retreating in front of the actors, it was considered the most technically difficult in the film, especially because of the time constraints imposed by the dim-out order.

The Tower Theater, Rosenberg's Department Store, and the Arrigoni Market, looking east down Fourth Street, 1941

Young Charlie with the Arrigoni Market behind her and the Tower Theater marquee in the upper right

Young Charlie's Growing Unease

Following her evening with Detective Graham, Young Charlie becomes increasingly suspicious of her uncle. Entering the house via the back staircase, she tries to piece together the newspaper article that Uncle Charlie had been trying to hide the evening before. When she is not successful, she rushes out of the house down the back staircase and heads to the library to do some research on the "Merry Widow" murderer. As mentioned earlier, the real Santa Rosa house had no back staircase, and thus this scene was clearly shot on a Hollywood set.

The next scene cuts to Young Charlie hurrying down a street crowded with evening strollers. There are a number of local buildings and businesses shown in the background.

Young Charlie is walking west down Fourth Street towards Courthouse Square. As she crosses D Street, there is a view east on Fourth Street briefly showing the vertical Tower

Contemporary view of Arrigoni Market on the left and Rosenberg's Department Store (now Barnes & Noble) on the right, looking east down Fourth Street

YOUNG CHARLIE HURRYING TOWARDS THE SANTA ROSA PUBLIC LIBRARY

Theater sign and fluorescent marquee in the upper right-hand corner of the frame. Young Charlie walks past a building with a striped canopy and square-patterned glass window panes on the northeast corner of D and Fourth Streets. This building housed the historic Arrigoni Market, located at 701 Fourth Street. This international grocery and wine store was founded in 1937 by the Arrigoni brothers. The brothers ran the store until 1975. Today, the building has been refurbished and the business, now a deli with new owners, retains the Arrigoni name.

After crossing D Street, Young Charlie is shown rushing by a number of glass storefronts. She then races into the intersection of Fourth Street and Mendocino Avenue, disobeying the traffic cop and nearly getting hit by a car. After a lecture from the police officer, Young Charlie hurries toward the grand, ivy-covered Santa Rosa Public Library.

In reality, if Young Charlie were walking to the library from her house on McDonald Avenue, she would have to walk to Third and E Streets where the library's main entrance once stood. In the film, she unrealistically goes several blocks out of the way down Fourth Street to Courthouse Square—a route that uses the bustling downtown as a backdrop.

The elegant stone library, located on Third and E Streets, had large rectangular windows and a striking Romanesque façade covered by ivy. The library scenes were done at night on August 14, 1942, with powerful lights attached to the trees. The shoot went so well, it was finished earlier than anticipated.

The Library was constructed in 1904 with a grant of $20,000 from steel mogul Andrew Carnegie. The distinctive "Free Public Library" sign over the library's front door identifies the building as funded by Andrew Carnegie. Between 1889 and 1923 Carnegie funded more than a thousand "free public libraries" across the United States, including dozens in California. Surviving Romanesque-style Carnegie libraries in California include San Luis Obispo, Nevada City, Chico, and Hanford.

The 1906 earthquake damaged the Santa Rosa Public Library extensively and, sadly, the building was condemned as unsafe in 1960. In 1965, the structure was finally demolished to make way for the modern main branch of the Sonoma County Library built on the same site.

An original Carnegie library still stands in the city of Petaluma, a few miles south of Santa Rosa, offering a hint of what the Santa Rosa Library would have looked like today, had it survived. The Petaluma Library, now a historical museum, was designed by Brainerd Jones in 1903 and is on the National Register of Historic Places. The building, located at 20 Fourth Street, has an exterior of sandstone and white Alameda rock, and fine interior paneling and woodwork. Although the Petaluma Library, built in the Classical Revival style, is architecturally distinct from the Santa Rosa Library, they were of similar scale and vintage. The Petaluma Library still has the "Free Public Library" words above the entrance.

CONTEMPORARY VIEW OF THE SONOMA COUNTY PUBLIC LIBRARY, BUILT ON THE SITE OF THE OLD SANTA ROSA PUBLIC LIBRARY

CONTEMPORARY VIEW OF THE PETALUMA LIBRARY, AN ORIGINAL CARNEGIE LIBRARY

Petaluma and the Remake of *Shadow of a Doubt*

THE SONOMA COUNTY TOWN OF PETALUMA HAS ITS own connection to the cinematic legacy of *Shadow of a Doubt*. The 1991 Hallmark Hall of Fame television remake of *Shadow of a Doubt* was filmed largely in Petaluma. A few scenes, however, were shot in nearby Santa Rosa, including a different "Newton" house on McDonald Avenue. According to the *Press Democrat*, the makers of the remake had wanted to use the house at 904 McDonald Avenue from the original *Shadow of a Doubt*, but Hitchcock's contract with the house's owners specified that the house never be used in a remake of the movie.

Petaluma was chosen instead of Santa Rosa because its downtown is better preserved. The film stars Mark Harmon as Uncle Charlie. Tippi Hedren even makes a brief appearance as one of the elderly widows being stalked by the Merry Widow murderer.

THE CAST OF THE *SHADOW OF A DOUBT* REMAKE

FILMING THE *SHADOW OF A DOUBT* REMAKE ON McDONALD AVENUE IN SANTA ROSA, 1990

Scenes in Petaluma for the *Shadow of a Doubt* remake were shot at the American Trust Company Building (now the Antique Collective), McNear's and the Mystic Theatre, the Old Petaluma Train Depot, the old Elks Lodge (now the Petaluma Hotel), the Women's Club, and Washington Street near Keller Street.

The next day, the film takes on a dark, heavy tone. Young Charlie seems to be avoiding Uncle Charlie by sleeping all day, coming down the back staircase and staying in the kitchen. The dinner scene is loaded with tension as the two Charlies engage in a subtext-filled dialogue that the other family members are not fully aware of. Young Charlie runs out of the house in distress and Uncle Charlie jumps up to go after her.

Young Charlie runs down a crowded Fourth Street followed closely by Uncle Charlie. She goes past the glass storefronts of F.W. Woolworth and Karl's Shoes in the Rosenberg Building toward the familiar intersection at Mendocino Avenue. As she approaches the intersection, the sign "Karl's" from Karl's Shoes is visible briefly in the upper-right portion of the frame.

YOUNG CHARLIE WALKING PAST GLASS STOREFRONTS AT THE ROSENBERG BUILDING, WITH KARL'S SHOES SIGN VISIBLE IN UPPER RIGHT. NOTE: AT NIGHT THE AWNINGS OF THE BUILDINGS WERE ROLLED UP.

VIEW OF FOURTH STREET STOREFRONTS IN THE ROSENBERG BUILDING, INCLUDING KARL'S SHOES AND F.W. WOOLWORTH AND COMPANY, 1949

YOUNG CHARLIE AT THE MENDOCINO AVENUE INTERSECTION; NOTE THE
NEON SIGN FOR THE HOTEL SANTA ROSA IN THE UPPER LEFT

Right before she arrives at the intersection, in the foreground, a tall neon sign is visible several blocks ahead. The sign is from the Hotel Santa Rosa, which is visible looking west down Fourth Street on the south side of the street between Exchange Avenue and B Street. The hotel building was torn down when the area was redeveloped in the 1960s.

Young Charlie nearly bumps into a police officer at the corner just as Uncle Charlie catches up with her and grabs hold of her arm. After the police officer scolds Young Charlie for "speeding" on the crowded sidewalk, she crosses the street with Uncle Charlie.

The two Charlies walk south on Exchange Avenue. In the background, there is a view of the J.C. Penney Company building at 537 Fourth Street, and Uncle Charlie guides Young Charlie into the seedy 'Til-Two bar.

YOUNG CHARLIE AND UNCLE CHARLIE WITH THE J.C. PENNEY BUILDING
IN THE BACKGROUND

THE SONOMA COUNTY COURTHOUSE WITH THE 'TIL-TWO BAR TO THE LEFT, 1959

The 'Til-Two bar's sign is shown in the foreground with the Bank of America clocktower building in the background. On the exterior, the "Tables for Ladies" sign, direct phone line to the Red Top Taxi company, and clock on the door set at 2:00 A.M. are authentic details of Santa Rosa during the 1940s.

The exterior scene was filmed in front of the actual 'Til-Two bar, a local institution where county employees met after work for drinks. The bar was located at the southwest corner of Santa Rosa Avenue and Third Street. During the 1960s, the building was torn down and the bar closed when the Courthouse was demolished. Today, the approximate site houses a modern commercial building, and is across the street from the new Bank of America building.

Inside, there is a long bar and a jukebox in the background; diamond-shaped light sconces and beer posters line the walls. Numerous military men enter and exit. The hardwood booth where Uncle Charlie and Young Charlie sit has a rough, uncomfortable look to it.

AD FOR RED TOP TAXI, 1941

YOUNG CHARLIE AND UNCLE CHARLIE IN A BOOTH AT THE 'TIL-TWO BAR

THE METHODIST EPISCOPAL CHURCH SOUTH, AS IT APPEARS IN THE FILM

We were not able to definitively confirm if the smoky interior bar shots were actually filmed inside the 'Til-Two or on a studio set. However, locals who patronized the bar believe the actual interior was used. In addition, *Life* magazine reports that Hitchcock helped keep the set production expenses within the limits set by the War Production Board by spending only $211 on the bar interior. Given the elaborate details of the scene, it appears likely that the actual bar's interior was used for filming and the studio only supplemented the scene with additional props. Additionally, as Uncle Charlie and Young Charlie enter the bar from outside, the scene appears to be filmed with a single continuous shot. There is no discernible cut from the exterior location to an interior set, suggesting the actual interior was used.

The interior provides an excellent example of a seedy downtown bar. It represents a small slice of big-city depravity within a Middle America setting. Clearly, this is not a place where the naive Young Charlie is comfortable.

During the scene, the waitress, a former classmate of Young Charlie's, mentions that she just lost her job at "Kern's." According to the Sonoma County Phone Directory, there was not a place named Kern's in Santa Rosa during the 1940s.

The movie then cuts to the next day, a Sunday morning. A group of well-dressed parishioners is standing in front of a Gothic-style church. Young Charlie, Anne, and Katherine are there, having just attended services.

The church used in this scene was the Methodist Episcopal Church South, located at Fifth and Orchard Streets. Hitchcock chose this location in part because it was no longer being used as a church. Thus, in filming, he would not offend any churchgoers. At the time, the building served as a recreation center for soldiers. Built in the 19th century, the church no longer exists. Instead, a modern parking garage and retail building now sit on the location.

The extras in this scene were residents of Santa Rosa. According to *Life*, Universal Studios reportedly used the Santa Rosa Chamber of Commerce as a casting office and paid extras $5 a day for their work.

CONTEMPORARY PHOTO OF A PARKING GARAGE AT FIFTH AND ORCHARD, FORMER LOCATION OF THE METHODIST EPISCOPAL CHURCH SOUTH

THE METHODIST EPISCOPAL CHURCH SOUTH, 1897

YOUNG CHARLIE WALKING WITH ANN AND KATHERINE
DOWN McDONALD AVENUE

HERBIE HAWKINS AND JOE NEWTON TALKING IN FRONT OF
THE NEWTON HOUSE

As the Newton girls and Katherine leave church, Detectives Saunders and Graham are waiting for them. Saunders tells Young Charlie they are about to receive confirmation that Uncle Charlie is the Merry Widow murderer. As the group strolls down McDonald Avenue back to the Newton home, the large weeping trees and vibrant gardens of the neighborhood are seen in all their glory.

Hitchcock takes some liberties with Santa Rosa geography in this scene. The Newton house is depicted as being just a few blocks from the church. In reality, the actual walk is over a mile.

When the Newton girls arrive home, Uncle Charlie is waiting outside on the porch, scowling at Young Charlie. Joe Newton and Herbie Hawkins walk by talking about how the police caught the Merry Widow murderer in Maine. Uncle Charlie's hostility towards Young Charlie remains, however.

YOUNG CHARLIE INVESTIGATES THE REAR STEPS

The Attempted Murders of Young Charlie

Young Charlie is soon shown walking down the rear steps on her way to run errands. She takes a violent fall, just barely avoiding serious injury by grabbing the railing. Young Charlie notices the steps may have been tampered with, and that evening she secretly investigates the stairs with a flashlight.

The next evening, Uncle Charlie makes his second attempt at killing Young Charlie. He starts the car in the garage, allows it to build up carbon monoxide, and removes the keys, leaving it running. When Young Charlie goes into the garage to investigate why the car is running, the door shuts behind her.

The family in the house remain unaware that Young Charlie is trapped in the garage. In the background, the radio is tuned to KSRO. The radio is playing soft music when a news bulletin comes in. The radio announcer says ". . .with studios in Vallejo and Santa Rosa, California." As the newscast begins, Uncle Charlie changes the station to a musical broadcast and turns up the volume to block out the noise of the car engine in the garage.

The use of KSRO was an authentic local touch. It would have been very common for households in Sonoma County to be listening to KSRO, because the station was the first and only Sonoma County–based radio station in the early 1940s. All other signals received in Sonoma County at this time were from San Francisco. KSRO was founded in 1936, and had studios in Santa Rosa and Vallejo. It featured symphony music, opera, and local news, and was well suited for the middle-class Newtons.

FILMING THE REAR STAIRCASE SCENE. HITCHCOCK CAN BE SEEN AT THE TOP OF THE STAIRS ALONG THE RAILING DIRECTING TERESA WRIGHT.

UNCLE CHARLIE COMING OUT OF THE SOON-TO-BE-EXHAUST-FILLED GARAGE

Neighbor Herbie Hawkins notices something odd in the garage, and the family and Uncle Charlie come rushing out to save Young Charlie. She narrowly avoids death, and Uncle Charlie is foiled once again. The family is scheduled to go see Uncle Charlie speak at a town function, but Young Charlie stays behind to recover. While home alone, Young Charlie tries to phone Detective Graham, who is staying at the Hotel Stewart located in Fresno.

Fresno is in California's Central Valley, 230 miles south of Santa Rosa. It is an odd choice as a location for Detective Graham to be staying, since the investigation was centered in Santa Rosa. Be that as it may, in reality there was no Hotel Stewart in Fresno in the early 1940s.

CONTEMPORARY VIEW OF GARAGE AT 904 McDONALD AVENUE

The Finale

Family and friends return to celebrate Uncle Charlie with a party at the Newton house. Uncle Charlie announces he will be leaving for San Francisco the next day, telling the group he will always miss the nice little town of Santa Rosa.

The following day, while the family is seeing Uncle Charlie off at the train depot, there are several views of the area around Railroad Square. As a group of local citizens is wishing Uncle Charlie farewell, there is a view of a large warehouse behind them. This building, located on the southwest corner of Fourth and Wilson Streets, is an old wooden storage facility used by the railroad. It was built in the 1930s and today houses a Chevy's Mexican Restaurant.

UNCLE CHARLIE SAYING GOODBYE TO THE CITIZENS OF SANTA ROSA AT RAILROAD SQUARE. NOTE THE STRUCTURE BEHIND THEM.

CONTEMPORARY VIEW OF THE SAME STRUCTURE AT FOURTH AND WILSON STREETS, NOW A CHEVY'S MEXICAN RESTAURANT

CONTEMPORARY VIEW FROM THE RAILROAD DEPOT LOOKING NORTH ACROSS THE TRACKS. THE TWO-STORY WOODEN VICTORIAN BUILDING SHOWN IN THE MOVIE NO LONGER EXISTS.

UNCLE CHARLIE SAYS GOODBYE TO EMMA NEWTON AT RAILROAD SQUARE

As Uncle Charlie is congratulated for donating money to the local hospital, the camera zooms in for a closer shot and rotates slightly counter-clockwise around the square. When Herbie Hawkins tells Uncle Charlie his train is approaching, the Lee Brothers Building (also seen during the first Railroad Square sequence at the beginning of the film) is visible in the background.

Uncle Charlie says goodbye to Emma. There is a view looking north up the railroad tracks, and a small two-story wooden Victorian building is visible in the background. This building no longer exists, and the site where it stood is an empty lot today.

As Uncle Charlie is saying his goodbyes, there is a shot of a troubled Young Charlie standing in front of the train tracks. A large warehouse is briefly visible in the background before Uncle Charlie's train arrives behind her traveling southbound toward San Francisco.

This large warehouse was built in 1915. It continues to stand today, as does a large metal-frame water tower, a reminder of Santa's Rosa's industrial days long past.

Building up to the harrowing climactic scene, Uncle Charlie keeps Young Charlie on the train with him as it begins to pull out of the station. He then moves her towards a door and starts to angle her off the accelerating train. Instead, she manages to shift her weight and maneuver Uncle Charlie to the door, pushing him out onto the neighboring tracks, where he is run over by an oncoming train.

CONTEMPORARY VIEW OF THE WAREHOUSE ACROSS THE TRACKS FROM THE RAILROAD DEPOT AT RAILROAD SQUARE

YOUNG CHARLIE WAITS FOR UNCLE CHARLIE TO LEAVE RAILROAD SQUARE. THE WAREHOUSE BEHIND HER STILL EXISTS TODAY.

AN OFF-CAMERA PHOTO OF UNCLE CHARLIE'S FUNERAL PARADE AT FOURTH STREET AND MENDOCINO AVENUE

The scene closes with one of the film's recurring motifs: a shot of couples dancing to the "Merry Widow Waltz" in a formal ballroom.

Uncle Charlie's funeral is the final sequence in the film. First, there is a procession with people lining Fourth Street and Mendocino Avenue at Courthouse Square. A motorcade of black cars heading west on Fourth Street turns right onto Mendocino Avenue and passes under the "Santa Rosa/Redwood Highway" arch. At the corner, the striped awning of the Rosenberg Building is shown. As the cars pass beneath the arch, the traffic officer removes his hat in respect for Uncle Charlie, who had made a powerful impression on the people of Santa Rosa.

A VIEW OF SANTA ROSA'S ROSE PARADE IN 1951. THE PARADE PASSES BY THE SAME CORNER AS UNCLE CHARLIE'S FUNERAL, BUT INSTEAD OF TURNING ONTO MENDOCINO AVENUE IT CONTINUES DOWN FOURTH STREET.

YOUNG CHARLIE AND DETECTIVE GRAHAM TALK IN FRONT OF THE METHODIST EPISCOPAL CHURCH SOUTH

This procession was filmed from Mendocino Avenue, looking south towards Fourth Street. Fourth Street near the Courthouse was the traditional focal point for parades and civic events in Santa Rosa, such as the Rose Parade. The parade has been held annually in Santa Rosa, sometime during the month of May, for 105 years.

The movie ends with Young Charlie and Detective Graham talking in front of the Methodist Episcopal Church South. As a result of Uncle Charlie's visit, the young woman — and indeed all of Santa Rosa — will never quite be the same.

Hitchcock in front of the Methodist
Episcopal Church South

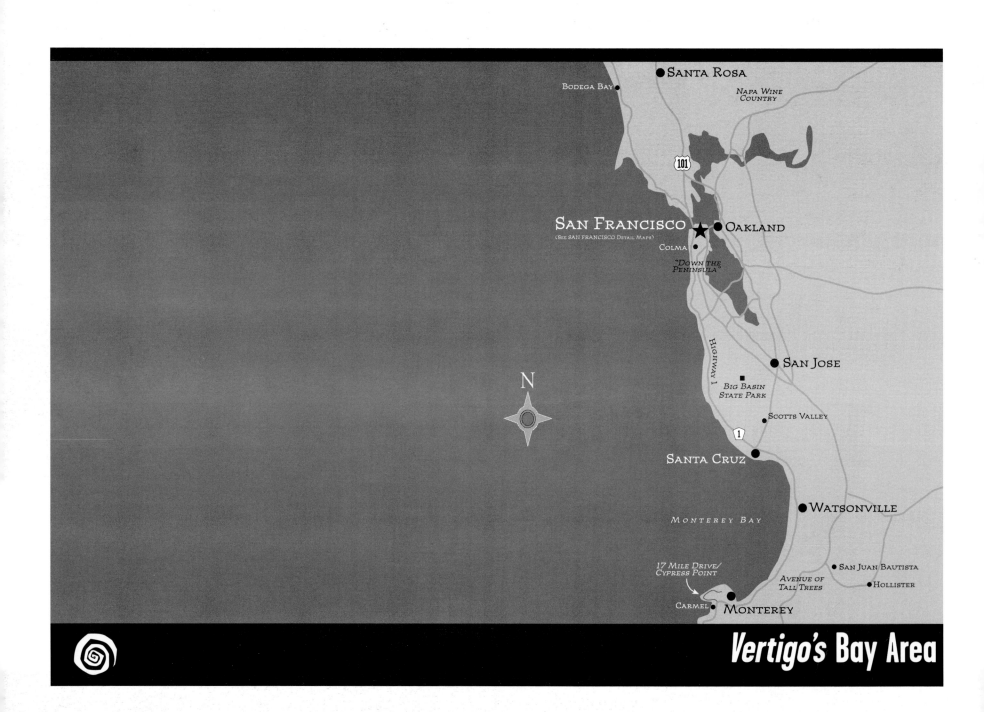

Vertigo's Bay Area

Vertigo

Hitchcock's Tortured Valentine to "The City"

"Well, San Francisco's changed. The things that spell San Francisco to me are disappearing fast."

– GAVIN ELSTER IN VERTIGO

Introduction

Gavin Elster's commentary on "The City," as locals call it, is even more relevant today than when he spoke those lines in this 1958 masterpiece. San Francisco is constantly reinventing itself as its architecture, industry, population, culture, and spiritual energy evolve with the times. The City has changed dramatically from the time when Hitchcock and his fictional *Vertigo* villain Gavin Elster walked the streets in the 1950s. Then again, San Francisco retains many of the buildings, monuments, and unique qualities it possessed at that time. Even when businesses have been closed or buildings torn down, their legacies live on,

FooTsTePs iN THe Fog

in films, books, photographs, and in the minds of those who remember San Francisco's not so distant past.

Hitchcock captured the romance, mystery, and elegance of The City in one of cinema's suspense classics, *Vertigo*, which was produced in 1957 and released in 1958. San Francisco's tall buildings, twisting staircases, and dramatic bridges make it an ideal setting for *Vertigo*. San Francisco's steep hills create winding streets, gorgeous vistas, and a jagged skyline. The coastline too is rugged, with dangerous cliffs and sharp curves which only add to the suspense. The blend of the city's unique character with Hitchcock's keen ability to weave a sinister tale creates a brilliant psychological suspense film.

In *Vertigo*, John "Scottie" Ferguson (James Stewart) is a police officer who develops a severe fear of heights after one of his colleagues falls to his death from a San Francisco rooftop. Scottie's emotional distress causes him to leave the force, but when his former classmate, Gavin Elster (Tom Helmore), asks him to follow Gavin's troubled wife Madeleine, Scottie accepts. Scottie is unknowingly pulled into a plot to kill Gavin's real wife when he follows an impersonator of Gavin's wife (Kim Novak), and stands powerless when she apparently falls to her death. Scottie's love for the Madeleine he knew results in a complete nervous breakdown. After his recovery, Scottie bumps into the Madeleine impersonator, Judy Barton (also played by Kim Novak), and when he learns her true identity, a chain of events is set in motion which ultimately leads to Judy's tragic death.

Vertigo seems like a travelogue of San Francisco and the surrounding area's famous historical sites, monuments, architecture, and luxurious businesses from the 1950s. Hitchcock had a remarkable ability to capture the subtleties of time, place, and spirit in his films. Even in cases where the actual filming occurred on a studio set far away from the original location, Hitchcock captured the essence of a setting by a meticulous use of authentic details. While *Vertigo* is a notable suspense masterpiece, it is also a remarkable testament to Hitchcock's passion for the San Francisco Bay Area.

VIEW OF DOWNTOWN SAN FRANCISCO FROM NOB HILL, 1947

KIM NOVAK BEING GREETED BY UNIVERSITY OF CALIFORNIA BERKELEY STUDENTS AS SHE ARRIVES IN SAN FRANCISCO FOR THE OPENING OF VERTIGO, MAY 9, 1958

The Stage Door Theater in San Francisco where Vertigo had its first public showing, 1964

Kim Novak arriving by train into San Francisco's Southern Pacific Depot for the opening of Vertigo, May 9, 1958

Prior to the premiere of *Vertigo*, Hitchcock held a weekend-long party and tour of film locations in San Francisco for more than 125 journalists. The event included dinner at Ernie's—a city landmark—with Hitchcock, James Stewart, and Kim Novak, followed by entertainment in the Fairmont Hotel's Venetian Room (which had been the inspiration behind the ballroom dancing scene in the film). *Vertigo* had its first public screening at San Francisco's Stage Door Theater at 420 Mason Street near Union Square on May 9th, 1958.

Setting the Stage: The Rooftops of Downtown San Francisco

Vertigo begins with a rooftop chase sequence set near downtown San Francisco. With sweeping views of the Bay, the Bay Bridge, Coit Tower, and the skyline of San Francisco, San Francisco Police Detective Scottie Ferguson runs from rooftop to rooftop after a fleeing criminal. The geography of San Francisco is immediately captured in panoramic fashion, conveying a sensation of height and depth while establishing a perfect backdrop and mood for a film featuring a character suffering from acrophobia.

Jumping from one roof to the next, the criminal is closely followed by a uniformed police-man and finally Scottie, who slips and falls, only barely holding on to the edge of a roof gutter. As Scottie peers down beyond his dangling feet to the street many stories below, the view suddenly becomes elongated and distorted, demonstrating Scottie's extreme fear of high places.

The opening scene in *Vertigo* was actually filmed on a studio stage in Los Angeles. The Bay Bridge and the San Francisco skyline were superimposed in the background. Nevertheless, the viewer is instantly captivated with and introduced to the city that hosts *Vertigo*.

The panoramic background footage of downtown San Francisco was shot from the Fairmont Hotel on Nob Hill (on Mason Street between California and Sacramento Streets), where the cast and crew stayed during the filming of the movie. During the opening scene, the camera moves in a sweeping 180-degree arc across the downtown skyline. As the chase proceeds across the rooftops, the view pans from south to north, showing the Montgomery Street skyscrapers, the Southern Pacific Railroad Building with the "SP" sign flashing, the Ferry Building, and then eventually Telegraph Hill.

As the criminal and uniformed police officer jump to the roof of a neighboring building, the background footage of San Francisco focuses in on a view down Sacramento Street looking east toward the San Francisco Bay. The street can be identified as Sacramento because it appears to intersect with Market Street between the Ferry Building on the left and the "SP" sign on the right. When the police officer pauses to help Scottie, there is a brief view of Coit Tower on Telegraph Hill over the officer's right shoulder.

SCOTTIE FERGUSON SLIPS AND FALLS ON A ROOFTOP ABOVE SAN FRANCISCO

SCOTTIE HANGING FROM A ROOFTOP GUTTER WITH A VIEW OF SAN FRANCISCO IN THE BACKGROUND

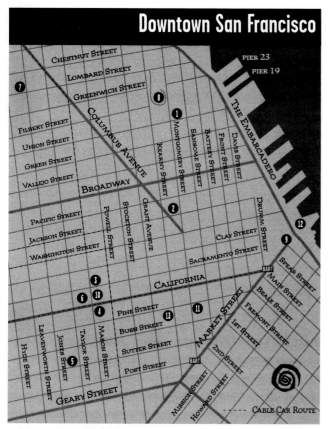

Downtown San Francisco

❶ 296 Union Street (the film location of Midge's studio apartment)
❷ Former location of Ernie's Restaurant
❸ Brocklebank
❹ Mark Hopkins Hotel and Top of the Mark
❺ Argonaut Book Shop (current location)
❻ Flood Mansion/Pacific Union Club
   (the film location of Gavin Elster's club)
❼ 900 Lombard Street (the film location of Scottie's apartment)
❽ Coit Tower
❾ Southern Pacific Building
❿ The Fairmont Hotel and the Venetian Room
⓫ Montgomery Street skyscrapers (B of A/Russ Buildings)
⓬ Ferry Building
⓭ Former location of Argonaut Book Shop

A subtle but interesting detail worth noting during this sequence is the lighting on the Ferry Building. When the camera pans across the skyline at the beginning of the sequence, the Ferry Building is lit up. When the scene cuts to the view down Sacramento Street, in the background, just before the criminal has jumped to the neighboring roof, the Ferry Building is dark. Then, after the criminal jumps to the neighboring roof and struggles to climb over the crest, the Ferry Building is lit in two stages from the bottom up. First the lower half of the building is lit, and then, a second later, the upper half and clock face are lit. After Scottie jumps to the roof, there is another cut in the footage and the Ferry Building is dark again.

The studio's "Catalog of Shots" from November 8, 1957 confirms these nighttime shots of downtown San Francisco were taken from a parapet on the Fairmont Hotel. The records also confirm shots were taken with the Ferry Building lights off and with the lights turned on. This indicates the lights of the Ferry Building were deliberately lit during the course of the scene—perhaps to provide a visual cue that the scene was taking place during twilight or dusk, or possibly to provide a subtle change to the background view to make the scene feel more authentic or visually appealing.

After the dramatic rooftop sequence, we are taken into the heart of San Francisco, where the plot—and additional views of the San Francisco Bay Area—begins to unfold.

The next scene in *Vertigo* occurs in the Telegraph Hill studio apartment of Midge (Barbara Bel Geddes), an artist and Scottie's former fiancée. Scottie is sitting on a chair watching Midge work, gazing out the window. The apartment has a dramatic, almost aerial view across town to Russian Hill. Although this scene was shot on a studio lot, the re-created view used on the set is authentic and geographically accurate.

CONTEMPORARY VIEW OF RUSSIAN HILL FROM A BUILDING ON THE CORNER OF UNION AND MONTGOMERY STREETS

Midge is seen sketching a cleverly engineered brassiere which, she explains, was built with the same design as a cantilevered bridge. This style of bridge was coincidentally used on the eastern span of the Bay Bridge. She tells Scottie that the bra was created by an aircraft engineer "down the peninsula" (i.e., in the South Bay) in his spare time. This piece of dialogue is as relevant and humorous today as it was in the 1950s. Even all those years ago, the area now known as Silicon Valley had the beginnings of entrepreneurial spirit and technological innovation.

BACKDROP SHOT OF BAY BRIDGE AND PIERS 19 AND 23 FROM THE CORNER OF UNION AND MONTGOMERY STREETS

Although the actual location of Midge's apartment was not explicitly specified in *Vertigo*, it is almost certainly intended to be situated on top of Telegraph Hill at 296 Union Street, on the northwest corner of Montgomery and Union Streets. Several facts lead to this conclusion. Interior scenes of the apartment (a studio set designed and furnished to look like an upscale artist's studio apartment in 1950's San Francisco) show a distinctive view looking west to the San Francisco neighborhood of Russian Hill, including the sloping Union and Filbert Streets. The view is clearly of Russian Hill from Telegraph Hill, because many of the distinctive apartment houses shown in the scene are still standing on Russian Hill today. Note that the contemporary photo on the previous page has almost the identical view as the one used on the studio set for Midge's apartment.

MIDGE IN HER TELEGRAPH HILL APARTMENT WITH A VIEW OF RUSSIAN HILL IN THE BACKGROUND

CONTEMPORARY VIEW OF BAY BRIDGE AND PIERS FROM THE CORNER OF UNION AND MONTGOMERY STREETS

Further evidence comes later in the film in the nighttime scene when Scottie drives Midge home from the Argosy Book Shop. There is a stunning backdrop shot of the western span of the Bay Bridge, Yerba Buena Island, Piers 19 and 23, and the San Francisco Bay. The only place on Telegraph Hill that has this precise bay view looking east is the 200 block of Union Street. The only place on this block of Union Street that also has westward views of Russian Hill consistent with the interior shots in Midge's apartment is the corner of Union and Montgomery Streets. Only at the very top of Union Street could you have views west to Russian Hill and east to the Bay Bridge. When you are any lower on the street, the views are restricted to one direction.

Since the film was made, the apartment building on the northeast corner of Union and Montgomery Street (i.e., 296 Union Street) was torn down, and a new four-story wood building with brown shingles was built on the site.

The Telegraph Hill neighborhood has some of San Francisco's steepest streets—several of which turn into staircases—as well as some of its most dramatic views. Scottie's attack of acrophobia on Midge's stepstool happens in a very appropriate neighborhood.

During the scene in Midge's apartment, the dialogue is flavored with local references. Scottie tells Midge that Gavin Elster, an old college friend from Stanford University (located 35 miles to the south in Palo Alto), has called and asked Scottie to pay him a visit. When Scottie explains that Elster has an address in the Mission District, Midge exclaims, "Well, that's Skid Row, isn't it?" This line is sure to cause laughter with audiences familiar with San Francisco today. While the Mission District has always been a working-class neighborhood of immigrants, from Germans and Swedes in the early days to Irish and Latinos more recently, today this multi-ethnic neighborhood is full of trendy restaurants and bars, as well as book, furniture, and used-clothing stores. It is also home to artists and high-tech workers.

CONTEMPORARY VIEW OF THE APARTMENT BUILDING AT 296 UNION STREET

A Shipyard in "The Mission"

After the scene with Midge, Scottie visits Gavin Elster, the villainous husband of Madeleine Elster—soon to become Scottie's obsession. Elster's Mission District address is actually an office at the San Francisco shipyards. In reality, the Mission is south of Market Street, but not on the water, and thus could not be home to a shipbuilding facility. Hitchcock is often very precise about using realistic geographic details to give his films authentic local flavor. Occasionally, however, as in this case, he takes artistic liberties.

The entrance to Elster's office (where Hitchcock makes his signature cameo appearance), as well as the office interior, were filmed at a studio in Los Angeles. However, the shipyard scene, with huge cranes visible through the window of Elster's office, was filmed in San Francisco at Bethlehem Shipyards at 20th and Illinois Streets in the Dogpatch neighborhood that borders the Mission Bay area (not the same as the Mission). The large mechanical cranes seen in the background of this scene, inserted via a process shot, are still operating today.

GAVIN ELSTER'S SHIPYARD OFFICE WITH CRANES IN BACKGROUND

The facility, the oldest working civilian shipyard in the United States, is currently owned by the San Francisco Dry Dock Company and is used to repair ships. The Dogpatch neighborhood is full of beautiful brick warehouses, some of which date to the late 19th century. Today the neighborhood has a quirky mix of businesses and people: high-tech companies, smokestack industries, the reputed San Francisco headquarters of the Hells Angels, and a number of well-preserved Victorian houses. The new baseball stadium where the San Francisco Giants play—Pacific Bell Park—is not far away.

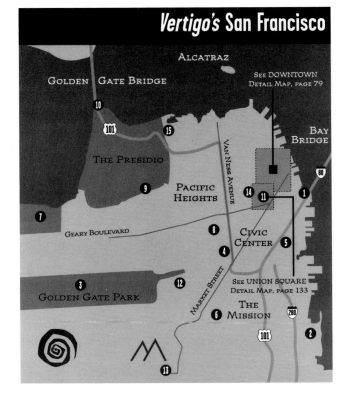

Vertigo's San Francisco

❶ Ferry Building
❷ SF Dry Dock Company and former location of the Bethlehem Shipyards
❸ Portals of the Past and Lloyd Lake
❹ War Memorial Opera House and Civic Center complex
❺ Podesta Baldocchi (current location)
❻ Mission Dolores church and cemetery
❼ Palace of the Legion of Honor
❽ Former site of Portman Mansion ("McKittrick Hotel" and St. Paulus Church
❾ Presidio Boulevard Entrance Gate
❿ Fort Point and the Golden Gate Bridge
⓫ Union Square
⓬ St. Joseph's Hospital
⓭ Twin Peaks
⓮ York Hotel (location of Judy's apartment in the "Empire")
⓯ Palace of Fine Arts

In Elster's wood-paneled, old-world-style office with leather chairs, ship models, and paintings of seafaring scenes, Scottie explains his acrophobia to Elster, saying he "can't climb stairs that are too steep or go to high places like the bar at the Top of the Mark…but there are plenty of street-level bars in this town." Verbal and visual references to famous city spots, such as the Top of the Mark, add an authentic feeling to *Vertigo*, and underscore Hitchcock's fondness for the Bay Area. The lounge at the Top of the Mark, with Coit Tower and the Bay in the background, would not be a good place to visit for someone with Scottie's affliction.

Elster convinces Scottie to follow his wife Madeleine, observe what she does, and watch out for her well-being. According to Elster, his wife is acting as if a long-dead Spanish relative named Carlotta Valdes possesses her. Elster expresses concern she may harm herself during her wanderings around San Francisco.

CONTEMPORARY VIEW OF CRANES AT THE SAN FRANCISCO
DRY DOCK COMPANY

VIEW OF THE SAN FRANCISCO BAY FROM THE TOP OF THE MARK BAR, 1959

Elster tells Scottie that Madeleine sits staring for hours at the Portals of the Past in Golden Gate Park. Although not shown in the movie, the Portals, near the middle of Golden Gate Park at Lloyd Lake, is a famous viewpoint containing a marble archway salvaged from the destroyed A.N. Towne mansion, which once stood where Nob Hill's Masonic Auditorium is currently located. The archway was moved to Golden Gate Park after the 1906 earthquake and fire consumed the mansion. Elster mentions that Madeleine travels five miles from their apartment to Golden Gate Park. In reality, this is almost the exact distance from California and Mason Streets—which we later learn is where the Elsters live—to Golden Gate Park.

During this conversation, Elster offers critical insights about the character of San Francisco. These comments also suggest the reasons why Hitchcock chose the city as the setting for *Vertigo*: "Well, San Francisco's changed. The things that spell San Francisco to me are disappearing fast....Yes, I should have liked to have lived here then…color, excitement, power, freedom."

In earlier versions of the film's screenplay, Elster gives a much longer soliloquy describing the hypnotic beauty and mystery of San Francisco and its ties to the past. This dialogue was removed from the final script, but it still offers a perfect synopsis of Madeleine's wanderings around San Francisco and hints at some of the later plot developments.

> GAVIN ELSTER: "You won't know what to look for at first, Scottie. Even I, who know her so well, cannot tell, sometimes, when the change has begun. She looks so lovely and normal. I realize now that the deep change began on the first day I brought her to San Francisco. You know what San Francisco does to people who have never seen it before. All of it happened to Madeleine, but with such an intensity as to be almost frightening.

> "She was like a child come home. Everything about the city excited her; she had to walk all the hills, explore the edge of the ocean, see all the old houses and wander the old streets; and when she came upon something unchanged, something that was as it had been, her delight was so strong, so fiercely possessive! These things were hers. And yet, she had never been here before. She had been born and raised in the East. I liked it at first, of course. I love this place; I wanted my bride to love it. But then it began to make me uneasy. Her delight was too strong; her excitement was too intense, it never faded; her laugh was too loud, her eyes sparkled too brightly; there was something feverish about the way she embraced the city. She possessed it.

PORTALS OF THE PAST MONUMENT IN GOLDEN GATE PARK, DATE UNKNOWN

EXTERIOR OF ERNIE'S AS SEEN IN *VERTIGO*
(THIS WAS FILMED ON A SOUND STAGE)

"And then one day she changed again . . . and a great sigh settled on her, and the cloud came into her eyes . . . I don't know what happened that day, where she went, what she saw, what she did. But on that day, the search was ended. She had found what she was looking for. She had come home. And something in the city possessed her."

The shipyard office scene concludes with Elster telling Scottie that he can see Madeleine at dinner that night at Ernie's, where they will be dining prior to attending the opera.

Dinner at Ernie's

Ernie's, a famous San Francisco restaurant, is the site Hitchcock chose for Madeleine's dramatic first appearance in *Vertigo*. The establishment was located at 847 Montgomery Street in a beautiful brick Victorian building that survived the 1906 earthquake.

As the next scene opens, there is a brief exterior shot of the restaurant and then a cut to the interior. Scottie sits at the curved bar of the finely appointed restaurant, waiting to catch a glimpse of Madeleine. Even from the bar, with its detailed brass work and dark stained wood, it is clear this is an elegant venue. As the camera pans across the room, it lingers on a woman who, after a time, gets up, revealing the full beauty of a stunning green dress set off against the ornate red-walled interior of the room.

While the actual filming of Ernie's interior and exterior occurred on Hollywood sound stages, the sets were carefully modeled after the real thing. Ernie's second-floor Ambrosia Room, with waist-high dark wood paneling and red velvet damask wallpaper with a Victorian rose-swirl design, antique light sconces, and finely detailed wood furniture, was almost perfectly replicated by Hitchcock's crew. The set included art work and table settings borrowed from the actual restaurant.

EXTERIOR OF ERNIE'S RESTAURANT AT 847 MONTGOMERY STREET, 1964

SCOTTIE AT THE UPSTAIRS BAR IN ERNIE'S (ON THE SOUND STAGE)

Hitchcock struck up a friendship with brothers Victor and Roland Gotti who had taken over the restaurant from their father in the 1940s. The brothers served as consultants to Hitchcock during the filming of *Vertigo*. Roland, and Ernie's maître d' Carlo Doto, each have cameos in *Vertigo*, serving as the maître d' and bartender respectively.

In fact, according to the *Los Angeles Examiner*, Hitchcock was so concerned with realism on the Ernie's set that the cast and extras actually ate a meal from Ernie's menu during the filming of *Vertigo* in Los Angeles. The food consisted of salad with Roquefort dressing, New York steaks, baked potatoes, vegetables, and banana fritters. After the cast had gorged themselves during the morning filming, Hitchcock jokingly suggested that they take an hour for lunch. Five years later, Victor and Roland Gotti joined Hitchcock as special guests in Bodega Bay to watch some of the filming of *The Birds*. In that film, Hitchcock would again use many locals— including the owner of the Tides Restaurant—in cameo roles.

After filming the Ernie's scenes, Hitchcock, who was a wine connoisseur and grape grower, sent a truckload of wine to the Gottis as a gift. The restaurant also profited financially from the publicity generated by its prominent role in *Vertigo* and the fact that its actual name was used in the film.

HOSTESS AT ERNIE'S SETTING FLOWERS, 1960

"MADELEINE ELSTER'S" FIRST APPEARANCE IN *VERTIGO*

INTERIOR SHOT OF PATRONS DINING AT ERNIE'S STUDIO SET

Hitchcock later hosted a *Vertigo* opening-weekend dinner at Ernie's for journalists. The dinner cost $75 a person, a truly extravagant sum for the 1950s. Hitchcock was quoted as saying, "the proprietors and chefs of Ernie's understate this fare as the $75 dollar gold-plate dinner. It is truly a festive board in the finest Lucullan tradition. It includes many French names I don't understand." The menu featured "L'Oisette de Boeuf Victoria Avec sa Sauce Madere" (Beef with Madera Sauce), among other enticing dishes.

Ernie's cuisine always had a distinctly continental flavor. It included French and Italian dishes like Chicken Cynthia (chicken breast baked in a champagne and Mandarin orange sauce), Braised Squab in a Mold of Vegetables, and Fricassee of Maine Lobster and Day Boat Scallops. In addition to the Ambrosia Room featured in *Vertigo*, Ernie's had the Elysian and Montgomery Rooms and an elegant bar downstairs. In the basement there was an enormous wine cellar. From bluebloods to the blue-collared, generations of San Franciscans looking for an elegant night on the town ate at Ernie's.

COUPLE BEING SERVED COFFEE IN THE AMBROSIA ROOM AT ERNIE'S, 1960

VICTOR (LEFT) AND ROLAND GOTTI AT ERNIE'S FIRST-FLOOR BAR, 1978

Hitchcock and his wife Alma frequently dined at Ernie's when they were staying at their Scotts Valley weekend home near Santa Cruz. They would be transported by limousine from the San Francisco airport or Scotts Valley for dinner. Other famous Ernie's customers included Marilyn Monroe, Joseph Cotten, Fred Astaire, Cary Grant, Frank Sinatra and Ava Gardner, Sammy Davis Jr., and politicians of all stripes. Ernie's closed in 1995 after 61 years and was replaced by the Essex Supper Club, which kept the Ernie's décor largely intact. The club went out of business in 1998 and much of the original furniture and fixtures from Ernie's were auctioned off in December 1998.

As Madeleine and Elster exit Ernie's, their stated destination is the San Francisco Opera House. Although not shown in *Vertigo*, the San Francisco War Memorial Opera House, located in the Civic Center at Van Ness Avenue and Grove Street, is one of the City's premier cultural institutions. The Opera House and its twin, the Veterans Building, are connected by a formal outdoor court and were designed by architects Arthur Brown and Albert Lansburgh. The two buildings, together known as the War Memorial complex, were built in the French Renaissance style and were completed in 1932. The complex has been the site of many famous events, including the conference where the United Nations Charter was signed by President Truman and other world leaders in 1945. In addition to the War Memorial buildings, the Civic Center also has San Francisco's distinctive new public library (opened in Spring of 1996), the recently refurbished Beaux-Arts style City Hall, Davies Symphony Hall, the Civic Auditorium, and other important public buildings.

CONTEMPORARY VIEW OF SAN FRANCISCO'S WAR MEMORIAL OPERA HOUSE

SCOTTIE WAITS OUTSIDE THE REAR OF THE FLOOD MANSION WITH GRACE CATHEDRAL IN THE BACKGROUND

CONTEMPORARY VIEW OF THE REAR OF THE FLOOD MANSION WITH GRACE CATHEDRAL IN THE BACKGROUND

Taking a Tour of San Francisco

The following day, Scottie takes up the task of trailing Madeleine, beginning at the home of Mr. and Mrs. Gavin Elster. Scottie waits in his car on Nob Hill. There is a brief view of the rear of the Flood Mansion where the Pacific Union Club is located; Grace Cathedral appears in the background.

CONTEMPORARY VIEW OF THE BROCKLEBANK

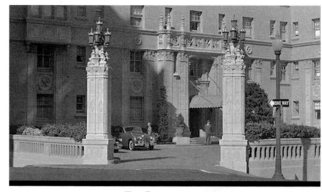

THE BROCKLEBANK, AS IT APPEARS IN VERTIGO

Next, we see an elegant "L"-shaped apartment building. The camera pans from the front pillars of the parking lot up to the top of the structure. The building we are looking at is the Brocklebank, a Nob Hill landmark, built in 1924 and located at 1000 Mason Street on the corner of Mason and Sacramento Streets. This was an appropriately exclusive place for the Elsters to live. Its real-life residents have included many wealthy and famous San Franciscans such as Herb Caen, Angela Coppola, and Michele and Joe Alioto. Parties at the building are a staple of the *San Francisco Chronicle*'s social column. Today, the Brocklebank looks virtually unchanged from the way it did in *Vertigo*.

As Madeleine's green Jaguar Mark IV pulls out from between the twin columns of the Brocklebank's entrance, going south on Mason Street, Scottie slides in behind her car, and the first of many tours of the streets of San Francisco begins. The sequence that follows has several geographically inaccurate parts and is one of the most difficult to identify in the film. The sequence shows a discontinuous route from Nob Hill to Union Square that includes a non-existent back alley and a back door that also did not exist.

MADELEINE DRIVES BY THE FAIRMONT HOTEL ON MASON STREET

First, Madeleine passes the Fairmont Hotel. Next, she turns left down California Street, which is undergoing road construction.

CONTEMPORARY VIEW OF THE FAIRMONT HOTEL

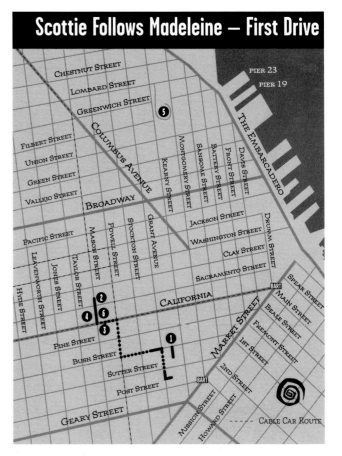

Scottie Follows Madeleine — First Drive

❶ Claude Lane
❷ Brocklebank
❸ Mark Hopkins Hotel and Top of the Mark
❹ Flood Mansion/Pacific Union Club
   (the film location of Gavin Elster's club)
❺ Coit Tower
❻ The Fairmont Hotel

━━━ DRIVE SHOWN IN THE MOVIE

•••• DRIVE IMPLIED BUT NOT SHOWN IN THE MOVIE

MADELEINE TURNS DOWN CALIFORNIA STREET FROM MASON STREET

Then there is a geographically discontinuous cut to a view west down the 500 block of Bush Street toward Grant Avenue with the Bay Bridge in the background. The steep pitch of the hill and the two "Hotel" signs on the north side of Bush Street help identify the location. Today, the Hotel Juliana (590 Bush) and Astoria Hotel (510 Bush) are still located on this block. Presumably, off camera, Madeleine and Scottie have taken a right onto Powell Street off California Street and then a left onto Bush Street. At the end of the 500 block of Bush Street, Madeleine, followed by Scottie, makes a right turn onto Grant Avenue.

MADELEINE TURNS DOWN BUSH STREET TOWARD GRANT AVENUE

CONTEMPORARY VIEW OF BUSH STREET LOOKING EAST TOWARD GRANT AVENUE. NOTICE THAT SKYSCRAPERS BUILT AFTER *VERTIGO* WAS FILMED BLOCK THE VIEW OF THE BAY BRIDGE TODAY.

The film cuts to a view looking south down Grant Avenue toward the corner of Post Street with the buildings on Market Street visible in the background. This shot is geographically discontinuous because after the turn off Bush onto Grant, Madeleine and Scottie are shown south of the Sutter Street intersection, a block further down Grant Avenue than the intersection of Bush and Grant. For those familiar with San Francisco, this discontinuity makes the scene slightly confusing. Presumably, off camera Madeleine and Scottie have traveled south along Grant Avenue from the intersection with Bush and across Sutter Street.

The corner of Post and Grant is identifiable by the letters "HOUSE" on the vertical White House Department Store sign and the two-pronged street lamp located near the corner of Grant Avenue and Post Street. The White House was a famed Gold Rush–era department store that closed in 1965. The building now houses a Banana Republic store.

EXTERIOR VIEW OF THE WHITE HOUSE DEPARTMENT STORE ON SUTTER STREET AND GRANT AVENUE. THE STREET LAMP AND STORE SIGN ARE VERY SIMILAR TO THE ONES SHOWN IN VERTIGO, WHICH WAS FILMED ON THE POST STREET AND GRANT AVENUE SIDE OF THE BUILDING, CIRCA 1950.

MADELEINE DRIVES DOWN GRANT AVENUE AFTER CROSSING SUTTER STREET. NOTE THE SIGN FOR TILLMAN PLACE ON THE RIGHT.

CONTEMPORARY VIEW OF GRANT AVENUE LOOKING SOUTH FROM SUTTER STREET TOWARD POST STREET. IN VERTIGO, THE FOOTAGE ON GRANT AVENUE BEGINS SLIGHTLY SOUTH OF SUTTER STREET.

MADELEINE TURNS LEFT FROM GRANT AVENUE ONTO ASHBURTON PLACE
AT THE WHITE HOUSE DEPARTMENT STORE, JUST BEFORE POST STREET

In addition, this location is identified by the briefly visible street sign Scottie passes on the right, earlier in the scene. The sign is for Tillman Place, a small alley intersecting Grant Avenue in the middle part of the block. Studio records confirm Hitchcock filmed driving footage along Grant Avenue.

Madeleine then turns left across Grant Avenue just before reaching Post Street. She appears to enter an alleyway. This is Ashburton Place—a narrow dead-end alley which served as a delivery entrance to the White House building. This alley is so small and obscure that it does not even appear on most detailed maps of downtown San Francisco.

The next scene cuts to a geographically discontinuous view south down Claude Lane toward Sutter Street, as if Ashburton Place were in fact a narrow street rather than a short delivery alley. Some Hitchcock authors have mistakenly identified this alley as Maiden Lane. However, studio records and careful observation suggest otherwise.

CONTEMPORARY VIEW FROM TILLMAN PLACE ACROSS GRANT AVENUE
TO ASHBURTON PLACE AT THE FORMER WHITE HOUSE DEPARTMENT
STORE BUILDING

The movie implies Madeleine turns left onto Claude Lane, a narrow alley running between Bush and Sutter Streets. In reality this is impossible because Claude Lane is a one-way street running south, and Bush Street, which leads to the northern entrance of Claude Lane, runs one-way to the west. So the only way to turn onto Claude Lane is to head west on Bush Street and turn right. Additionally, Claude Lane is about three blocks away from the White House Department Store at Grant Avenue and Post Streets, where Madeleine makes her left turn, so she could not have turned from Grant Avenue onto Claude Lane. Despite the geographic inconsistencies in this sequence, it still retains an authentic San Francisco ambiance because all of the locations are within a few blocks of each other and all show the architecture and density of traffic which characterize the area surrounding Union Square.

MADELEINE DRIVES DOWN CLAUDE LANE

Madeleine enters the alley heading south at Bush Street, between Grant and Kearny Streets. Today, the Bush Street end of Claude Lane—part of San Francisco's loosely defined French Quarter—is home to salons, boutiques, and cafés and is closed off during business hours. The section near Sutter Street looks much the same as it did when *Vertigo* was filmed.

ALFRED HITCHCOCK WITH LONGTIME PERSONAL ASSISTANT AND *VERTIGO* SCRIPT SUPERVISOR PEGGY ROBERTSON ON LOCATION AT CLAUDE LANE

CONTEMPORARY VIEW OF CLAUDE LANE LOOKING SOUTH
TOWARD SUTTER STREET

Madeleine parks her car (today there are café tables in the street and "No Parking at Any Time" signs in the alley) and walks through an old wooden door on the east side of the alley surrounded by an arched brick doorway. Scottie soon follows her, walking through the door into a dark, dirty passage that opens up into another door—revealing the stunning beauty of the Podesta Baldocchi flower shop.

Hitchcock took geographic liberties in filming the flower shop scene. Podesta was not actually located off Claude Lane and, at the time of filming, the store did not have a back entrance. However, the store was located on Grant Avenue right next to Ashburton Place— the alley Madeleine turned into before the scene cut to Claude Lane.

The wood doorway with brick framing Madeleine and Scottie walk through, depicted as the back entrance to Podesta, is indeed on Claude Lane. It's the first door down from the Bush Street entrance on the east side of the alley and, though now closed off with iron bars, it is still there today.

From his position peering through the opened door, Scottie watches Madeleine peruse the shop, magnificently appointed with vivid colors and flower arrangements. Madeleine purchases a nosegay of flowers.

SCOTTIE ENTERS THROUGH THE DOOR ON CLAUDE LANE

CONTEMPORARY VIEW OF THE NOW-BARRED DOOR ON CLAUDE LANE

Podesta Baldocchi

PODESTA BALDOCCHI WAS—AND STILL IS—AN ELEGANT SAN FRANCISCO florist. The shop was located at 224 Grant Street (between Sutter and Post Streets) for almost 40 years. It used to be well known for offering complimentary boutonnières in a bucket out on the street as a promotion to attract male customers. Tiffany's preceded Podesta at this location, but now the space is occupied by a leather store. The striking black and white tile floors captured in *Vertigo*, acquired from the Panama-Pacific Exposition, have been removed since Podesta moved to a new location in the 1980s.

The current home of Podesta is 508 Fourth Street near the corner of Bryant Street in a distinctive old brick building. Even after 50 years in business, the florist is still the place to go for the most elegant flowers in San Francisco. Kim Novak returned to the store many years after filming *Vertigo*, "simply because," she told the *San Francisco Chronicle*, "it was so fragrant, I had to have another whiff."

According to biographer Donald Spoto, during filming, florists at Podesta had to change flowers several times because the set lights caused the flowers to wilt. At one point it was so hot that the sprinkler systems went off. Nevertheless, Hitchcock persevered—remaining meticulous about small details. For example, he personally selected the cars and trucks that were filmed in the background through the store windows. The cast and crew spent 12 hours shooting at the flower shop to get less than a minute of footage used in the final version of the film.

EXTERIOR OF PODESTA BALDOCCHI AT 224 GRANT STREET, CIRCA 1950

CONTEMPORARY VIEW OF THE EXTERIOR AT 224 GRANT STREET

Podesta Baldocchi

CONTEMPORARY VIEW OF THE EXTERIOR OF THE CURRENT
LOCATION OF PODESTA BALDOCCHI AT 508 FOURTH STREET

THIS OFF-CAMERA STILL FEATURES KIM NOVAK AND MILIZA MILO
INSIDE PODESTA BALDOCCHI

CONTEMPORARY VIEW OF THE FRONT EXTERIOR OF MISSION DOLORES CHURCH

MADELEINE'S CAR PARKED IN FRONT OF MISSION DOLORES

After Madeleine leaves Podesta Baldocchi, Scottie follows her to the historic Mission Dolores, for which the Mission District of San Francisco is named. Madeleine parks her car and disappears into the building.

Scottie enters the church through a side door, and then goes out into the graveyard and gardens. The cemetery garden of yellow, red, and pink roses is in full bloom, and Scottie stares through the foliage at Madeleine as she looks at the gravestone of Carlotta Valdes, the ancestor who is supposedly haunting Madeleine's mind and body.

ALFRED HITCHCOCK IN FRONT OF MISSION DOLORES, 1957

Alfred Hitchcock and James Stewart reviewing the script on the set in the Mission Dolores graveyard

The Mission, located at the corner of 16th and Dolores Streets, is built of whitewashed adobe brick and tile. It was founded in 1776 and is the oldest intact building in San Francisco. The beautiful graveyard, one of only two cemeteries left in San Francisco, still has the romantic character and lovely, muted shades of color shown in *Vertigo*.

The Carlotta Valdes gravestone created for *Vertigo*, once a major tourist attraction at the graveyard, has been removed because it was not "authentic" enough to reside in the hallowed grounds of the Mission cemetery. Many early Spanish Californians are buried here, including the first governor of Northern California.

SCOTTIE IN THE MISSION DOLORES GRAVEYARD WITH THE STEEPLE FROM THE MISSION DOLORES BASILICA VISIBLE IN THE BACKGROUND

SCOTTIE VIEWING THE VALDES GRAVE

MADELEINE IN THE MISSION DOLORES GRAVEYARD

CONTEMPORARY VIEW OF THE APPROXIMATE LOCATION WHERE SCOTTIE STOOD VIEWING THE VALDES GRAVE. NOTE THE PLACEMENT OF THE CROSS IN BOTH OF THE PHOTOS.

CONTEMPORARY VIEW NORTH ON CASTRO STREET AT THE INTERSECTION OF CASTRO, MARKET, AND 17TH STREETS

SCOTTIE DRIVING NORTH ON CASTRO STREET AT THE INTERSECTION OF CASTRO, MARKET, AND 17TH STREETS

After departing from Mission Dolores, Scottie follows Madeleine's car north on Castro Street, turning left onto 17th Street at the intersection of Castro, Market, and 17th Streets. Presumably, after leaving Mission Dolores, Madeleine has headed southwest to Castro Street.

Hitchcock then cuts to Scottie following Madeleine going west on 17th Street toward a steep hill. Although not the fastest route, the 17th Street hill is one of the most dramatic slopes in San Francisco and could be taken to the Richmond District, which we learn in the next scene is Madeleine's destination.

CONTEMPORARY VIEW WEST ON 17TH STREET FROM MARKET STREET

SCOTTIE DRIVING WEST ON 17TH STREET TOWARD THE STEEP PART OF THE STREET

SCOTTIE APPROACHES THE FRONT OF THE PALACE OF THE
LEGION OF HONOR

The majestic Roman-style pillars of the Palace of the Legion of Honor appear in the next scene. Set in Lincoln Park near the Presidio, the Legion of Honor has a spectacular view of the Golden Gate Bridge and the surrounding landscape. This small museum has an interesting permanent collection including Picassos, Rodins, and Impressionist works, as well as excellent traveling exhibitions. The galleries were earthquake retrofitted and expanded in 1996.

CONTEMPORARY VIEW OF THE
FRONT OF THE PALACE OF THE
LEGION OF HONOR

SCOTTIE WATCHES MADELEINE IN A GALLERY AT THE PALACE OF
THE LEGION OF HONOR

The current location of the Portrait of Carlotta, painted for and shown in the film, is unknown. However, an earlier version for which Vera Miles (Hitchcock's original choice for Madeleine, who could not do the role because she became pregnant) modeled sits in the Southern California offices of Robert Harris and James Katz, who restored *Vertigo* in 1996. Several of the other paintings seen in the background of the *Vertigo* scene are still on display in Gallery Six of the Legion of Honor where *Vertigo* was filmed.

Madeleine, with Scottie following, next drives to the Gothic-Victorian McKittrick Hotel near the northwest corner of Eddy and Gough Streets. As Scottie arrives and parks, a large church that resembles the French cathedral at Chartres is shown in several shots. The church is diagonally across the street from the McKittrick Hotel.

This was the St. Paulus Lutheran Church (950 Gough Street), a Gothic redwood structure built in 1894, that survived the 1906 earthquake, but sadly burned down in 1995. The lot has been vacant since the fire.

There are also shots looking east past the south side of Eddy Street between Gough and Franklin Streets showing the large four-story Edwardian build-ing. This building remains today.

SCOTTIE IN FRONT OF ST. PAULUS LUTHERAN CHURCH

SCOTTIE ON THE SOUTH SIDE OF EDDY STREET BETWEEN GOUGH AND FRANKLIN STREETS, WITH THE FOUR-STORY EDWARDIAN BUILDING BEHIND HIM

CONTEMPORARY VIEW OF THE FOUR-STORY EDWARDIAN BUILDING

ST. PAULUS LUTHERAN CHURCH, 1940

Scottie watches Madeleine walk into the McKittrick Hotel. Soon, she appears in the window of an upper-story room. The "hotel" is actually the historic twenty-room Portman Mansion, owned at one time by Henry J. Portman. Never actually a hotel, the mansion was built in 1890 and located at 1007 Gough Street on the northwest corner of Eddy and Gough Streets. The two-story wood building, with tall narrow windows, an eerie ornamental façade, and short black spiked fence, creates a sense of unnerving mystery. Scottie's cautious facial expression adds to this feeling. The use of a "California Gothic" or "California Gingerbread" Victorian house to create mystery and suspense was a technique Hitchcock would repeat a few years later in *Psycho*. Hitchcock himself used the terms California Gothic and California Gingerbread when referring to the style of the Bates Mansion in an interview with Truffaut.

EXTERIOR OF THE "McKittrick Hotel"

EXTERIOR VIEW OF THE PORTMAN MANSION, CIRCA 1950

Scottie soon follows Madeleine into the hotel, walking through the large wooden doors, revealing a stunning example of Victorian San Francisco architectural design.

The production crew chose this location for filming in part because of the architectural details: the cascading wood staircase with the tall newel post on the banister, sharply pointed crystal torchier hanging above the post, and lush, dark wood paneling and Victorian flower-patterned wallpaper throughout. At the end of the special-edition letterbox version of *Vertigo*, there are a series of production storyboard sketches of various scenes in the film, including one of the interior of the McKittrick highlighting the architectural details of the site.

The mansion was torn down in 1959 shortly after *Vertigo* was filmed. Today, tennis courts for the nondescript Normandy apartment building sit on the site.

This highly memorable segment of *Vertigo* ends when Madeleine mysteriously vanishes from Scottie's trail.

INTERIOR OF THE McKITTRICK HOTEL AS SEEN IN *VERTIGO*

CONTEMPORARY VIEW OF THE NORTHWEST CORNER OF EDDY AND GOUGH STREETS, WHERE THE PORTMAN MANSION FORMERLY STOOD

STORYBOARD SKETCH OF THE INTERIOR OF THE McKITTRICK HOTEL

INTERIOR STAIRWAY, NEWEL POST, AND TORCHIER AT THE PORTMAN MANSION, CIRCA 1950

The Argosy Book Shop

Scottie returns to Midge's apartment and asks her where he can find an expert on San Francisco history. Midge leads him to Pop Leibel, the owner of the Argosy Book Shop on Union Square in San Francisco. At the Argosy, Scottie and Midge learn the tragic story of Madeleine's great-grandmother, Carlotta Valdes, who was the discarded lover of a rich and powerful man in San Francisco's early years.

ARGOSY BOOK SHOP WITH VIEW OF REAR PROJECTION FOOTAGE AND FRONT ENTRANCE IN THE BACKGROUND. NOTE THE "MACINTOSH SWISS CHOCOLATES" SIGN BEHIND POP LEIBEL'S HEAD.

VIEW FROM THE CORNER OF POWELL AND O'FARRELL STREETS LOOKING NORTHEAST ON POWELL, 1955. NOTE THE "MACINTOSH SWISS CHOCOLATES" SIGN WHICH IS ALSO VISIBLE IN THE REAR PROJECTION FOOTAGE.

CONTEMPORARY VIEW OF 343 POWELL STREET

The fictitious Argosy Book Shop, filmed on a studio set, was supposedly located at 343 Powell Street (the street number is visible backwards above the store's door) near Union Square (notice the cable cars and the ringing of their bells as Scottie and Midge enter and leave the store). In the real world, 343 Powell Street is located directly on Union Square between Geary and Post Streets, and the view from the storefront is not of other businesses across Powell (as shown in *Vertigo*), but of the square itself. This is one of many examples where Hitchcock tweaks real-world geography for cinematic purposes. The actual street-level storefront at 343 Powell Street is attached to the Westin St. Francis Hotel.

The view of Powell Street shown in the background of the *Vertigo* scene was a process shot created using rear projection footage and was filmed on the 200 block of Powell Street, one block lower than the fictitious address. You can tell the rear projection footage was filmed on the 200 block of Powell Street because throughout the latter part of the scene there is a view of the Macintosh Swiss Chocolates sign behind Pop Leibel at 222 Powell Street (now an antique store). Hitchcock must have taken this rear projection footage from the Villa Florence Hotel located at 225 Powell, across the street from Macintosh Chocolates.

There is considerable confusion and disagreement over the real-world inspiration for *Vertigo*'s Argosy. According to Samuel Taylor, the primary screenwriter for the film, as quoted in Dan Auiler's book about the making of *Vertigo*, the store was inspired by a bookstore on the corner of Stockton and Maiden Lane, down the street from the City of Paris department store where Mr. Taylor worked when he was in college. Mr. Taylor said the store owner in *Vertigo*, Pop Liebel (played to great effect by Konstantin Shayne), was based on the owner of a San Francisco candy store near where he grew up. Other Hitchcock scholars have completely given up finding the inspiration for the Argosy.

CONTEMPORARY VIEW OF 222 POWELL STREET, FORMER HOME OF MACINTOSH SWISS CHOCOLATES

EXTERIOR OF THE ARGONAUT BOOK SHOP AT 350 KEARNY STREET IN SAN FRANCISCO (WITH ROBERT D. HAINES, SR. AND HIS BUSINESS PARTNER, RIGHT TO LEFT), 1945

EXTERIOR OF THE ARGOSY BOOK SHOP IN *VERTIGO*

INTERIOR OF THE ARGOSY BOOK SHOP, WITH MIDGE IN FRONT OF THE
BOOK CABINETS

However, there is convincing evidence that the Argosy was a thinly veiled reference not to the bookstore mentioned by Mr. Taylor, but instead to the Argonaut Book Shop on Kearny Street. The Argonaut, founded in 1941, specializes in rare manuscripts documenting California history, including early settlement and the Gold Rush (just like the Argosy in *Vertigo*). The Argonaut's original owner, Robert D. Haines, Sr., was also a founding member of the Antiquarian Booksellers Association of America. The shop was located at 350 Kearny Street until the early 1950s when it moved down a couple of storefronts to 336 Kearny Street.

According to the shop's current owner, Robert D. Haines, Jr., Hitchcock actually visited the 336 Kearny Street store, run at the time by Robert, Sr., prior to filming *Vertigo* and exclaimed: "This is what a bookstore should look like." Hitchcock sent his film crew to shoot the interior of the store in great detail so they could re-create it back at the studio. Many of the details in the interior photographs of the Argonaut (such as the mezzanine-level office, horizontal book displays, glass bookcases, storefront window, and the shape of the glass transom above the front door with the street address visible backwards through the glass) were included in the Argosy set in *Vertigo*. The gold-lettered store name on the window at the 336 Kearny address was also copied on the Argosy set.

INTERIOR OF THE ARGONAUT BOOK SHOP WITH A CUSTOMER AND ONE-TIME CO-OWNER BOB ROSE (LEFT TO RIGHT) AT 336 KEARNY STREET IN SAN FRANCISCO, 1952

INTERIOR OF THE ARGONAUT BOOK SHOP WITH ROBERT B. HAINES, SR., SMOKING A CIGARETTE. NOTE THE VIEW OF THE MEZZANINE LEVEL IN THE BACKGROUND, 1952.

The name "Argonaut" derives from the Greek myth of Jason and the Argonauts. The story tells of the search for the Golden Fleece by Jason and his companions. An argonaut is a traveler over water seeking precious treasure. Thus, the shop's name also alludes to the men and women who came to California seeking treasure during the Gold Rush. The Argonaut's current owner speculates that Hitchcock changed the name in *Vertigo* to avoid any legal complications. There is an Argosy Book Store located in New York City (116 East 59th Street) that was founded in 1925. The Argosy sells rare manuscripts, first editions, and other antique books and is a likely source for the use of the Argosy name in the movie.

The Argonaut moved from Kearny Street to its current location at 786 Sutter Street around 1969. The junior Mr. Haines is convinced that Hitchcock borrowed mannerisms from his father for the character of Pop Leibel, particularly the way in which Leibel lit and smoked his cigarettes.

Even today, the store is a treasure trove of California history, with beautiful rare editions of books and prints dating back to the 19th century. Its bookshelves and other furnishings, many from the original store, still closely resemble those used by Hitchcock in the studio set for the Argosy.

POP LEIBEL, HOLDING HIS CIGARETTE

CONTEMPORARY VIEW OF ROBERT D. HAINES, JR., STANDING OUTSIDE THE ARGONAUT BOOK SHOP AT 786 SUTTER STREET IN SAN FRANCISCO

Following their departure from the Argosy Book Shop, Scottie drops Midge at her apartment. Scottie's DeSoto automobile turns left from Calhoun Street onto Union Street toward Montgomery Street, with Piers 19 and 23 and the Bay Bridge in the background. This footage implies that Scottie is driving up Telegraph Hill from downtown San Francisco. However, this is impossible, and is another example of how movie geography may differ from the real world. Calhoun is a short dead-end street and is not accessible from downtown San Francisco. The scene concludes with Scottie sitting in his car and pondering the information from the Argosy; a view of the Bay Bridge is perfectly framed behind him out of the rear window.

CONTEMPORARY VIEW EAST ON UNION STREET FROM THE CORNER OF MONTGOMERY STREET IN THE TELEGRAPH HILL NEIGHBORHOOD

VIEW EAST ON UNION STREET OF THE BAY BRIDGE AND PIERS NEAR MIDGE'S APARTMENT

VIEW OF HUNTINGTON PARK ON NOB HILL WITH THE PACIFIC UNION CLUB (FLOOD MANSION) IN THE LEFT CENTER, THE
FAIRMONT IN THE LEFT REAR, AND THE MARK HOPKINS HOTEL IN THE CENTER REAR, 1951

CONTEMPORARY VIEW OF THE PACIFIC UNION CLUB ON NOB HILL

In the following scene, Scottie meets Elster in the lounge of an elegant men's club to report the information he has discovered from following Madeleine and investigating Carlotta. This segment was shot on a studio stage, and the club was not specifically identified in the movie. However, there are numerous private clubs throughout the city frequented by wealthy San Franciscans. According to Tom Wolfe, the Chief Concierge at the Fairmont Hotel on Nob Hill, and an expert on local lore, the nearby Pacific Union Club, one of the most exclusive, was a likely inspiration for the setting used in *Vertigo*. The club—located in the Flood Mansion, a large brownstone building at 1000 California Street between Grace Cathedral and the Fairmont Hotel—sits diagonally across Sacramento Street from the Brocklebank, so it would have been a very convenient place for Gavin Elster to frequent, just seconds from his apartment.

Along with the Fairmont, the mansion, modeled after brownstones on the East Coast, is one of the few Nob Hill structures to at least partially survive the 1906 earthquake and fire. Although the interior was destroyed, the brownstone shell still stands and, with a refurbished interior, serves as the Pacific Union Club.

This very private and exclusive club has always been home to captains of industry such as railroad executives and shipping magnates like Gavin Elster. It is impossible to gain entry into the club without escort from a member. Photography of its interior is also strictly prohibited. The following description of the interior, from a pamphlet provided by the club, gives an indication of the club's elegance and is fully consistent with the idea that the club served as Hitchcock's inspiration for Elster's club in *Vertigo*: "The first floor of the clubhouse features a beautiful dining room, lounge, bar, card rooms, reading rooms, and private dining rooms . . . . The second and third floors house a formal library, and sixteen elegant bedrooms and offices."

The scene in *Vertigo* with Elster sitting in a lounge drinking cocktails with an enormous marble fireplace in the background, reminiscent of an English gentlemen's club, may well have been inspired by the first-floor lounge of the Pacific Union Club.

A Leap into the Bay

The next day, Scottie follows Madeleine northwest on Presidio Boulevard into the Presidio. There is a brief view of the dome on the Palace of Fine Arts, the Marina district and the bay in the background. At the time *Vertigo* was filmed, the Presidio was a military base located in San Francisco; today it's a scenic urban national park.

GAVIN ELSTER AND SCOTTIE AT ELSTER'S MEN'S CLUB

VIEW OF THE PALACE OF FINE ARTS FROM SCOTTIE'S CAR AS HE DRIVES DOWN PRESIDIO BOULEVARD

THE PALACE OF THE LEGION OF HONOR AS SEEN IN *VERTIGO*

CONTEMPORARY VIEW OF THE PALACE OF THE LEGION OF HONOR

CONTEMPORARY VIEW OF THE PALACE OF FINE ARTS FROM PRESIDIO BOULEVARD

Driving northwest down Presidio Boulevard today, this same view of the Palace of Fine Arts and the Marina District is largely obscured by a fence and overgrown foliage, but the dome of the Palace is still briefly visible from a car. This is a logical way to get to the Palace of the Legion of Honor. Presidio Boulevard intersects with Lincoln Boulevard, which turns into El Camino Del Mar, outside the Presidio and leads directly to the Legion of Honor.

The scene then returns to the Palace of the Legion of Honor where Madeleine again visits her ancestor's portrait. After she leaves, Scottie once again follows Madeleine. The driving scene that unfolds next occurs along part of San Francisco's scenic and famous 49-Mile Drive. They travel east on El Camino Del Mar with its dramatic view of the Golden Gate Bridge, offering a hint of what is coming in the next scene. The view of the Golden Gate Bridge shown in the film is only a few yards down El Camino Del Mar, just past the museum.

VIEW OF THE GOLDEN GATE BRIDGE FROM EL CAMINO DEL MAR AS SEEN IN *VERTIGO*

CONTEMPORARY VIEW OF THE GOLDEN GATE BRIDGE FROM EL CAMINO DEL MAR

SCOTTIE DRIVING NORTH ON PRESIDIO BOULEVARD TOWARD THE
PRESIDIO GATE

Next, Madeleine and Scottie re-enter the Presidio. Logically, they would have driven through the entrance near 24th Avenue where El Camino Del Mar turns into Lincoln Boulevard. However, in a geographic inconsistency, the film shows them entering the Presidio going west through the Presidio Boulevard gate (near Pacific Avenue). Hitchcock may have used this entrance to the Presidio because it is very picturesque, with the Victorian row houses of Presidio Heights on the down-sloping block of Presidio Boulevard, and the tunnel-like trees immediately inside the Presidio. This gate is also distinctive because of its narrow roadway and squat white concrete obelisk gateposts (compared to the taller stone posts at the Arguello Avenue and Lombard Street entrances). The footage of this entrance was taken near the same section of Presidio Boulevard shown in the earlier scene with the view of the dome of the Palace of Fine Arts.

CONTEMPORARY VIEW SOUTH ON PRESIDIO BOULEVARD TOWARD
JACKSON STREET

CONTEMPORARY VIEW OF THE PRESIDIO BOULEVARD GATE INTO THE PRESIDIO. NOTE THAT THE PRESIDIO
EMBLEMS HAVE BEEN REMOVED FROM THE STONE PILLARS.

SCOTTIE APPROACHES THE PRESIDIO BOULEVARD ENTRANCE GATE
INTO THE PRESIDIO

SCOTTIE FOLLOWS MADELEINE THROUGH THE GATE AT THE ENTRANCE TO MARINE DRIVE IN THE PRESIDIO

CONTEMPORARY VIEW OF THE GATE AT THE ENTRANCE TO MARINE DRIVE IN THE PRESIDIO

MARINE DRIVE (WITH SAN FRANCISCO IN THE BACKGROUND) AS SEEN IN *VERTIGO*

CONTEMPORARY VIEW OF MARINE DRIVE WITH SAN FRANCISCO IN THE BACKGROUND

Scottie follows Madeleine to Lincoln Boulevard, and then to Long Avenue and through the gate to Marine Drive. Eventually they reach Fort Point at the foot of the looming Golden Gate Bridge, with a view of Marin County across the Bay. Fort Point, a former military base with brick defensive walls, sits under the southern span of the Golden Gate Bridge.

SCOTTIE'S AND MADELEINE'S CAR AT FORT POINT

When the famous San Francisco fog rolls in and covers part of the bridge, Fort Point becomes a mysterious and romantic place. The first military installation on this site was built in 1794 by the Spanish. The current brick structure was built by the Army Corps of Engineers between 1853 and 1861 to protect ships carrying Gold Rush–era cargo. The fort was put on alert during military conflicts from the Civil War through World War II, but was never involved in battle. It is now a part of the Golden Gate National Recreation Area.

CONTEMPORARY VIEW OF THE GOLDEN GATE BRIDGE AND FORT POINT

In one of the film's most dramatic moments, Madeleine makes her famous suicide attempt by jumping into San Francisco Bay. Contrary to popular myth, Kim Novak did not have to do repeated takes of this scene to please a perfectionist Hitchcock. A stunt double was filmed jumping off the seawall onto a stretched parachute. The steps leading down to the water shown in *Vertigo* do not actually exist at Fort Point and were instead filmed on a studio stage. Novak did spend a limited amount of time in a studio water tank for this scene. It's a good thing no one actually jumped into the bay from Fort Point because it's a long drop to the rocky waters below. The swirling tides beneath the bridge could easily drag a person out into the Pacific Ocean, and local surfers report that sharks can occasionally be seen in the area.

MADELEINE STANDS BY THE WATER AT FORT POINT

After saving Madeleine from the rough waters of the Bay, Scottie takes her back to his apartment at 900 Lombard Street. This duplex from the 1950s sits near the corner of Lombard and Jones Streets, a few blocks below the famous twists and turns of Lombard Street—the "crookedest street in the world." At the time *Vertigo* was filmed, this was a modern building.

The interior of Scottie's apartment was filmed on a Hollywood sound stage. The actual apartment windows do not have the Coit Tower views shown in *Vertigo*, but the outside street corner does have a nice view of the tower. According to Henry Bumstead, studio set designer for *Vertigo*, the views of the tower from the apartment were included in the film because Hitchcock believed it was a phallic symbol and would add sexual tension to the scenes in Scottie's apartment.

SCOTTIE CARRIES MADELEINE AFTER HER JUMP INTO THE SAN FRANCISCO BAY

In *Vertigo*, Elster calls Scottie's apartment while Scottie and Madeleine are talking about her apparent "slip" into the bay. As Scottie talks on the phone with Elster, Madeleine quietly leaves.

A LATER SCENE IN SCOTTIE'S APARTMENT WITH COIT TOWER VISIBLE IN THE BACKGROUND

Scottie Follows Madeleine — Second Drive

- ❶ Brocklebank
- ❷ Mark Hopkins Hotel and Top of the Mark
- ❸ Flood Mansion/Pacific Union Club
  (the film location of Gavin Elster's club)
- ❹ 900 Lombard Street
  (the film location of Scottie's apartment)
- ❺ Coit Tower
- ❻ The Fairmont Hotel and the Venetian Room

━━ *Drive shown in the movie*

●●●● *Drive implied but not shown in the movie*

Scottie and Madeleine Fall in Love

The next day, the action again starts in front of the Brocklebank apartment building, as Scottie begins to follow Madeleine once more.

At the beginning of the scene, right after Madeleine pulls out of the Brocklebank and passes the Fairmont, road construction is briefly visible at the intersection of California and Mason Streets. This roadwork was also visible in the earlier driving sequence,

CONSTRUCTION ON CALIFORNIA STREET AT MASON STREET, AS SEEN IN VERTIGO

the first time Scottie follows Madeleine from the Brocklebank. The *Vertigo* footage that was filmed in the summer and fall of 1957 captures the rebuilding of the California Street cable car line that occurred at the same time as the filming. According to cynical local observers, this and other San Francisco intersections shown in *Vertigo* seem to still be under construction today.

VIEW OF THE FAIRMONT HOTEL LOOKING NORTHEAST AT THE CORNER OF CALIFORNIA AND MASON STREETS SHOWING CABLE CAR LINE CONSTRUCTION, 1957

SCOTTIE FOLLOWS MADELEINE DOWN CALIFORNIA STREET FROM MASON STREET

CONTEMPORARY VIEW WEST DOWN CALIFORNIA STREET FROM MASON STREET

With Scottie in pursuit, Madeleine turns right on California Street and takes a circuitous and zigzagging route from Nob Hill to Russian Hill.

SCOTTIE FOLLOWS MADELEINE DOWN CUSHMAN STREET, TRAVELING NORTH FROM CALIFORNIA STREET

CONTEMPORARY VIEW OF CUSHMAN STREET LOOKING NORTH FROM CALIFORNIA STREET

SCOTTIE FOLLOWS MADELEINE DOWN SACRAMENTO STREET, TRAVELING WEST FROM CUSHMAN STREET

SCOTTIE FOLLOWS MADELEINE DOWN TAYLOR STREET, TRAVELING NORTH FROM SACRAMENTO STREET

From California Street, Madeleine takes a right on Cushman Street immediately after passing the entrance to the Pacific Union Club at the Flood Mansion (her husband's men's club). She turns left on Sacramento Street and then right on Taylor Street. Next, she takes a

CONTEMPORARY VIEW OF TAYLOR STREET LOOKING NORTH FROM SACRAMENTO STREET

CONTEMPORARY VIEW OF CLAY STREET, LOOKING EAST FROM TAYLOR STREET

SCOTTIE FOLLOWS MADELEINE DOWN CLAY STREET, TRAVELING EAST
FROM TAYLOR STREET

right on Clay Street (the Bay Bridge is partially visible behind the buildings in the background); then left on Mason Street ("L"-shaped cable car tracks are visible at the intersection
of Mason and Washington Streets); then right on Washington Street (the Bay Bridge is
partially visible behind the buildings in the background and the "T"-shaped cable car tracks
can be seen at the intersection of Washington and Powell Streets).

SCOTTIE FOLLOWS MADELEINE DOWN MASON STREET, TRAVELING NORTH
FROM CLAY STREET

CONTEMPORARY VIEW OF MASON STREET, LOOKING NORTH
FROM CLAY STREET

SCOTTIE FOLLOWS MADELEINE DOWN WASHINGTON STREET, TRAVELING
EAST FROM MASON STREET

CONTEMPORARY VIEW OF WASHINGTON STREET, LOOKING EAST FROM MASON STREET, WITH THE BAY BRIDGE
IN THE BACKGROUND

Madeleine then turns left on Powell Street, but Powell Street is not shown after the turn. Instead, the scene becomes geographically discontinuous. Without ever showing Powell Street, there is a cut to Madeleine on Filbert Street turning left onto Leavenworth Street.

According to the studio's "Daily Production Report" from December 4, 1957, they also filmed Scottie following Madeleine from Jackson to Polk Streets. Jackson intersects with Powell Street on the next block heading north after Washington Street and then intersects with Polk Street. Polk Street intersects with Filbert Street. This footage, which was cut from the film, would explain the geographical progression, i.e., how Madeleine and Scottie get to Russian Hill from Nob Hill, a little more than a mile away from the intersection of Powell and Washington Streets.

On Leavenworth Street, there is a dramatic view west from the corner of Filbert Street of the famous Alcatraz Island in San Francisco Bay. At the time *Vertigo* was filmed, Alcatraz still served as a maximum-security prison holding some of the most dangerous convicts in the United States.

SCOTTIE FOLLOWS MADELEINE NORTH ON LEAVENWORTH STREET FROM FILBERT STREET WITH ALCATRAZ ISLAND IN THE BACKGROUND

CONTEMPORARY VIEW NORTH ON LEAVENWORTH STREET FROM FILBERT STREET WITH ALCATRAZ ISLAND IN THE BACKGROUND

SCOTTIE FOLLOWS MADELEINE TO THE CORNER OF LEAVENWORTH AND FILBERT STREETS

CONTEMPORARY VIEW OF THE CORNER OF LEAVENWORTH AND FILBERT STREETS

SCOTTIE FOLLOWS MADELEINE EAST DOWN LOMBARD STREET, TRAVELING FROM LEAVENWORTH STREET

CONTEMPORARY VIEW OF THE FRONT ENTRANCE TO THE APARTMENT BUILDING AT 900 LOMBARD STREET (CORNER OF JONES AND LOMBARD STREETS)

SCOTTIE APPROACHES MADELEINE OUTSIDE OF HIS APARTMENT AT 900 LOMBARD STREET

SCOTTIE AND MADELEINE OUTSIDE THE FRONT ENTRANCE TO SCOTTIE'S APARTMENT

CONTEMPORARY VIEW EAST DOWN LOMBARD STREET FROM LEAVENWORTH STREET

Leaving Leavenworth Street, Madeleine turns right onto Lombard Street (at the foot of the famous crooked block). Scottie, still trailing Madeleine, sees her pull over by his apartment.

Scottie watches as Madeleine leaves a thank-you note at his door. After approaching her, the two of them have a conversation, with Coit Tower framed in the background. This San Francisco landmark, situated at the top of Telegraph Hill, is visible in a number of scenes in *Vertigo*, including the opening rooftop chase sequence. It was visible from Scottie's apartment window the night before and is the landmark that allows Madeleine to find Scottie's apartment. As Scottie wryly notes, "That's the first time I've been grateful for Coit Tower."

Lillie Hitchcock Coit

LILLIE
HITCHCOCK
COIT

CONTRARY TO POPULAR BELIEF, COIT TOWER was not built at the behest of Elizabeth Wyche "Lillie" Hitchcock Coit (no relation to Alfred). Instead, it was constructed after her death in 1933 with funds she left to the city of San Francisco. Her instructions were to use one-third of her fortune to "add to the beauty of the city I have always loved." However, because she was the "patroness" of all the firemen in San Francisco—this according to Frederick J. Bowlen, Battalion Chief of the San Francisco Fire Department—and because of her standing as an honorary member of the Knickerbocker Engine Company No. 5, the tower was dedicated as a monument to Mrs. Coit as well as to the city's firefighters. While the Art Deco-style tower was not intentionally designed to portray the nozzle of a firehose, many people believe it does indeed resemble one. A second memorial to Mrs. Coit was unveiled in Washington Square on December 3, 1933; it is a sculpture featuring three firemen, one of whom is carrying a woman in his arms.

SCOTTIE AND MADELEINE TALKING, WITH A VIEW EAST OF COIT TOWER AND TELEGRAPH HILL

SKYLINE BOULEVARD (HIGHWAY 35) AS SEEN IN *VERTIGO*

With their attraction to each other growing by the moment, Scottie and Madeleine decide that "wandering" together is far more enjoyable than going it alone, and so they get into Madeleine's green Jaguar and set off on a day trip. There is a wide-angle view of the two of them driving south on Skyline Boulevard (Highway 35) near Big Basin Highway, a logical route to the redwoods south of San Francisco.

They arrive at a redwood forest; the enormous trees make the scene dark and shady, giving it a feeling of impending doom. Although the location is never identified in the film, it is frequently assumed to have been Muir Woods, about 20 miles north of San Francisco. However, the scene was actually filmed at Big Basin Redwoods, about 70 miles south of San Francisco, but fairly close to Hitchcock's weekend retreat in Scotts Valley. Several members of the cast and crew stayed at Hitchcock's ranch during the filming at Big Basin.

Big Basin is the oldest state park in California, founded in 1902. Today the park covers more than 16,000 acres with thousands of *Sequoia sempervirens*, the classic redwood tree, and miles of beautiful hiking trails. According to Auiler, much of the *Vertigo* footage appears to be filmed on what is known today as the Redwood Trail. The site may have been selected over Muir Woods because of its natural lighting. Also, Hitchcock was no doubt familiar with this location because of its proximity to his Scotts Valley property.

SCOTTIE AND MADELEINE AMONG THE REDWOODS AT BIG BASIN

SCOTTIE AND MADELEINE KISS AS WAVES CRASH IN THE BACKGROUND

MADELEINE STANDING AT CYPRESS POINT ON 17-MILE DRIVE

After departing the woods, Scottie and Madeleine walk along a rocky ocean shore, with waves breaking in the background and a twisted Monterey cypress tree standing hauntingly in the middle of the shot. Madeleine seems to want to throw herself into the ocean again but she is stopped by Scottie. The tortured kiss between Scottie and Madeleine (dressed in a flowing white coat with a shimmering black scarf) as the waves crash behind them is a dramatic Hitchcock touch.

This scene was filmed at Cypress Point—a classic Northern California coastal location on 17-Mile Drive near Carmel. The point is named after the twisted Monterey cypress trees that litter the landscape. According to Dan Auiler, the cypress tree shown in *Vertigo* was actually brought in by the film crew for optimal placement and for easy reproduction on a studio stage where close-ups were filmed. Other points of interest on the drive include the Lone Cypress Tree and the Pebble Beach Golf Course.

Vertigo's Union Square and Vicinity

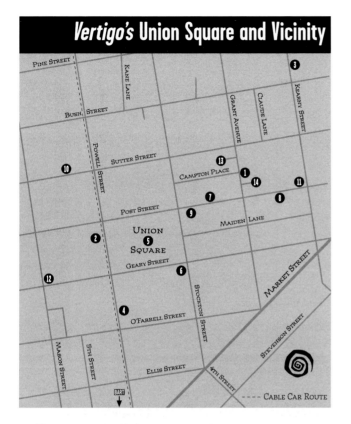

❶ Podesta Baldocchi (original location)
❷ Westin St. Francis
(the fictitious address of the "Argosy" Book Shop)
❸ Argonaut Book Shop (original location)
❹ Location from which rear projection footage was taken and
used in the "Argosy"
❺ Dewey Monument in Union Square
❻ I. Magnin department store
❼ Retail storefront and flower cart (Gump's former location)
❽ Gump's (current location)
❾ Escada (former location of Ransohoffs)
❿ Elizabeth Arden Salon (original location)
⓫ Elizabeth Arden Red Door Salon & Spa (current location)
⓬ Stage Door Theater
⓭ Tillman Place
⓮ White House Department Store and Ashburton Place

SCOTTIE WALKS THROUGH PRE-DAWN UNION SQUARE

The Death of Madeleine

The next scene is back at Midge's apartment where Midge, jealous of Madeleine, tries to humorously get Scottie's attention by painting herself into a portrait of Carlotta. Scottie is not amused and leaves her apartment looking distressed and is then shown walking through a deserted pre-dawn Union Square. Union Square, enclosed by Powell, Post, Geary, and Stockton Streets, is the heart of San Francisco's shopping and theater district. Scottie walks through the square and then crosses Stockton Street going east along Geary Street.

CONTEMPORARY VIEW OF UNION SQUARE, THE DEWEY MONUMENT AND THE ST. FRANCIS HOTEL

John White Geary donated the land used to make Union Square; the Square was named for the speeches and rallies held there in support of national unity after the Civil War. The tall column with the statue at the top is the Dewey Monument, commemorating Admiral Dewey who led the U.S. Navy to victory over Spain at Manila Bay in 1898. The column was installed in 1902.

VIEW OF UNION SQUARE LOOKING NORTHWEST, 1955

SCOTTIE AND MADELEINE DRIVING THROUGH THE ROCKY HILLSIDES
NEAR WATSONVILLE

SCOTTIE AND MADELEINE DRIVING THROUGH THE AVENUE OF TALL TREES

CONTEMPORARY VIEW OF THE AVENUE OF TALL TREES, LOOKING SOUTH

The day after the Union Square scene, Madeleine shows up at Scottie's apartment haunted by the dreams she had the night before. Scottie drives her to San Juan Bautista in an attempt to help her overcome her anxiety by visiting the place that appeared in her dreams. On the way there, Scottie and Madeleine drive past a rocky hillside. According to studio records, this scene was filmed along Highway 1 near Watsonville, which is only about 15 miles from San Juan Bautista. Watsonville would not have been on the most direct route from San Francisco to San Juan Bautista, which is straight down Highway 101, but it is very scenic.

Just prior to arriving at San Juan Bautista, Madeleine and Scottie drive through the distinctive grove of eucalyptus trees known as the Avenue of Tall Trees, on Highway 101. However, in another slight Hollywood distortion of geography, the grove is actually immediately south of the cutoff to San Juan Bautista off Highway 101, and you do not pass through it coming from San Francisco to San Juan Bautista.

The small town of San Juan Bautista, founded in 1797, is 91 miles south of San Francisco off Highway 101. The church at San Juan Bautista is the largest of the 21 mission churches in California.

The mission grounds are virtually unchanged from the time when *Vertigo* was filmed. The mission transports the visitor back hundreds of years to pre–Gold Rush Spanish California. The grounds are a state park with a historic plaza, church, white adobe arches, Plaza Stables, Plaza Hall, Plaza Hotel, and other buildings.

CLOISTERS, CHURCH, AND BELL TOWER AT MISSION SAN JUAN BAUTISTA AS SEEN IN *VERTIGO*. THE BELL TOWER WAS ADDED TO THE SCENE USING SPECIAL EFFECTS.

KIM NOVAK IN FRONT OF CHURCH CLOISTERS AT MISSION SAN JUAN BAUTISTA DURING THE FILMING OF *VERTIGO*

CONTEMPORARY VIEW OF THE CLOISTERS AT MISSION SAN JUAN BAUTISTA

THE CLOISTERS AT MISSION SAN JUAN BAUTISTA AS SEEN IN *VERTIGO*

The opening shot of the sequence starts with a view down the white adobe arches. The camera then pans to the right and reveals the Plaza, with the Plaza Hall and Stables. These arches—also known as cloisters—are the exterior of the monastery wing of the mission church building. The construction of the church began in 1803 and the building has been in continuous use since 1812. It is still owned and run by the Catholic Church. Along the northeast wall of the church there is an old cemetery where thousands of local Native Americans and Spanish Californians are buried. It is easy to imagine Carlotta Valdes having ancestors buried there.

CONTEMPORARY VIEW DOWN THE CLOISTERS AT MISSION SAN JUAN BAUTISTA

VIEW THROUGH THE CLOISTERS TOWARD THE PLAZA HALL AND STABLES AT MISSION SAN JUAN BAUTISTA AS SEEN IN *VERTIGO*

CONTEMPORARY VIEW THROUGH THE CLOISTERS TOWARD THE PLAZA HALL AND STABLES AT MISSION SAN JUAN BAUTISTA

Finally, the camera focuses in on the Plaza Stables. The Stables, full of plastic horses and old wagons, is where Scottie and Madeleine speak just before she rushes across the plaza, into the church, and to the top of the bell tower. The Stables were built in 1861 to accommodate the extensive stagecoach traffic passing through San Juan Bautista, a major stop on the Coast Line Stage Company's San Francisco-to-Los Angeles route. A blacksmith's shop with tools is located behind the Stables. Today the Stables look much the same as they did when *Vertigo* was filmed, with many of the same props inside.

After the scene in the Stables, Madeleine runs into the plaza, followed by Scottie. She tells him to let her go and to remember that she loves him. She then pulls away and dashes into the church.

SCOTTIE AND MADELEINE IN THE PLAZA STABLES AT MISSION SAN JUAN BAUTISTA

CONTEMPORARY VIEW OF THE PLAZA STABLES AT MISSION SAN JUAN BAUTISTA

CONTEMPORARY VIEW OF THE PLAZA STABLES WITH THE HORSE AND WAGON USED IN *VERTIGO*

ALFRED HITCHCOCK AND KIM NOVAK DURING THE FILMING AT
MISSION SAN JUAN BAUTISTA

SCOTTIE TRIES TO PREVENT MADELEINE FROM RUNNING AWAY IN THE
PLAZA AT MISSION SAN JUAN BAUTISTA

There is then a dramatic looming view of the bell tower from below as Scottie looks up and realizes Madeleine's intent. The tower did not exist at the time the movie was filmed and was added to the scene using special effects. Hitchcock had seen the original tower before it was removed in 1949 due to dry rot. Reportedly, he was not very pleased to find it gone when he came to film in 1957. Today, there is a new bell tower that was built in 1976. The new tower is short and built on the right side of the church compared to the original taller tower that was built on the left side of the church.

THE CHURCH BELL TOWER AS SEEN IN *VERTIGO*. THE TOWER WAS ADDED USING SPECIAL EFFECTS.

ANOTHER VIEW OF THE CHURCH AND BELL TOWER AS SEEN IN *VERTIGO*. NOTE: THE TOWER IS TO THE LEFT OF THE CHURCH.

CONTEMPORARY VIEW OF THE CHURCH WITH THE BELL TOWER ON THE RIGHT SIDE. THE CURRENT BELL TOWER IS SMALLER THAN THE ORIGINAL AND WAS BUILT AFTER *VERTIGO* WAS FILMED.

CONTEMPORARY VIEW OF THE LEFT SIDE OF THE CHURCH. NOTE THE ABSENCE OF THE BELL TOWER SHOWN IN *VERTIGO*.

VIEW OF THE CHURCH AT MISSION SAN JUAN BAUTISTA WITH DAMAGED BELL TOWER CIRCA 1900. THE ORIGINAL BELL TOWER LOST THE TOP OF ITS CONICAL SPIRE IN A HEAVY WINDSTORM IN 1897. THE TOP OF THIS TOWER WAS REPLASTERED IN 1923 AND THE TOWER WAS TORN DOWN IN 1949 DUE TO DRY ROT.

Scottie hurries into the church, looks to the right at an arched doorway, then left where he sees a staircase. He realizes Madeleine has already headed up to the tower. The arched doorway shown to the right is actually a view of the church looking left if you are facing the pulpit from the entrance—the opposite direction from what the movie implies. The view shown in the film when Scottie looks left did not exist in the church because the church did not have the bell tower shown in the movie. The arched doorway with stairs shown in *Vertigo* was filmed on a studio set. Hitchcock spliced shots of the church's actual interior with a studio set to give the scene an authentic feel.

CONTEMPORARY VIEW OF THE INTERIOR OF THE CHURCH AND PULPIT AT MISSION SAN JUAN BAUTISTA

INTERIOR OF THE CHURCH AND PULPIT AT MISSION SAN JUAN BAUTISTA
AS SEEN IN *VERTIGO*

CONTEMPORARY VIEW OF THE ARCHED DOOR LOOKING LEFT FROM THE FRONT ENTRANCE IN THE MISSION CHURCH

The footage of Scottie and Madeleine climbing the bell tower was filmed on a studio stage. When Scottie has almost reached the top, straining under the effects of his vertigo, he sees Madeleine fall past the window in an apparent suicidal leap to her death.

VIEW OF THE ARCHED DOORWAY IN THE MISSION CHURCH WHEN SCOTTIE LOOKS TO THE RIGHT. THIS ACTUALLY EXISTS IN THE CHURCH WHEN LOOKING LEFT.

VIEW OF THE ARCHED DOORWAY WITH THE BELL TOWER STAIRS WHEN SCOTTIE LOOKS TO THE LEFT. THIS WAS FILMED ON A STUDIO SET AND DOES NOT EXIST IN THE CHURCH.

CONTEMPORARY VIEW OF THE EXTERIOR OF PLAZA HALL

EXTERIOR OF PLAZA HALL AS SEEN IN *VERTIGO*

THE INQUEST INTO MADELEINE'S DEATH

The next sequence again opens with a view from the cloisters at San Juan Bautista, only this time as the camera pans around the plaza it stops at Plaza Hall, a two-story wooden building. There is an inquest into Madeleine's death going on. According to studio records, the scene was filmed in a Hollywood studio. However, the set was a finely detailed re-creation of the actual room, with its large rectangular windows and second-floor views.

Plaza Hall was built in 1868. The first floor was used as a private residence for the family of Angelo Zanetta, the man who built and ran the Plaza Hotel. The upper floor was used as a public meeting space for dances, political rallies, temperance groups, and civic associations.

Members of the cast of *Vertigo* ate at La Casa Rosa Mexican restaurant during the location filming, and Kim Novak has returned several times since then. The restaurant has a small collection of memorabilia from the film. During the week of filming in San Juan Bautista, Kim Novak and the film crew stayed at the now defunct Watsonville Register Hotel. According to Dan Auiler, Hitchcock, James Stewart, and key members of the production team such as Associate Producer Herbert Coleman and Script Supervisor Peggy Robertson stayed at Hitchcock's Scotts Valley home during the filming in San Juan Bautista.

Scottie's Breakdown

While trying to locate Madeleine's small rectangular gravestone, Scottie passes a distinctive tall white marble column with a small cross on top. This cross-topped grave marker was the main clue for identifying the location of this scene.

This is one of the most difficult and mysterious locations to track down from *Vertigo*, and it has not been identified in any previous writings on the movie. According to studio correspondence, the graveyard was located in San Mateo, but it was not specified whether it was the City or County of San Mateo. In San Mateo County, the city of Colma, located south of San Francisco, has 16 cemeteries. Colma is known as the "City of the Dead" because more people are buried in the city than live there. Because of the high land values in San Francisco, most graves there were disinterred and moved to Colma after 1901. To this day, Colma remains the most common place for San Franciscans to be put to rest, making it a likely candidate for the *Vertigo* scene.

In the cemetery scene, it is noteworthy that the tall cross-topped marker is the only gravestone with a clearly visible cross. Because Catholic cemeteries tend to be full of tombstones with crosses, it can be concluded that Madeleine's grave was unlikely to be in a Catholic cemetery, despite her Spanish heritage.

With the reasonable assumption that the scene was therefore filmed in a nonsectarian cemetery with large, old grave markers, the choices narrow down considerably. The only grave marker resembling the one in *Vertigo* is found in the Cypress Lawn Memorial Park (1370 El Camino Real) in Colma. It is a 19th-century monument in Section I. The vegetation (a variety of trees, including some palms) and the spacing of the nearby tombstones fit the scene from the film.

The tall grave marker with the cross on top is for Julia Hubbard (d. 1871), her husband James McMillian Shafter, and other family members. As a side note, the *Vertigo* site is located across the road from the grave of Steve Silver, the creator of San Francisco's famous musical spoof of pop culture, *Beach Blanket Babylon,* which plays at Club Fugazi in North Beach and has been running for more than 25 years.

CONTEMPORARY VIEW OF THE TALL GRAVE MARKER WITH A CROSS ON TOP IN CYPRESS LAWN CEMETERY IN COLMA, CALIFORNIA

CONTEMPORARY VIEW OF DOWNTOWN SAN FRANCISCO LOOKING EAST DOWN CALIFORNIA STREET FROM THE MARK HOPKINS HOTEL

VIEW OF DOWNTOWN SAN FRANCISCO LOOKING EAST DOWN CALIFORNIA STREET FROM THE MARK HOPKINS HOTEL AS SEEN IN VERTIGO

While several films have been shot at this cemetery, including *Harold and Maude*, we did not find records or history confirming *Vertigo* was shot there. Famous gravesites at Cypress Lawn include: Lillie Hitchcock Coit, of Coit Tower fame; William Randolph Hearst, publishing giant and founder of the *San Francisco Examiner*; Charles De Young, founder of the *San Francisco Chronicle*; and Frank J. "Lefty" O'Doul, National league batting champ and manager of the San Francisco Seals baseball team.

After Scottie visits the cemetery, there is a gloomy nighttime shot of fog-filled downtown San Francisco. There are a number of large skyscrapers partially illuminated by flashing signs and a span of the Bay Bridge faintly visible in the background.

The view is looking east down California Street from Nob Hill, showing the downtown skyscrapers of Montgomery Street. The old Bank of America building at 315 Montgomery Street (on the northeast corner of Pine and Montgomery) and the Russ Building at 235 Montgomery Street (on the southeast corner of Pine and Montgomery) are seen in the fog. The 31-story Russ Building, built in 1926, was the tallest building in San Francisco when it opened.

VIEW OF THE SOUTHERN PACIFIC BUILDING WITH "SP" SIGN ON MARKET STREET AT THE EMBARCADERO, 1955

The Southern Pacific Building at 65 Market Street near the corner of the Embarcadero is lit up at the end of the shot, with the large initials "SP" in red and then white lights on a huge sign. We were not able to conclusively identify two other neon signs shown in the shot, but they may include the Mobil Gas and the Sheraton Palace Hotel signs near the foot of Market Street. The "SP" sign was also visible in the opening sequence of the film.

Today, both the Bank of America and the Russ Buildings still stand, but from Nob Hill the view of the Bank of America Building is totally blocked by the new headquarters of Bank of America, the 52-story building at 555 California Street which was built in 1969. The Southern Pacific Building also remains at the foot of Market Street, but the sign is long gone and the railroad, now part of the Union Pacific, is no longer headquartered there.

VIEW OF DOWNTOWN SAN FRANCISCO LOOKING EAST DOWN CALIFORNIA STREET FROM THE MARK HOPKINS HOTEL. THIS OLDER PHOTO FROM 1947 FEATURES THE SAME SKYSCRAPERS SHOWN IN THE VERTIGO NIGHTTIME SHOT.

This brief scene is ominously foreboding as it foreshadows Scottie's breakdown. The shot was taken from the Mark Hopkins Hotel, across California Street from the Fairmont Hotel—which was where the opening shots of downtown San Francisco (used as background footage for the rooftop chase sequence) were filmed. We believe this view of downtown San Francisco was shot from the Mark Hopkins as opposed to the Fairmont because it was taken from a location on the south side of California Street (i.e., California Street is to the left of where the camera was positioned). Note: The shot from Vertigo is almost identical to the historical photograph—taken from the Mark Hopkins Hotel in the 1940s—featured above.

After the footage of downtown San Francisco, Scottie is shown in bed twisting and turning in an agonizing nightmare that apparently leads to his breakdown. There is a brief exterior shot of a hospital and a sequence with Scottie inside recovering.

The exterior of the hospital was filmed at St. Joseph's Hospital (351-355 Buena Vista Avenue East). The hospital exterior is identifiable by the distinctive view of San Francisco in the background, the giant doorway, and the staggered wide horizontal stripes decorating the exterior of the salmon-colored building. The Catholic hospital closed and the building was converted into a condominium complex in the early 1980s. This huge structure sits on top of Park Hill and is visible from many parts of the city. According to studio correspondence, Hitchcock also considered shooting this scene at the University of California hospital located in the Sutro Heights neighborhood. The interior hospital scenes were filmed on a studio set in Southern California.

EXTERIOR OF ST. JOSEPH'S HOSPITAL AS SEEN IN VERTIGO

EXTERIOR OF ST. JOSEPH'S HOSPITAL ON BUENA VISTA AVENUE, 1929

CONTEMPORARY VIEW OF THE EXTERIOR OF THE FORMER ST. JOSEPH'S HOSPITAL, NOW A CONDOMINIUM COMPLEX

VIEW OF SAN FRANCISCO FROM TWIN PEAKS AS SEEN IN *VERTIGO*

CONTEMPORARY VIEW OF SAN FRANCISCO FROM TWIN PEAKS

Scottie's recovery from a fog-filled world of mental illness and depression is signaled in *Vertigo* by a brief scene that shows a 180-degree-plus pan across San Francisco from high above. According to studio records, this shot was taken from the top of Twin Peaks, on Twin Peaks Boulevard at the top of Market Street. Being the highest point in San Francisco, it has sweeping, unobstructed views of the city. Not every day is as sunny as it was in the scene. More often, when the fog rolls in, the city seems to disappear under a blanket of gray, and visibility on Twin Peaks is reduced to almost zero.

SCOTTIE STANDING IN FRONT OF THE FAIRMONT AND MARK HOPKINS HOTELS ON MASON NEAR SACRAMENTO STREET

SCOTTIE WITH A WOMAN HE HAS MISTAKEN FOR MADELEINE, LOOKING NORTH ON MASON STREET FROM THE BROCKLEBANK

The Introduction of Judy Barton

After his release from the hospital, Scottie is shown wandering morosely around San Francisco: at the Brockle-bank, Ernie's, the Palace of the Legion of Honor, and Podesta Baldocchi, trying to conjure Madeleine back to life.

CONTEMPORARY VIEW OF THE FAIRMONT AND MARK HOPKINS HOTELS FROM MASON NEAR SACRAMENTO STREET

CONTEMPORARY VIEW NORTH ON MASON STREET FROM THE BROCKLEBANK

JUDY BARTON AND FRIENDS WALKING NORTH ON GRANT AVENUE, NEAR PODESTA, WITH POST STREET BEHIND THEM

SCOTTIE WALKING NORTH ON GRANT AVENUE, NEAR PODESTA, TOWARD SUTTER STREET

CONTEMPORARY VIEW SOUTH ON GRANT AVENUE TOWARD POST STREET

CONTEMPORARY VIEW NORTH ON GRANT AVENUE TOWARD SUTTER STREET

The sequence begins in front of the Brocklebank with a view of the Fairmont and Mark Hopkins Hotels. There is also a view north down Mason Street from the Brocklebank toward Fisherman's Wharf showing a large apartment building at 1750 Taylor Street. Later in the sequence, Scottie sees a women who reminds him of Madeleine in front of Podesta. She is walking north on Grant Avenue, chatting with a group of young women who appear to be heading home from their jobs downtown. Later in the film, we learn this is Judy Barton, a second role played by Kim Novak. Judy turns west on Sutter Street followed by Scottie.

EXTERIOR OF THE EMPIRE HOTEL AS SEEN IN *VERTIGO*

They arrive at the Empire Hotel, where Judy lives. The hotel is a somewhat seedy place for a single young woman to be residing. As Judy walks in the hotel's front door, there is a good shot of the huge half-oval windows on the ground level of the hotel.

The Empire Hotel, at 940 Sutter Street (between Hyde and Leavenworth Streets), has been renamed the York Hotel and renovated to its early splendor. The giant green neon "Empire" sign is gone, but the name "Empire" is still stamped above the Plush Room bar entrance. During Prohibition the bar was a notorious speakeasy.

The neighborhood where the York is located, at the edge of Nob Hill near the Tenderloin Red Light District, has a mixture of Nob Hill grandeur and Tenderloin decay. The area around Sutter Street still has many older hotels, some of them slightly seedy, providing a flavor for the atmosphere captured by Hitchcock's film. The Commodore Hotel (at 825 Sutter Street) and the Carleton Hotel (at Sutter Street between Hyde and Larken Streets) retain giant neon signs that are similar to the Empire Hotel's dramatic green neon sign.

CONTEMPORARY VIEW OF THE EXTERIOR OF THE YORK HOTEL

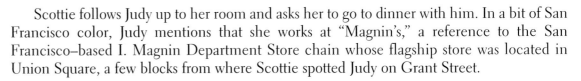

Scottie follows Judy up to her room and asks her to go to dinner with him. In a bit of San Francisco color, Judy mentions that she works at "Magnin's," a reference to the San Francisco–based I. Magnin Department Store chain whose flagship store was located in Union Square, a few blocks from where Scottie spotted Judy on Grant Street.

JUDY SITTING AT HER DESK INSIDE THE EMPIRE HOTEL (ACTUALLY A STUDIO SET)

Although no filming was actually done in the hotel's interior, York Hotel management points out that rooms 501 and 502 were used as models for the *Vertigo* studio set. Today, these rooms are known as the *"Vertigo* rooms," and retain the same look as shown in the film.

CONTEMPORARY VIEW OF ROOM 502 IN THE YORK HOTEL

CONTEMPORARY VIEW OF THE EXTERIOR OF THE COMMODORE HOTEL WITH NEON SIGN

SCOTTIE AND JUDY WALKING IN FRONT OF THE DOME AT THE PALACE OF FINE ARTS

The Second Romance

Judy reluctantly accepts Scottie's invitation to dinner. Before they head off to Ernie's, Judy reveals to the audience that she is the woman with whom Scottie fell in love. Judy was impersonating Madeleine as part of a plot by Elster to murder the real Madeleine Elster, who was thrown off the bell tower at San Juan Bautista.

Scottie and Judy dine at Ernie's and return to the Empire Hotel where Judy is shown bathed in the green neon light from the hotel's sign. The scene cuts to the new couple strolling down the street on a sunny day at the romantic Palace of Fine Arts, passing the lovely lagoon where other couples are lounging on the grass.

The scene was filmed along Baker Street near Marina Boulevard where the Palace is located. The structure, designed by architect Bernard R. Maybeck to resemble a Roman ruin, was originally constructed for the Panama-Pacific Exhibition in 1915 as a temporary plaster building. It was rebuilt as a permanent concrete structure in 1966. This replica is the only architectural remnant from the Exhibition.

During their walk by the Palace, there is a view south down Baker Street toward Geary Street. This is a typical block in San Francisco's famous Marina District and looks much the same today as when *Vertigo* was filmed.

CONTEMPORARY VIEW OF THE DOME AT THE PALACE OF FINE ARTS

SCOTTIE AND JUDY WALKING NORTH DOWN BAKER STREET TOWARD GEARY STREET

CONTEMPORARY VIEW SOUTH DOWN BAKER STREET TOWARD GEARY STREET

Later, the couple is briefly shown waltzing in an ornate ballroom. According to studio records, the ballroom in which they danced was intended to replicate the Venetian Room at the elegant Fairmont Hotel. The scene was actually shot on a studio stage. Again Hitchcock took great pains to create a realistic portrayal of the Venetian Room's ornate decor, even using actual ashtrays from the Fairmont Hotel on the studio set to maintain a realistic atmosphere during the filming of this scene.

SCOTTIE AND JUDY DANCING IN A BALLROOM

CONTEMPORARY VIEW OF THE VENETIAN ROOM AT THE FAIRMONT HOTEL

The Venetian Room at the Fairmont Hotel

THE FAIRMONT IS ONE OF SAN FRANCISCO'S WORLD-CLASS HOTELS. LOCATED ATOP NOB HILL at 950 Mason Street, it was a favorite of Hitchcock's. The cast and crew of *Vertigo* stayed at the hotel during location filming in San Francisco and Hitchcock returned many times, including during the publicity tour surrounding the opening of *The Birds*. Kim Novak also stayed there when she returned to San Francisco for the re-release of *Vertigo* in 1996. This five-star landmark is a byword for luxury and grandeur, and is one of San Francisco's best-known and most historically significant hotels. The hotel had been almost completed when the 1906 earthquake and fire largely destroyed it. It was the first hotel reconstructed after the earthquake and its opening symbolized San Francisco's ability to rebuild from the devastation of 1906.

THE FAIRMONT HOTEL, 1957

The Venetian Room itself has a colorful history. In 1947 the room was redecorated by Dorothy Draper and began to serve as a supper and dancing club. The club subsequently became one of the premier venues for ballroom dancing in San Francisco. In 1958, during a *Vertigo* preview party for journalists, Hitchcock hosted an evening of entertainment there with Dorothy Shay, a popular singer of the time. The room remains today, but is no longer regularly used as a supper club and ballroom.

During its storied tenure as a performance venue, the room hosted such legendary entertainers as Ella Fitzgerald, Frank Sinatra, Milton Berle, Marlene Dietrich, B.B. King, and Tony Bennett. Bennett first sang his signature song "I Left My Heart in San Francisco" in the Venetian Room. The singer reportedly buried a Baccarat red crystal heart in a time capsule beneath the room's floor to commemorate the event.

Many of the Fairmont's public spaces, including the lobby and Venetian Room, were restored to their original decor in 1999. Today, the Venetian Room—which is used for business meetings, weddings, and other social functions—has many of its original decorative features, including 24-foot-tall ceilings, elaborate gold leaf wall ornamentation, and elegant wall sconces.

KAY THOMPSON PERFORMING IN THE VENETIAN ROOM AT THE FAIRMONT HOTEL, 1954

CONTEMPORARY VIEW OF THE FLOWER STAND IN FRONT OF 250 POST STREET (FORMERLY GUMP'S)

SCOTTIE AND JUDY WALKING TOWARD A FLOWER STAND
IN FRONT OF GUMP'S

After the scene at the Venetian Room, Scottie buys Judy a bouquet of flowers at a stand located in front of Gump's, the San Francisco art and housewares store. After buying the flowers, Scottie leads Judy across Post Street to Ransohoffs Department Store where he begins his obsessive attempt to turn Judy into Madeleine. According to studio records, in order to maintain some sense of anonymity in busy Union Square, the flower stand scene was filmed using a hidden camera inside a specially constructed box built along the wall that separated Gump's from its next door neighbor, the fur clothier Schneider's.

Gump's began as a holiday gift store in the 1840s and became known as an exclusive luxury goods store specializing in home furnishings, jewelry, and Asian antiques. In an interesting side note, Alfred Hitchcock personally shopped at Gump's and gave Tippi Hedren a gift from the store (see the chapter on *The Birds* for more details).

CONTEMPORARY VIEW OF THE OLD GUMP'S BUILDING. THE LOCATION IS NOW HOME TO ALFRED DUNHILL AND EDDIE BAUER, BUT STILL FEATURES A FLOWER STAND IN FRONT OF THE STORE.

ORIGINAL GUMP'S STORE AT 250 POST STREET WITH FLOWER STAND, DATE UNKNOWN

When *Vertigo* was filmed, Gump's was located at 250 Post Street, between Stockton and Grant Streets in a beautiful pre-1906 building. In 1995, the store moved out of 250 Post Street to a new location one block away at 135 Post Street between Grant and Kearny Streets. The new Gump's includes touches from the original store, such as the big 18th-century red and gold Buddha from Tibet, but has been updated and modernized to reflect contemporary tastes. Today, the original building at 250 Post Street is home to the Alfred Dunhill and Eddie Bauer stores. However, one thing remains the same: There is still a flower cart regularly situated in front of the building.

A.P. Giannini and San Francisco's Flower Shops

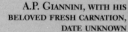

A.P. GIANNINI, WITH HIS
BELOVED FRESH CARNATION,
DATE UNKNOWN

BY INCLUDING THE FLOWER STAND SCENE IN *Vertigo*, Hitchcock touched on an interesting bit of San Francisco history: There is an abundance of flower stands adorning the streets of San Francisco. According to local lore, the presence of the stands can be traced directly back to A.P. Giannini, founder of the Bank of Italy (later the Bank of America). In 1918, Giannini requested a local florist provide him with a fresh carnation daily to wear in his buttonhole. When the florist tried to get a permit for setting up an outdoor flower stand in the financial district, the city refused. After intervention by the powerful Giannini, flower stands were permitted to operate in San Francisco, and they have been a downtown fixture ever since.

During the scene at the flower stand, the exterior of Ransohoffs Department Store, including the sign above its entrance, is visible in the background. Ransohoffs, an upscale women's clothing store, was located at 259 Post Street between Stockton Street and Grant Avenue. The store closed in 1976, and its space is now occupied by Escada, an Italian clothing designer. Like Ransohoffs, Escada has an elegant white décor and an upper floor that is reached by a curving central staircase. The brief view of the letters "nsohoffs" as Scottie and Judy walk through the entrance of the store was actually filmed on a studio set.

SCOTTIE AND JUDY APPROACH RANSOHOFFS, ACROSS THE STREET FROM
THE FLOWER STAND IN FRONT OF GUMP'S

CONTEMPORARY VIEW OF ESCADA (FORMERLY RANSOHOFFS) ACROSS THE STREET FROM
THE FLOWER CART AT 250 POST STREET

EXTERIOR OF RANSOHOFFS, 1930

EXTERIOR OF THE ENTRANCE TO RANSOHOFFS, AS RE-CREATED ON A STUDIO SET

EXTERIOR OF RANSOHOFFS DURING A WAR BOND DRIVE, 1943

CONTEMPORARY VIEW OF ESCADA (FORMERLY RANSOHOFFS)

For customers who could afford it, Ransohoffs offered incredibly attentive, individualized service in elegant surroundings and a formal atmosphere. The store had different clothing departments, such as shoes, dresses, jackets, etc., each with its own salon where staff members personally modeled the merchandise for customers. The interior shots in *Vertigo* were filmed on a studio set, but Hitchcock's crew spent three days taking measurements and copying the designs of the Ransohoffs dress and shoe salons, even noting the store's lighting, according to Donald Spoto. The décor shown in the interior photograph of a Ransohoffs salon (including colors, light fixtures, and furniture) is remarkably similar to the studio set shown in the *Vertigo* scenes.

SCOTTIE AND JUDY ON A STUDIO SET MODELED AFTER THE DRESS SALON
AT RANSOHOFFS

A GROUP OF WOMEN IN RANSOHOFFS SALON. THIS SALON IS VERY SIMILAR TO THE STUDIO SET OF THE
DRESS SALON IN *VERTIGO*, CIRCA 1930

ELIZABETH ARDEN PUTTING MAKEUP ON A CUSTOMER IN THE SAN FRANCISCO STORE, 1951

SCOTTIE SPEAKS TO A STYLIST ON A SET RE-CREATING THE INTERIOR OF
ELIZABETH ARDEN'S SALON

Scottie and Judy return to Scottie's apartment. They leave again to take Judy to a fashionable salon to have her hair dyed blond and styled the way Madeleine's was. After telling the stylist what he wants Judy to look like, Scottie leaves.

Studio records confirm this set was intended to replicate the Elizabeth Arden Salon. In the late 1950s, Elizabeth Arden was an extremely popular figure, appearing regularly in the press. Her salons represented upscale urban sophistication and pampering, and catered to the established crowd, a perfect fit for re-creating a figure like Madeleine Elster.

At the time *Vertigo* was filmed, the salon was located at 550 Sutter Street (between Powell and Mason) in a building set back from the street behind a wrought-iron fence. Today, this building houses an art gallery. In 1970 the salon moved to 230 Post Street and then closed in 1991. Elizabeth Arden reopened a salon in San Francisco in 1998 at 126 Post Street at the corner of Kearny Street. The new salon has Arden's trademarked "red door" at the front entrance.

CONTEMPORARY VIEW OF THE EXTERIOR OF THE ELIZABETH ARDEN SALON AT 126 POST STREET

SCOTTIE FORCES JUDY TO CLIMB UP THE STAIRS . . .

After Judy is transformed again into Madeleine, she returns to her room at the Empire Hotel where Scottie is anxiously waiting. In a famous and technically brilliant scene, Scottie and Judy kiss as the camera circles them in a 360-degree arc with the Empire Hotel fading into the San Juan Bautista Plaza Stables.

Afterwards, Judy unintentionally reveals to Scottie that she actually was the woman he fell in love with when she puts on the family heirloom locket she wore during the first part of the movie, when she was pretending to be Madeleine Elster. Scottie does not tell Judy he knows the secret.

Scottie sullenly drives Judy along the same highway shown earlier in the film during his original trip with Madeleine to San Juan Bautista. When they pass the Avenue of Tall Trees, an increasingly uncomfortable Judy realizes they are definitely headed back to San Juan Bautista. After they arrive, Scottie tells Judy about his previous trip there with Madeleine. Scottie explains he needs to go back to the past one more time. He cruelly forces Judy to climb up the stairs to the church bell tower. Near the top, in a state of anger, Scottie confronts Judy with his deduction that she had impersonated the real Madeleine Elster and participated with Gavin Elster in a plot to murder Madeleine. Judy is terrified as Scottie drags her to the top of the tower.

WHILE FIGHTING THROUGH HIS ACROPHOBIA.

HE DRAGS JUDY TO THE TOP OF THE TOWER . . .

AND CONFRONTS HER WITH THE TRUTH ABOUT ELSTER AND
THE REAL MADELEINE . . .

Judy begs Scottie to take her back and the two kiss near the ledge of the tower. A dark shadowy figure climbs up to the bell platform. Judy sees the ghost-like woman and, lurching backward in fear, falls off the tower. The figure is a nun who has come to investigate the voices she heard. Scottie has tragically lost his love for the second time. The film concludes with the nun ringing the Mission's church bells and a devastated Scottie staring down off the tower.

According to Dan Auiler, in an interesting side note, the soundtrack of the bells ringing at the end of the film was actually from an authentic California mission. It was a recording of the three bells at the Mission Dolores in San Francisco which was made during the filming of the graveyard sequence. And so ends Hitchcock's tortured valentine to "The City."

ONLY TO SEE JUDY FALL TO HER DEATH.

BODEGA BAY
(See BODEGA BAY
Detail Maps, Page 180)

• Bodega

● Santa Rosa

Valley Ford

Petaluma

1

101

San Francisco ★

"The city dump" ■

80

580

880

N

17

Scotts Valley

1

101

Santa Cruz ● • Capitola

The Birds' Bay Area

cHApTeR ThrEE

The Birds

A Flight of Terror Along the Remote Sonoma Coast

"How do you like our little hamlet? . . . Well, I suppose it doesn't offer much to a casual visitor unless you're thrilled by a collection of shacks on a hillside."

— ANNIE HAYWORTH IN *THE BIRDS*

The Birds (1963) is an ambiguous, multi-faceted film. On the one hand, it is a psychological drama about human frailty and personal growth in the face of powerful natural forces. On the other hand, it is a mix of science fiction, horror, and fantasy—a precursor to the Academy Award–winning *Jaws*. The setting for the movie is a recurring theme in Hitchcock's work: a small provincial town that is only a short drive from the big city, but seems to be a world away.

The Birds begins on the streets of 1960's San Francisco, before moving north along the rugged California coast to Bodega Bay and the hamlet of Bodega in Sonoma County.

The movie was filmed and edited between 1961 and 1963, with the location filming done in the spring and summer of 1962. As always, Hitchcock and his team paid very close attention to the area's geography, locations, actual businesses, and flavor to give the film a rich, authentic feel. As Hitchcock explained to Truffaut: "You know, there's a lot of detail in this movie; it's absolutely essential because these little nuances enrich the overall impact and strengthen the picture." He did modify one important aspect of local geography: He combined various locations spread around the Bodega Bay region with studio footage into a single compressed "downtown" Bodega Bay which did not actually exist.

In an interview with *Cinema* magazine, reprinted in *Hitchcock on Hitchcock*, the director says that he visited Bodega Bay before the movie's script was even written. Based on the geography of the bay discovered on this visit, Hitchcock developed the scene where Melanie takes the boat to the Brenners' house. Before finalizing the script, Hitchcock even sent an advance team to photograph local residents and school children so the cast's wardrobes would accurately reflect how residents dressed.

"In order to get the characters right, I had every inhabitant of Bodega Bay—man, woman, and child—photographed for the costume department." The Bodega Bay Historical Society still has copies of many of these photos.

In addition to San Francisco and Bodega Bay, *The Birds* has wider references to Northern California, including Santa Rosa, Sebastopol, and Santa Cruz. The film fits into Hitchcock's pattern of using Northern California venues for inspiration, plot setting, and filming location.

Tippi Hedren plays wealthy young socialite Melanie Daniels. She meets attorney Mitch Brenner, played by Rod Taylor, in a San Francisco pet store. The cheeky Melanie drives up to the Brenner family home in Bodega Bay to play a practical joke on Mitch. In Bodega Bay, she gets caught up in a series of increasingly violent and dangerous bird attacks of unknown origin. Ultimately, she and the Brenners barely escape with their lives.

HITCHCOCK ON TIDES PIER IN BODEGA BAY, 1962

A CABLE CAR IN UNION SQUARE PASSES BY MELANIE

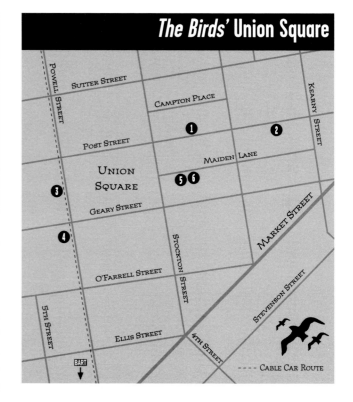

The Birds' Union Square

❶ Gump's (location at the time of the filming)

❷ Gump's (current location)

❸ Westin St. Francis Hotel

❹ "Davidson's Pet Shop" (fictitious location)

❺ Formerly Robison's House of Pets (location at the time of filming — currently Jil Sander boutique)

❻ Formerly Robison's House of Pets (currently Marc Jacobs)

A Chance Meeting in a San Francisco Pet Shop

The Birds opens with a shot of a San Francisco cable car, a symbol of "The City," and the unmistakable clanging of a cable car bell. After the cable car passes by, there is a wide-angle shot of a bustling urban scene—San Francisco's busy and fashionable Union Square. There is a camera pan of the western side of the square showing its palm trees and landscaping, prominently featuring the Dewey Monument, which stands proudly in the middle of the square.

The audience is soon introduced to Melanie Daniels, a well-dressed, attractive young woman. She is shown walking west on Geary Street across Powell Street, and then turning south on Powell. Before entering Davidson's Pet Store on the southwest corner of the intersection, she passes by a bus stop featuring a poster advertising San Francisco. The film crew modified the corner slightly for the filming, removing a newspaper vendor's booth.

UNION SQUARE, 1955

HITCHCOCK MAKES HIS CAMEO WITH HIS SEALYHAM TERRIERS GEOFFREY AND
STANLEY IN FRONT OF DAVIDSON'S PET SHOP

During the walk, Melanie is whistled at and turns to smile and wave at her admirer. This sequence is a re-creation of the role Tippi Hedren played in a diet drink TV commercial from which Hitchcock "discovered" her.

Just before Melanie enters the pet store, there are several more cable car bell rings. It is at this moment that Hitchcock makes his cameo, walking out of the pet shop and turning south on Powell Street with his beloved Sealyham terriers, Geoffrey and Stanley. At this point in his career, Hitchcock tried to make his cameos early in his films so the audience would not be distracted waiting to see the signature appearance for which he was known.

Hitchcock opened the film in San Francisco on a typical day with people walking the streets, working, and shopping in order to create a sense of normal human activity—a normalcy he would shatter with the forthcoming bird attacks.

Because Hitchcock drew such large crowds when he was in San Francisco, he directed this particular scene while hidden in a studio truck that was disguised as a furniture van. The use of this hidden camera was similar to a technique Hitchcock used in *Vertigo* to film near crowded Union Square. In that film, Hitchcock disguised a camera in the wall of a store next door to Gump's to film the scene where Scottie buys Judy flowers from a curbside florist cart. The *Vertigo* scene was filmed on Post Street a couple of blocks away from the location of the pet store in *The Birds*.

CONTEMPORARY VIEW FROM GEARY AND POWELL STREETS OF
UNION SQUARE WITH A CABLE CAR

MELANIE WALKING UP THE STAIRS TO THE MEZZANINE LEVEL OF DAVIDSON'S PET SHOP

NOTE THE TWO DOGS IN THE PAINTING BEHIND MITCH. THEY BEAR AN UNCANNY RESEMBLANCE TO STANLEY AND GEOFFREY. ANOTHER SLY JOKE BY HITCHCOCK?

MELANIE, MITCH, AND A PAIR OF LOVEBIRDS

Melanie enters the pet shop and walks upstairs to the mezzanine level of the store, just as Mitch Brenner makes his first appearance in the movie. Mitch pretends to mistake Melanie for a sales clerk and asks for her help finding lovebirds. Melanie plays along, but is caught by Mitch who recognizes her from stories in the gossip columns. Mitch then leaves the store while Melanie plots revenge. Mitch Brenner is a very fortunate man in this scene. His car is parked right on Geary Street just outside the door to the pet store, something a parking-obsessed San Franciscan could wait a lifetime for, particularly in the crowded Union Square area.

MEZZANINE LEVEL OF DAVIDSON'S PET SHOP WITH MITCH, MELANIE, AND THE SALES CLERK

EXTERIOR OF ROBISON'S HOUSE OF PETS AT 125 MAIDEN LANE IN SAN FRANCISCO, 1953

The Gump's Bird Pin

HITCHCOCK INFORMED TIPPI HEDREN HE WAS casting her as the lead in *The Birds* during a dinner at Chasen's restaurant in Los Angeles. To celebrate the occasion, he gave her a small gold pin showing three birds in flight decorated with seed pearls. The pin was from Gump's in San Francisco, near the Union Square location of the pet shop in *The Birds*.

In December of 2000, as part of a fundraising effort for her ROAR foundation, which supports a wildlife sanctuary for big cats such as lions and tigers, Tippi Hedren made an appearance at Gump's in San Francisco where she launched the sale of a commemorative bird pin that was inspired by the gift Hitchcock gave her forty years earlier.

TIPPI HEDREN'S BIRD PIN FROM GUMP'S

Although the outdoor part of this scene was filmed on location in San Francisco, the exterior façade and interior of Davidson's were filmed in a studio in Los Angeles. Davidson's was closely based on Robison's House of Pets, a historic business located near Union Square, first at 125 Maiden Lane, and later at 135 Maiden Lane.

Robison's, founded in 1850, was the oldest pet store in the United States at the time of the filming of *The Birds*. It was originally a produce store, but it also carried a few exotic animals, such as goldfish, canaries, and monkeys, all brought to San Francisco by the Chinese sailors who worked on the produce ships. The animals were allowed to wander freely around the store—an approach that was popular with the customers. The owners soon realized that selling pets was a better business than selling fruits and vegetables. They became famous for importing rare and exotic species of birds. This is reflected in dialogue in *The Birds* when the sales clerk tells Melanie that Myna birds are hard to find and are imported directly from India.

OWNER ANSEL ROBISON HOLDING A PAIR OF SQUIRREL MONKEYS, 1953

AN AFGHAN RECEIVES A NEW COLLAR AT ROBISON'S HOUSE OF PETS, 1953

The store also supplied big-game animals to zoos, circuses, and private collectors like William Randolph Hearst who kept big-game animals from Africa at Hearst Castle. The famous big-game hunter and safari leader Frank Buck, the originator of the phrase "bring 'em back alive," got his start trapping and importing exotic animals for the store's owners. Mr. Buck met the Robisons in San Francisco while he was in town for the Panama Pacific Exposition in 1915. The House of Pets closed in 1995.

The interior of Robison's was similar to the studio set of Davidson's in *The Birds*. Both were packed with a variety of animals in cages and had interior mezzanine levels. The Marc Jacobs boutique now occupies the Robison's location at 125 Maiden Lane, while the Jil Sander boutique has taken over the space where Robison's was located at the time *The Birds* was filmed at 135 Maiden Lane. The interior of this latter location has been completely redone and the mezzanine level from Robison's has been removed. Meanwhile, the Marc Jacobs building has replaced the Robison's structure shown in the earlier photograph.

Hitchcock's use of Robison's is reminiscent of the Argosy Book Shop shown in *Vertigo*. Both were fictitiously renamed but reflected the look and feel of actual long-standing San Francisco stores. Hitchcock took artistic license and relocated both businesses in each movie to Powell Street near Union Square.

LEFT TO RIGHT: UNKNOWN, CHIMPANZEE, MRS. FRANK BUCK, AND MR. FRANK "BRING 'EM BACK ALIVE" BUCK, 1940

CONTEMPORARY VIEW OF THE EXTERIORS OF THE MARC JACOBS AND JIL SANDER BOUTIQUES, FORMER LOCATIONS OF ROBISON'S HOUSE OF PETS

Looking for Mitch Brenner

The film cuts to a portable bird-cage with two lovebirds being carried by Melanie through a front door into the elegant marble-floored lobby of a San Francisco apartment building. Melanie is attempting to get revenge on Mitch for embarrassing her in the pet store. When she blithely leaves the birds with a note outside Mitch's door, a nosey neighbor (Richard Deacon) explains to her that Mitch spends his weekends in Bodega Bay sixty miles to the north of San Francisco, "an hour and a half by freeway or two hours if you take the coast highway."

FRONT ENTRANCE TO MITCH BRENNER'S APARTMENT BUILDING

The neighbor's directions are quite precise. This is the first of many verbal references which help set up the location of Bodega Bay in relation to San Francisco, near enough for a weekend trip but far enough away to feel like it's another world.

We could not definitively confirm where the brief interior and exterior scenes at Mr. Brenner's San Francisco apartment were filmed. According to studio correspondence, Hitchcock considered using the six-story Nob Hill apartment building at 1155 Jones Street (at the corner of Jones and Sacramento Streets) and actually got permission from the owner to film at the location. However, the exterior of the building could not have been used in the film because its entrance has steps outside the front door and the scene in the movie shows a flat entrance leading directly out to the sidewalk.

In all likelihood, these scenes were filmed on a studio set inspired by the elegant Nob Hill neighborhood where 1155 Jones Street was situated. Even if it was not used in the film, 1155 Jones Street provides a good example of the style and atmosphere Hitchcock wanted to have for this scene. Mitch Brenner, a successful attorney, lived in an elegant apartment building with a marble-floored lobby. It is a place where well-to-do San Francisco bachelors could hang their hats. However, the building does not convey a permanent homey feeling like Mitch's family house in Bodega Bay. 1155 Jones Street is located 11 blocks east of another bachelor's apartment filmed by Hitchcock. In *Vertigo*, Scottie Ferguson lived at Jones and Lombard Streets.

CONTEMPORARY VIEW OF 1155 JONES STREET IN SAN FRANCISCO. NOTE THE STAIRS AS OPPOSED TO THE FLAT ENTRANCE SHOWN IN THE FILM.

The next scene cuts to a shot of the two lovebirds in a cage sitting in the passenger-side foot well of a car. We hear the noise of an engine and the squeal of tires as the car zooms around a corner. As the view widens, Melanie is driving a light green Aston-Martin convertible, enjoying the freedom of racing her sports car aggressively along a scenic coastal road, presumably on her way to Bodega Bay.

State Route 1 (or Highway 1) is a two-lane road that hugs the coast of California for much of the length of the state and offers sweeping panoramas of the Pacific Ocean as well as the cliffs that delineate the rugged edge of the continent. More than twenty years earlier, Hitchcock had filmed on Highway 1 (about 120 miles to the south of Bodega Bay) for the Monte Carlo and English coast sequences used in *Rebecca* and *Suspicion*.

However, Highway 1 was not used in the filming of *The Birds* because the California State Highway Department denied Hitchcock permission to stop traffic on the highway. Instead, aerial shots from a helicopter, and ground-level driving footage, were taken along the northern part of Bay Hill Road, a short four-mile connector road.

VIEW OF MELANIE DRIVING ON BAY HILL ROAD TOWARDS BODEGA BAY. THIS FOOTAGE WAS TAKEN FROM A HELICOPTER.

CONTEMPORARY VIEW OF BODEGA BAY FROM NORTHERN SEGMENT OF BAY HILL ROAD, HALF A MILE ABOVE TOWN

MELANIE DRIVING ON THE NORTHERN SEGMENT OF BAY HILL ROAD, ABOVE BODEGA BAY

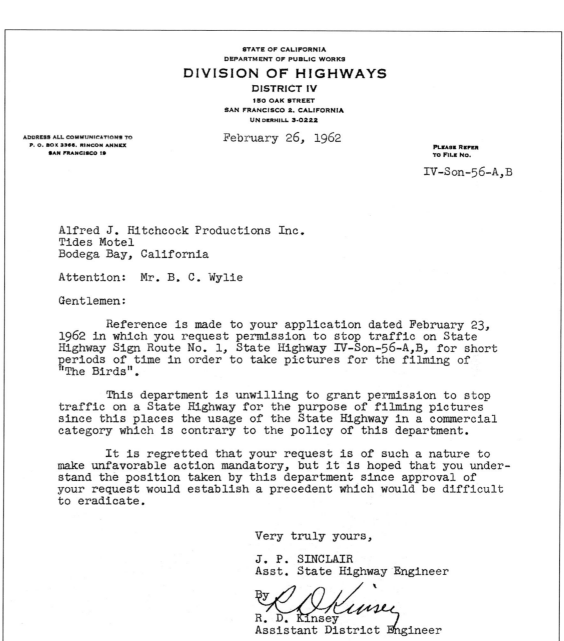

STATE OF CALIFORNIA
DEPARTMENT OF PUBLIC WORKS

DIVISION OF HIGHWAYS

DISTRICT IV

150 OAK STREET
SAN FRANCISCO 2, CALIFORNIA
UNderhill 3-0222

ADDRESS ALL COMMUNICATIONS TO
P. O. BOX 3366, RINCON ANNEX
SAN FRANCISCO 19

February 26, 1962

PLEASE REFER
TO FILE NO.

IV-Son-56-A,B

Alfred J. Hitchcock Productions Inc.
Tides Motel
Bodega Bay, California

Attention: Mr. B. C. Wylie

Gentlemen:

Reference is made to your application dated February 23, 1962 in which you request permission to stop traffic on State Highway Sign Route No. 1, State Highway IV-Son-56-A,B, for short periods of time in order to take pictures for the filming of "The Birds".

This department is unwilling to grant permission to stop traffic on a State Highway for the purpose of filming pictures since this places the usage of the State Highway in a commercial category which is contrary to the policy of this department.

It is regretted that your request is of such a nature to make unfavorable action mandatory, but it is hoped that you understand the position taken by this department since approval of your request would establish a precedent which would be difficult to eradicate.

Very truly yours,

J. P. SINCLAIR
Asst. State Highway Engineer

By *R. D. Kinsey*

R. D. Kinsey
Assistant District Engineer

LETTER DENYING PERMISSION TO STOP TRAFFIC AND FILM ON
HIGHWAY 1, 1962

AERIAL VIEW OF SONOMA COAST SHOWING BODEGA BAY AND BODEGA HEAD, 1960

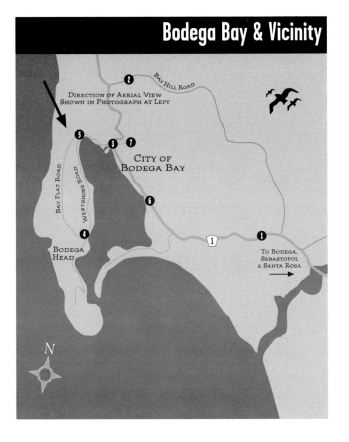

Bodega Bay & Vicinity

❶ California coastal highway (State Highway 1)
❷ Bay Hill Road
❸ "Brinkmeyer's post office and store"/Diekmann's
❹ "Brenner farm"
❺ Bay Flat and Westshore Roads
❻ The Tides Wharf Restaurant/Inn at the Tides
❼ Taylor Street hill

The Geography of Bodega Bay and Bodega

The Birds is primarily set in and around Bodega Bay on the picturesque Sonoma Coast, a collection of jagged cliffs and rocky beaches 60 miles north of San Francisco on Highway 1. The three small villages of Bodega Bay, Bodega Head, and Bodega (a few miles inland from the bay itself), were used to convey a sense of quiet rural isolation. These locations were masterfully blended by Hitchcock, as he combined the rough forces of nature with an isolated, rural setting. This created the perfect atmosphere for a movie about human frailty in the face of natural disaster.

The Birds is based on a novel by Daphne du Maurier that was set in the Cornish countryside in England. Hitchcock, however, wanted to make a movie featuring attractive city dwellers and not rural folk, and the Bodega Bay region gave him the solution he sought. Hitchcock explained his choice of locations to the *San Francisco Chronicle*:

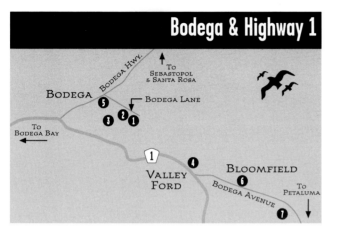

Bodega & Highway 1

1. "Annie Hayworth's cottage set"
2. "Bodega Bay School"/The Potter Schoolhouse
3. St. Teresa de Avila's Church
4. "Fawcett farmhouse"/Bianchi ranch
5. The Casino
6. Downtown Bloomfield
7. "Brenner driveway"/Nosecchi Dairy

VIEW OF BODEGA LOOKING EAST, 1960

"Many filmmakers forget how important geography is to a story. I chose Bodega Bay because I wanted an isolated group of people who lived near an articulate community. Bodega Bay is a place where sophisticated San Franciscans drive to spend the weekend. The location provided the combination we wanted."

In *The Birds*, the sleepy hamlet of Bodega Bay is designed to contrast sharply with busy San Francisco just as small-town Santa Rosa contrasts with the dirty, crowded Newark, New Jersey in *Shadow of a Doubt*. Later in the film, Annie Hayworth (Suzanne Pleshette), the schoolteacher, tells Melanie Daniels, "There is a lot of spare time in Bodega Bay," and later describes Bodega Bay as "a little hamlet . . . a collection of shacks on a hillside." In contrast, Mitch's sister, Cathy Brenner (Veronica Cartwright), quotes Mitch as describing San Francisco as "an anthill located at the foot of a bridge."

A newspaper account from Santa Rosa's *Press Democrat* also quotes Hitchcock explaining why he chose Bodega Bay as the setting for *The Birds*:

"I chose Bodega Bay because it's small, intimate, isolated, colorful—the sort of place made for this picture," he said. "The people are just right for the scenes I need. San Francisco's mud-flats, the Monterey Peninsula—they wouldn't do at all."

Also, he explained, the film crew needed an area with low land, and not a lot of mountains or trees so they could easily film birds in the sky. Bodega Bay met these criteria perfectly. One problem with Bodega Bay, however, was it was so bright and picturesque that it was too cheery for the mood Hitchcock was trying to achieve. The technicians actually had to dampen the colors during the editing process.

Finally, Hitchcock's personal connection to Northern California and previous filmmaking in the area contributed to his selection of the Sonoma Coast as the location for the film. Hitchcock had visited Bodega Bay in June 1942, just prior to filming *Shadow of a Doubt* in Santa Rosa. He took a daylong fishing trip with local dignitaries off the coast of Bodega Bay aboard a boat from the Smith Brothers fishing fleet, and reportedly became quite fond of the area. Hitchcock's use of a Northern California location for *The Birds* allowed him to reference a famous bird incident that occurred near Santa Cruz, one which is mentioned during the long scene inside the Tides Restaurant.

Over the years, Bodega Bay and Bodega have become very closely associated with *The Birds*. To this day, thousands of tourists visit the town each year looking for locations from the movie. Sadly, many of the buildings filmed in Bodega Bay were old wooden structures that have been destroyed by fires since the movie was made, while others were simply temporary sets that were torn down after the completion of the filming. Nevertheless, intriguing locations featured in the movie still remain.

MELANIE DRIVING PAST THE TIDES MOTEL

Melanie Arrives in Bodega Bay

Melanie drives north on Highway 1 into a small town, passing several white wooden buildings beside the road. This is the first appearance of the Tides Wharf complex in the movie. The first building she drives by is the Tides Motel. Then she passes the driveway leading down to the Tides parking lot and there is a view of the Tides Restaurant—also along Highway 1, but slightly north of the motel.

MELANIE DRIVING PAST THE TIDES' PARKING LOT AND RESTAURANT

TIDES MOTEL AND RESTAURANT IN BODEGA BAY, 1963

The footage near the Tides is a "process shot," created using rear projection technology. Tippi Hedren sat in a car on a studio stage and background footage of Bodega Bay was projected on a transparent screen behind her. A process shot was a technique that Hitchcock and other directors frequently used with varying degrees of success to make it appear as if action were occurring on location when in reality the actors were being filmed on a studio stage where the production team could have complete control over sound, lighting, and weather. The close-up shots of Melanie riding in the boat across the bay, Mitch and Melanie talking on a hill above the birthday party, and the children running down the hill after the schoolhouse attack are among the other process shots used in *The Birds*.

The Tides Wharf complex in Bodega Bay plays a key role in *The Birds*. It is included in many scenes, serves as a central point in the geography of Hitchcock's Bodega Bay, and is a place to which the characters continually return.

MITCH STANDING ON TOP OF THE TIDES PIER. NOTE THE OUTBUILDING WITH THE DISTINCTIVE ROOF BEHIND HIM.

MELANIE AND MITCH WALKING PAST THE TIDES GIFT SHOP AND THE TIDES RESTAURANT

TIDES PARKING LOT, LOWER BUILDINGS, AND WHARF AREA IN BODEGA BAY, 1963

At the time the movie was filmed, the complex consisted of the Tides Motel and the Tides Restaurant (also known as the "Upper Tides") with a phone booth located outside. These two buildings were situated along Highway 1 with a driveway in between them leading to the parking lot and lower buildings. The lower buildings consisted of a café which served snacks to the fishermen (known as the "Lower Tides"), a fish market and bait store, a boat rental building, a gift store, and a wharf with a pier.

Mitch Zankich, who owned the Tides at the time of the filming, cut a deal with Hitchcock: In exchange for his not charging for the use of the Tides as a setting in the film,

TIDES OWNER MITCH ZANKICH'S CAMEO IN *THE BIRDS*

MITCH ZANKICH ON A PIER BEHIND THE TIDES. THIS WAS A RESEARCH PHOTO TAKEN BY HITCHCOCK'S LOCATION SCOUTING TEAM, 1962.

Hitchcock gave the owner a line in the movie, used the actual name of the Tides Restaurant in the film, and named the male lead (played by Rod Taylor) "Mitch." Zankich's speaking part, which occurs after the first attack on Melanie, is: "Mitch! What happened, Mitch?" The Tides' association with *The Birds* proved to be a great benefit for the restaurant's business. Inspired by *The Birds*, many visitors come to Bodega Bay to dine at the restaurant. Hitchcock's use of the Tides in *The Birds* is similar to Ernie's in *Vertigo*: In both cases, he used an actual restaurant by name in multiple scenes in a film and featured the owners and staff in bit parts.

HITCHCOCK LEADING THE CAST AND CREW IN SWEARING NOT TO REVEAL THE ENDING OF THE MOVIE (WHICH, INCIDENTALLY, HAD NOT BEEN SETTLED AT THIS POINT), 1962. THIS WAS ESSENTIALLY A PUBLICITY STUNT PLAYING ON HITCHCOCK'S REPUTATION FOR SECRECY CONCERNING THE ENDINGS OF HIS FILMS.

BODEGA BAY RESIDENTS WATCHING THE ACTION ON THE SET AT THE TIDES, 1962

During the six weeks of filming, the cast and crew frequently ate lunch at the Tides. As reported in the April 2, 1998 *Press Democrat* by a waitress who was present at the time of filming:

"I took the crew and Hitchcock in the banquet room at noon time . . . Hitchcock would never stay for dinner, he would go back to San Francisco. But Rod Taylor and Suzanne Pleshette would stay, and Tippi. . . . Hitchcock was very reserved . . . but he was always very pleasant. He ate the same thing every day. . . . You know how precise he was with his pictures and all—every day he would say 'I'm going to have a piece of sole, my dear, about so big, and a cup of green beans and a few pieces of lettuce. And don't put anything else on the plate.'"

187

Hitchcock's Fictitious Geography of Bodega Bay

THE FOOTAGE IN *THE BIRDS* IMPLIES that the Tides buildings are just below the large fish market building and the Bodega Bay General Store and Post Office in the center of the town. In reality, there was no downtown directly above the Tides complex. The fish market building and the General Store and Post Office were filmed on a studio set and spliced into the location. Hitchcock was modifying Bodega Bay's geography to make it appear more dense and bustling.

To make matters even more confusing, in later scenes, buildings from the nearby village of Bodega—the schoolhouse, church, Druids Hall, and the Casino—are cinematically relocated into Bodega Bay to make it appear that the two hamlets are a single location.

In reality, at the time of filming, the area around the Tides consisted of only a few scattered wooden buildings. Bodega is seven miles inland of Bodega Bay. Despite the artistic license taken by Hitchcock, the fictitious layout of "downtown" Bodega Bay is internally consistent throughout the film.

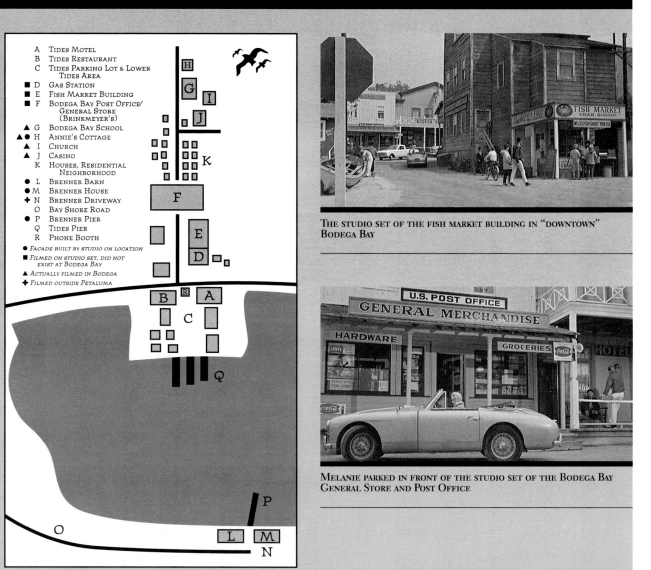

A TIDES MOTEL
B TIDES RESTAURANT
C TIDES PARKING LOT & LOWER TIDES AREA
■ D GAS STATION
■ E FISH MARKET BUILDING
■ F BODEGA BAY POST OFFICE/ GENERAL STORE (BRINKMEYER'S)
▲ G BODEGA BAY SCHOOL
▲●▲ H ANNIE'S COTTAGE
▲ I CHURCH
▲ J CASINO
K HOUSES, RESIDENTIAL NEIGHBORHOOD
● L BRENNER BARN
● M BRENNER HOUSE
✚ N BRENNER DRIVEWAY
O BAY SHORE ROAD
● P BRENNER PIER
Q TIDES PIER
R PHONE BOOTH

● *FACADE BUILT BY STUDIO ON LOCATION*
■ *FILMED ON STUDIO SET, DID NOT EXIST AT BODEGA BAY*
▲ *ACTUALLY FILMED IN BODEGA*
✚ *FILMED OUTSIDE PETALUMA*

THE STUDIO SET OF THE FISH MARKET BUILDING IN "DOWNTOWN" BODEGA BAY

MELANIE PARKED IN FRONT OF THE STUDIO SET OF THE BODEGA BAY GENERAL STORE AND POST OFFICE

MELANIE WALKING TO THE PIER AT THE TIDES WHARF COMPLEX WITH
THE OUTBUILDING AND HOTEL IN THE BACKGROUND

The Tides Wharf complex has been expanded and the restaurant rebuilt twice since *The Birds* was filmed. Where the Tides Restaurant once stood there is now a driveway leading to the new Tides restaurant, gift store, and fish market. The Inn at the Tides Motel is located above the current restaurant across Highway 1. Today, only a single outbuilding remains from the original Tides Wharf complex.

CONTEMPORARY VIEW OF THE OUTBUILDING

CONTEMPORARY VIEW OF THE RECONSTRUCTED TIDES WHARF RESTAURANT

Front view of Hellwig's Store and Post office (later named Diekmann's Bay Store) in Bodega Bay, California, 1922

Diekmann's General Store and Post Office

After passing the Tides Motel, Melanie makes a right turn off Highway 1 into a small downtown area with a large three-story wood-plank building with a "Fish Market" sign and several other buildings. She parks in front of the Bodega Bay General Store and Post Office.

Melanie gets out of her car and heads into the General Store and Post Office to ask where Mitch Brenner lives. The store's interior is a colorful and cluttered mess, crowded with food, hardware, fishing tackle, and post office boxes.

Although the interior and exterior were studio sets, they were closely modeled on Diekmann's store, an actual business in Bodega Bay. The "Sonoma County Dog Licenses Available Here" sign on the exterior of the front door is an example of Hitchcock's meticulous efforts to add very subtle elements of local flavor into his studio sets.

Contemporary view of the front of Diekmann's Bay Store

The set for the General Store and Post Office was inspired by an actual business in Bodega Bay called Diekmann's, which served as a grocery store and post office. The building also had an attached hotel. Diekmann's was located just off Highway 1 at the foot of the Taylor Street hill in the northern part of Bodega Bay, a half-mile north of the Tides Wharf complex.

The General Store and Post Office was not specifically named during the scene where Melanie arrives in Bodega Bay. However, several times later in the movie, "Brinkmeyer's" store is mentioned in the dialogue. It is where the Brenners and Fawcetts bought chicken feed and where Melanie tells Annie Hayworth she bought her nightgown.

Brinkmeyer's never existed in Sonoma County. It is assumed the name is a reference to Diekmann's, a business in Bodega Bay. Just as Davidson's Pet Shop was a take-off on Robison's House of Pets, and the Argosy Book Shop in *Vertigo* was based on the Argonaut Book Shop, Brinkmeyer's was a renamed version of Diekmann's.

Diekmann's—still owned by the Diekmann family—is in business today in the same location. No longer a post office, the store is still packed full of a wide variety of merchandise. However, due to a fire, the building has been completely rebuilt and relocated slightly north since *The Birds* was filmed.

INTERIOR OF BRINKMEYER'S GENERAL STORE AND POST OFFICE WITH THE POSTMASTER

INTERIOR OF BRINKMEYER'S GENERAL STORE, PACKED WITH GROCERIES AND SUPPLIES

INTERIOR OF DIEKMANN'S GENERAL STORE WITH MR. DIEKMANN. THIS WAS A RESEARCH PHOTO TAKEN BY HITCHCOCK'S LOCATION SCOUTING TEAM, 1962.

The postmaster walks outside the store with Melanie. He points to an area across the water where Mitch Brenner's house is located. The view is past the buildings of "downtown," through the Tides Wharf parking lot, and across the bay.

The view across Bodega Bay shown in the film is of Bodega Head, located on an out-cropping of land which continues around the bay. However, the view shown was not the actual view from Diekmann's store. The view was shot from the hill above the Tides Wharf complex. Again, Hitchcock "splices" the Tides Wharf complex right below the general store in the film's geography.

The image of the Brenner house location, as seen from "downtown," was produced using a process shot. In this instance, the fish market building was filmed on a studio stage and combined with background footage of the view across the Tides' parking lot to the other side of Bodega Bay. The combined image was then augmented by the matte painter, Al Whitlock, who enhanced the sky and blended in the area between the fish market and the parking lot. A "matte" refers to a partial painting of an existing image to modify, highlight, or retouch the scene. This was the first of numerous mattes created by Mr. Whitlock that helped establish the fictitious geography of Bodega Bay in the movie.

Melanie asks the postmaster if there is a back road leading to the Brenner house and learns that the only way to the house, apart from the main road, is to take a boat straight across the water. Melanie then orders a boat. She also asks for the name of Mitch's sister. When the postmaster is not sure, he suggests Melanie ask Annie Hayworth, the local schoolteacher.

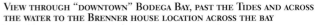

VIEW THROUGH "DOWNTOWN" BODEGA BAY, PAST THE TIDES AND ACROSS THE WATER TO THE BRENNER HOUSE LOCATION ACROSS THE BAY

CONTEMPORARY VIEW ACROSS BODEGA BAY FROM ABOVE THE TIDES WHARF COMPLEX

MELANIE DRIVING ON BODEGA HIGHWAY WITH A VIEW OF THE
CASINO RESTAURANT

CONTEMPORARY VIEW OF THE CASINO RESTAURANT. THIS VIEW IS FROM
THE OPPOSITE SIDE OF THE ONE SHOWN IN *THE BIRDS*

A Visit to Annie Hayworth's

Melanie drives to Annie Hayworth's home. She passes a wooden building on Bodega Highway, an old house at the intersection of Bodega Highway and Bodega Lane, and turns right onto Bodega Lane. She then drives past the Bodega Bay School and stops in front of the schoolteacher's small, charming cottage.

The location of this scene is actually in the tiny town of Bodega, with a current population of about 300. Bodega is seven miles northeast of Bodega Bay. However, Hitchcock blends the two tiny towns into a single hamlet for the purposes of this movie. The first wooden building Melanie passes on Bodega Highway is the Casino, a restaurant where the cast and crew ate meals during location filming in Bodega.

The cottage was a set with a false front constructed specifically for *The Birds*. The film crew took down the schoolteacher's cottage set shortly after shooting concluded.

Melanie introduces herself to Annie (Suzanne Pleshette) and finds out that Mitch's sister is named Cathy. Annie seems unhappy that Melanie has driven up from San Francisco to visit Mitch.

MELANIE AND ANNIE IN FRONT OF ANNIE HAYWORTH'S COTTAGE

HITCHCOCK AND TIPPI HEDREN IN FRONT OF ANNIE HAYWORTH'S COTTAGE

VIEW OF THE TEMPORARY SET OF ANNIE HAYWORTH'S COTTAGE, 1963

The Potter School and St. Teresa's Church

THE CHARMING ONE-ROOM POTTER SCHOOLHOUSE, LOCATED IN the village of Bodega on Bodega Lane, was fictitiously called the Bodega Bay School in *The Birds*. The school was built in 1873. By the time Hitchcock was picking locations, it was dilapidated and scheduled for demolition. Hitchcock had the school partially rebuilt for the filming, and the crew added a temporary fence surrounding the adjoining yard and jungle gym.

In the 1980s, the schoolhouse was briefly converted into a bed and breakfast, and then became a restaurant. Along with St. Teresa de Avila's Church, the schoolhouse is one of the few original buildings shown in *The Birds* that still exists today. The schoolhouse is now a private residence, with a gift store on the ground floor. It is an officially documented "classic haunt" with a resident ghost and a history of paranormal events and sightings.

St. Teresa de Avila's is a scenic little country Catholic church located near the Potter Schoolhouse in Bodega, off Bodega Highway. Although never specifically named in the film, it is shown several times in the background during scenes filmed at the schoolhouse. The church was built of redwood in 1859 by shipmakers from New England. It was dedicated in 1861, and has served Bodega continuously since then. At one time, Ansel Adams photographed it for its rural charm.

The church is named after St. Teresa, a Spanish nun born in 1515 in Gotarrendura, near Avila, Spain. She was famous for her visions, including one in which her heart is pierced by an angel. St. Teresa went on to found a reform movement to re-establish purity and poverty as central features of convent life.

MELANIE'S CAR PARKED IN FRONT OF THE POTTER SCHOOLHOUSE WITH ST. TERESA'S CHURCH VISIBLE IN THE BACKGROUND

MELANIE'S CAR APPROACHING THE BODEGA BAY SCHOOL

CONTEMPORARY VIEW OF THE POTTER SCHOOLHOUSE

CONTEMPORARY VIEW OF ST. TERESA DE AVILA'S CHURCH

A Trip Across the Bay

The next scene cuts to Melanie writing Cathy Brenner's name on a note, with the general store/post office in the background. Melanie then drives down to the Tides Wharf complex and gets in a small motorboat. Rumor has it that, while filming the boat rental scene, Tippi Hedren slipped off the boat and fell in the water wearing a full mink coat and holding the birdcage with the lovebirds.

Although the Tides Wharf complex has been almost completely rebuilt since *The Birds* was filmed, the piers shown in the scene with Melanie are nearly identical today.

Melanie is helped into the boat by a dockhand and heads straight across Bodega Bay toward the Brenner house on Bodega Head. When she gets halfway across the bay there is a view back toward the town of Bodega Bay showing the Tides Wharf complex and dozens of other buildings clustered together, as well as the schoolhouse and church on a hill above town.

MELANIE DRIVING THROUGH "DOWNTOWN" BODEGA BAY TOWARD THE TIDES WHARF COMPLEX

MELANIE ON THE PIER AT THE TIDES

CONTEMPORARY VIEW OF THE PIER AT THE TIDES

MELANIE CROSSING THE WATER WITH "DOWNTOWN" BODEGA BAY IN THE BACKGROUND. THIS SHOT WAS PRODUCED WITH MATTE TECHNOLOGY, AND MOST OF THE BUILDINGS WERE PAINTED ONTO THE IMAGE.

CONTEMPORARY VIEW OF THE TIDES AND BODEGA BAY FROM BODEGA HEAD

This view was a matte where most of the buildings—including the church and schoolhouse—were painted onto what was basically an empty landscape (with the exception of the Tides Wharf complex). In effect, the matte artist created a town where none actually existed. However, this arrangement of buildings is internally consistent with other parts of the film.

AERIAL VIEW OF TIDES WHARF COMPLEX IN BODEGA BAY, 1963

AERIAL VIEW OF BODEGA BAY, NORTH OF THE TIDES COMPLEX, 1960. NOTE THAT THE AREA NORTH OF THE TIDES WAS THE MOST DENSELY POPULATED PART OF BODEGA BAY, CONTRARY TO THE GEOGRAPHY PORTRAYED BY HITCHCOCK.

ALFRED HITCHCOCK WALKING WITH MEMBERS OF THE CREW ON THE BRENNER PIER

MELANIE WALKING ALONG THE BRENNER PIER

In her boat, Melanie approaches the Brenner family home. An old white house with a vibrantly painted red barn is visible. After docking her boat on the Brenner pier, Melanie drops the lovebirds off in the house. Then she takes the boat back out into the water.

The actual site did not have a pier, so Hitchcock needed to get special permission from the Coast Guard to construct one. After the filming was done, the film crew was required to remove it.

The Brenner farmhouse depicted in the movie was located across the bay from the main part of Bodega Bay on Bodega Head. The actual property was not much of a ranch when Hitchcock's advance team arrived. It consisted of several broken-down old shacks, and was owned at the time of filming by Rose Gaffney.

Ms. Gaffney, an elderly woman at the time *The Birds* was filmed, was locally famous for leading a successful grassroots movement to prevent Pacific Gas & Electric from building a nuclear power plant on Bodega Head. Locals who knew her describe her as "an old-fashioned pioneer woman." Ms. Gaffney had never heard of Mr. Hitchcock and only reluctantly agreed to rent him her property for filming. The film crew built facades for the farmhouse, the barn, and other buildings.

THE GAFFNEY PROPERTY AS IT EXISTED AT THE TIME *THE BIRDS* WAS FILMED, 1962

CLOSE-UP OF THE GAFFNEY HOUSE AS IT EXISTED AT THE TIME *THE BIRDS* WAS FILMED, 1962

According to Hitchcock, the facades were very close copies of a nearby Russian farmhouse built in the 1800s, perhaps located in Sebastopol about 16 miles to the northeast of Bodega Bay. The crew also built the gazebo used in the party scene and tidied up the surrounding yard and landscape.

The Gaffney structures burned down in the late 1960s and the land is now owned by the Bodega Marine Laboratory. The site where the Brenner house was located during filming is identifiable today by a grove of cypress trees on the right side of Westshore Road and the "Restricted Access – Bodega Marine Laboratory Housing" sign.

The Bodega Marine Laboratory and Marine Reserve on Bodega Head are run by the University of California at Davis and staffed by scientists, college students, and volunteers who study marine habitats and biology.

CLOSE-UP VIEW OF THE BRENNER RANCH WITH FARMHOUSE AND BARN. THESE BUILDINGS WERE ONLY FACADES BUILT BY THE MOVIE CREW.

DISTANT VIEW OF THE BRENNER RANCH WITH FARMHOUSE AND BARN

Herb Caen and *The Birds*

HERB CAEN, THE LEGENDARY AND BELOVED SAN Francisco newspaperman, wrote his column for almost sixty years from 1938 to 1997, when he passed away. If you lived in the Bay Area, Caen's six-day-a-week column was required reading to know what was going on around town. For many, Caen personified San Francisco. Caen met with and wrote about innumerable people, famous and ordinary, who lived in and visited the city. Naturally, Caen socialized with Hitchcock when the director was in town. The two lunched together at Jack's restaurant and Caen mentioned the "Master of Suspense" in his columns.

On a promotional tour for *The Birds*, Hitchcock met the columnist in Union Square for a brief interview. Caen's *San Francisco Chronicle* column from April 3, 1963 described the encounter.

"As the pigeons fluttered about our heads and shoulders, we talked about 'The Birds', which Mr. Hitchcock described as 'a fowl epic, if ever I made one. Biggest cast of extras I ever had, too. Over 28,000 birds. Of course, they all worked for chicken feed except for the buzzards which had agents' . . . .

" 'The ads,' I said, 'quote you as calling it 'the most terrifying picture I have ever made.' Is that true?'

" 'Oh indubitably,' he replied. 'I financed it myself, and I'm terrified at the thought of losing all my money.'"

HITCHCOCK AND HERB CAEN DINING AT JACK'S, 1951

The First Bird Attack

Mitch goes into the family house from the yard and runs back out after seeing the lovebirds Melanie left for his sister Cathy. He spots the boat with Melanie in it out in the bay, and jumps into his car and makes the curving shoreline drive around the bay back towards "downtown."

Mitch is actually driving on both Bay Flat Road and Westshore Road. These two roads connect Bodega Head to Bodega Bay, running largely parallel to each other with Bay Flat Road being the older and higher one. Westshore Road was constructed by Pacific Gas & Electric as part of the proposed plan to build a nuclear power plant on Bodega Head. PG&E actually went so far as to dig out a foundation for the plant, a gaping excavation known by locals as "the hole in the head."

MITCH DRIVING ALONG BAY FLAT ROAD

CONTEMPORARY VIEW OF BAY FLAT ROAD

MITCH ESCORTS MELANIE TO A TABLE IN THE TIDES RESTAURANT

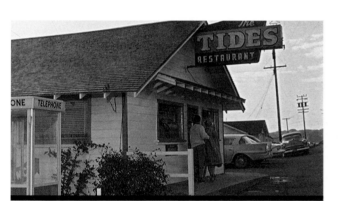

MITCH AND MELANIE WALKING INTO THE TIDES RESTAURANT

Mitch arrives at the Tides Wharf complex by car as Melanie approaches by boat. At that moment, a sea gull swoops down and pecks Melanie in the head, causing her to bleed. Mitch helps Melanie out of the boat. They go first to the boat charter building which is "closed for lunch," walk past the gift store, and enter the Tides Restaurant.

Mitch tends to Melanie's wound in the restaurant. Mitch's mother, Lydia Brenner (Jessica Tandy), arrives, and coldly scrutinizes Melanie. At the end of the scene, Mitch invites Melanie over for dinner that night.

The scene inside the Tides Restaurant was filmed on a studio sound stage, which was modeled on the actual interior of the Tides Restaurant. The set even had a view of the water and other buildings at the Tides Wharf complex.

Following the scene in the Tides, the action returns to Annie Hayworth's house where Melanie convinces Annie to let her stay in Annie's "room for rent" for the night.

Dinner at the Brenners' Home

Melanie drives up the Brenners' front driveway that evening on her way to dinner. The bright red barn and Brenner house are at the end of the road.

The driveway is another example of Hitchcock taking artistic license with Sonoma County's actual geography in order to achieve cinematic aims. Despite appearances, some shots of the driveway were not filmed at the Gaffney property on Bodega Head.

Studio *Daily Production Reports* record that the Brenner driveway was filmed at an unspecified ranch outside of Petaluma. It is highly probable the site was located off Bodega Avenue, a 25-mile-long stretch of road that starts in Petaluma as Washington Street, then turns into Bodega Avenue and eventually becomes Highway 1 near Bodega Bay.

MELANIE DRIVING UP THE BRENNER DRIVEWAY

CONTEMPORARY VIEW OF THE DRIVEWAY LEADING TO THE NOSECCHI DAIRY

LYDIA DRIVING DOWN THE BRENNER DRIVEWAY AWAY FROM THE RANCH

Hitchcock and his crew were very familiar with this stretch of road because all of the Sonoma County locations in the film are located off of it: downtown Bloomfield (filmed but not used in the final cut), the Bianchi ranch in Valley Ford, and Bodega and Bodega Bay. The cast and crew of the film traveled the road every day when they came to Bodega Bay from their hotel in Santa Rosa. The only problem with filming the scene on Bodega Avenue, near Petaluma, was that the road is landlocked. Water from the bay and other elements such as the Brenner barn were added using a matte.

There are many dairy farms and ranches outside of Petaluma off Bodega Avenue. A number of these farms have long unpaved driveways that look similar to the one used in the film. The one that most closely matches the "Brenner" driveway is the Nosecchi Dairy driveway north of Petaluma at 5345 Bodega Avenue. The Nosecchi property contains a long, flat, straight driveway; a three-rail white fence; and phone lines running parallel to the fence on the same side of the driveway as shown in the film.

The current owners of the property owned the farm when *The Birds* was filmed but do not recall Hitchcock filming their property. The exact location of filming remains unconfirmed, but, at a minimum, the Nosecchi property illustrates similar elements to those shown in the film and provides an example of the type of property that inspired the filmmakers' model for the Brenner driveway.

When she arrives, Melanie walks up to the Brenner house and rings the doorbell. Instead of coming to the door, the Brenners walk up from the rear of the barn with Cathy Brenner leading the way. The Brenners have been looking at their chickens, who are not eating. Lydia Brenner, Mitch's mother, suspects it's the feed she purchased from Brinkmeyer's. After calling Fred Brinkmeyer, Lydia learns that another local farmer, Dan Fawcett, is also having trouble getting his chickens to eat. Fawcett purchased a different brand of feed than Lydia did.

The inside of the Brenner house was filmed on a Hollywood sound stage. Hitchcock gave the house an authentic Sonoma County charm. The interior feels slightly old-fashioned with country-style touches in the furniture and décor, but yet was not completely rustic or unfinished.

After dinner, Melanie plays the piano and converses with Cathy. Melanie learns that Mitch works as a defense lawyer at San Francisco's Hall of Justice. The Hall, an imposing stone building not shown in the film, is San Francisco's police headquarters. It is located at 850 Bryant Street between 7th and 8th Streets.

CONTEMPORARY VIEW OF THE HALL OF JUSTICE IN SAN FRANCISCO

The Technology Behind *The Birds*

FILMING *THE BIRDS* WITH 1960'S TECHNOLOGY WAS QUITE A CHALLENGE. THE BIRD ATTACK sequences in the film were produced using a number of different techniques. The shots of the birds swooping down onto Bodega Bay during the gas station fire were obtained by filming seagulls that were chasing food thrown off the cliffs of Santa Cruz Island off the coast of Southern California.

The bird images were individually "rotoscoped" one-by-one onto the actual film celluloid. Rotoscoping is an animation technique where images of previously shot live-action footage—in this case birds diving after food—are projected onto a drawing board or another piece of film, such as the matte of Bodega Bay from above. This allows the artist to trace the existing images onto the new medium and produce realistic animation in a relatively short period of time.

The shots of the birds over Union Square, in the sky above the Brenner house, and at Cathy's birthday party were actually obtained by filming gulls at the San Francisco City Dump (located in South San Francisco off Tunnel Road). Crew members attracted the birds by raking large piles of spoiled food and garbage from local bakeries. According to the studio's *Daily Production Reports*, problems with fog and overcast weather reportedly made shooting at the dump difficult. The crew spent three days shooting more than 20,000 feet of film of gulls flying and diving into the piles of garbage.

The production team—led by animal handler Ray Berwick—also captured and acquired numerous live birds which were used in the filming of the movie. It took many months of work to capture and train all the birds used in the film. Some of these animals were kept in Bodega Bay during the filming, and Hitchcock's production team was cited with a misdemeanor offense and fined $400 for having more birds in their possession than were permitted by law. Officials from the American Humane Association, who were present during the entire filming, reported that the birds were not being mistreated.

In other parts of the film, such as the final scene when the Brenners and Melanie drive away from the bird-infested Brenner farm, dummy birds were mixed in with actual birds. The crew also experimented with some mechanical birds, but they turned out to be unrealistic-looking and were only used in a few scenes, such as the chimney sequence when the sparrows get into Lydia Brenner's hair.

VIEW OF THE INTERIOR OF ANNIE'S HOUSE, WITH ANNIE AND MELANIE

MITCH AND MELANIE WALKING ON A SANDY HILLSIDE.
THIS WAS A PROCESS SHOT FILMED ON A STUDIO SET.

The Birds Appear All Over Bodega Bay

After leaving the Brenner home, Melanie walks into Annie Hayworth's cottage where she has rented a room for the night. The cottage interiors were filmed on a Southern California sound stage. The outside of the house has the quaint country charm of a small-town schoolteacher's cottage. As pointed out by Camille Paglia in her book *The Birds*, the interior is decorated in a sophisticated, slightly Bohemian manner with modernistic wall prints and an avant-garde lamp.

Hitchcock intended the house to portray the complexity of the Hayworth character: part lonely, rural schoolteacher, part sophisticated former city dweller. Annie reveals to Melanie that she used to date Mitch in San Francisco. Annie moved to Bodega Bay to be closer to Mitch, hoping to rekindle their romance. As Melanie prepares to retire for the evening, a gull kills itself by flying into Annie Hayworth's door, establishing an ominous mood.

Cathy Brenner's birthday party the next day takes place on a a bright and sunny afternoon. Mitch and Melanie walk on a sandy hillside above the Brenner house. There is a view of the sky, the bay, and the coastal hills.

As they walk up the hillside, there is a slow dramatic pan of the bay, filmed on location. However, once the couple nears the top of the hillside, the camera pulls in and the background somewhat abruptly changes to rear projection footage which was filmed on a studio set.

THE SAME SCENE, FILMED ON LOCATION

The events of the party are interrupted by a flock of seagulls that swoop down and attack the children. After the attacking birds are chased away, Mitch convinces Melanie to stay for dinner. As dinner is finishing, hundreds of sparrows suddenly fly down the Brenners' chimney and invade the house. While Mitch chases out the birds, Melanie escorts Lydia and Cathy to safety.

The scene then cuts to the Brenner living room after the attack, with broken teacups, upset furniture, spilled food on the floor, and tilted picture frames. The local sheriff investigating the scene refuses to believe anything is amiss.

Melanie decides to spend the night with the Brenners instead of driving back to San Francisco via Santa Rosa and the freeway. Hitchcock uses Santa Rosa, about 25 miles from Bodega Bay and the seat of Sonoma County, to represent Bodega Bay's nearest connection to civilization, a place of safety with police, hospitals, and freeways. This is ironic given Santa Rosa's role as the quintessential small town, a haven from the evils of big cities, in *Shadow of a Doubt*.

The next day, Mitch rakes a fire outside, while Melanie awakens and puts on her make-up. Lydia tells Mitch she is going over to the Fawcett farm. The camera follows Lydia as she drives a green pickup truck slowly along the Fawcetts' dirt driveway. The Fawcett farmhouse is framed by a grove of tall shade trees.

Lydia finds Dan Fawcett lying on the floor in bloody and torn clothing with his eyes gouged out amid a smashed-up bedroom. Lydia flees, and drives very quickly back to the Brenner farm. As she leaves the Fawcett farm, she kicks up rolling clouds of dust, which contrast dramatically with the calm dust-free approach she made to the farm just moments earlier.

DISTANT VIEW OF THE FAWCETT RANCH FRAMED BY A GROVE OF TREES AS SHOWN IN THE FILM

CONTEMPORARY VIEW OF THE BIANCHI RANCH

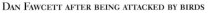

DAN FAWCETT AFTER BEING ATTACKED BY BIRDS

In Truffaut's interview with Hitchcock, Hitchcock explained he actually watered down the driveway for filming Lydia's approach to make sure there was no dust kicked up to enhance the contrast with her panicked exit. Also, the inspiration for showing the dead farmer with gouged-out eyes came from contemporaneous news reports during the filming of *The Birds*. A flock of crows killed a farmer's young lamb in Bodega Bay by gouging out its eyes and pecking it to death.

The interior shots of the Fawcett farm were filmed on a studio set carefully modeled on the original house. According to Hitchcock:

> "The house of the farmer who's killed by the birds is an exact replica of an existing farm up there: the same entrance, the same halls, the same kitchen. Even the scenery of the mountain that is shown outside the window of the corridor is completely accurate."

The outdoor shots of the Fawcett farm scene were actually filmed at the Bianchi ranch, located in Valley Ford about nine miles southeast of Bodega Bay. The ranch, visible from Bodega Avenue, is the first farm on the right side of the highway heading north on Bodega Avenue after the village of Valley Ford.

Today, the ranch is a working dairy, still owned by the same family who lived there when *The Birds* was filmed. After the filming, there was a fire on the property and the main house was damaged. It has since been partially rebuilt and connected to a smaller building that was separate at the time of filming. However, many elements of the ranch—the grove of tall trees behind the house, the long dirt driveway, the outbuildings, the barn, and even the green John Deere tractor—are unchanged from the time of filming.

VIEW OF THE FAWCETT BARN AND LYDIA'S TRUCK

CONTEMPORARY VIEW OF THE BIANCHI BARN

THE GREEN JOHN DEERE TRACTOR SHOWN IN THE FILM . . .

STILL EXISTS TODAY!

The Bodega Bay School Attack

After Lydia arrives back at the Brenner farm, there are additional scenes of the inside of the Brenner house. In her book on *The Birds*, Camille Paglia points out that the ormolu clock, London city prints, and heavy gilt mirror decorating Lydia's bedroom suggest the sophistication and wealth of Lydia and the Brenner family.

In the next scene, Melanie drives to the Bodega Bay School. Melanie is checking on Cathy Brenner, to make sure she is safe. She parks in front of the schoolhouse, and the sounds of singing children can be heard. Melanie sits down on a bench, elegantly smoking a cigarette as she waits for the children's song to end. The camera cuts from Melanie to a wider shot of a jungle gym and an outbuilding where crows begin to gather ominously as the children continue to sing. Eventually, Melanie notices the buildup of birds and runs inside the schoolhouse to warn Annie and the children.

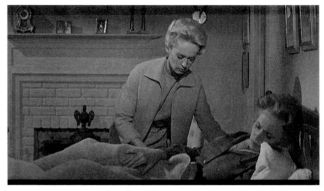

MELANIE AND LYDIA IN LYDIA'S BEDROOM

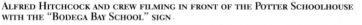

ALFRED HITCHCOCK AND CREW FILMING IN FRONT OF THE POTTER SCHOOLHOUSE WITH THE "BODEGA BAY SCHOOL" SIGN

MELANIE SITTING ON A BENCH OUTSIDE THE SCHOOLHOUSE WITH THE JUNGLE GYM BEHIND HER

THE BODEGA BAY SCHOOL AND PLAYGROUND WITH DUMMY BIRDS DURING THE FILMING OF *THE BIRDS*, 1962

CHILDREN FLEEING THE SCHOOLHOUSE DURING THE BIRD ATTACK. THIS PART OF THE SCENE WAS FILMED IN BODEGA ON BODEGA LANE; THE BIRDS WERE ADDED LATER USING SPECIAL EFFECTS.

VIEW UP BODEGA LANE OF CHILDREN FLEEING THE SCHOOLHOUSE DURING THE BIRD ATTACK

CONTEMPORARY VIEW LOOKING UP BODEGA LANE TOWARD THE POTTER SCHOOLHOUSE IN BODEGA

The Potter Schoolhouse shown in the film looks remarkably similar to the way it does today. While the jungle gym and bench are gone, a well-preserved main building remains.

Once Melanie alerts Annie to the danger, Annie asks the children to silently exit the school and go home or to the hotel at the bottom of the hill. As the children leave the schoolhouse, the birds swoop down to attack. Several children are run down by the pecking birds. A red-haired girl falls and breaks her glasses, and needs Cathy Brenner's help to get back up.

CHILDREN FLEEING THE SCHOOLHOUSE DURING THE BIRD ATTACK. THIS PART OF THE SCENE WAS FILMED IN BODEGA BAY ON THE TAYLOR STREET HILL.

The scene with the children running away from the schoolhouse as the birds attack is one of the most memorable in the film. During this scene, Hitchcock cinematically splices inland Bodega and coastal Bodega Bay into a single city. The children are initially shown running down Bodega Lane in the city of Bodega away from the schoolhouse and St. Teresa de Avila's church. So far the scene is geographically accurate.

The scene then cuts back and forth several times between Bodega Lane in Bodega and the Taylor Street hill in the city of Bodega Bay where the children are shown running past the houses that line Taylor Street.

The splicing of the two cities is most evident when Melanie, Cathy, and the red-haired girl seek refuge from the birds in a white station wagon parked on Taylor Street. The view through the car's rear window is of the schoolhouse in Bodega. The view out the car's front windshield is of Bodega Bay, making it appear as if the schoolhouse were located at the top of Taylor Street.

This sequence is the only time Bodega Bay's real general store/post office—Diekmann's—is shown in the film (as opposed to the studio set). The views down the Taylor Street hill show the store across Highway 1, overlooking the bay.

Annie's instructions to the children to "run to the hotel" would have to be a reference to the Tides Motel in order to be consistent with the film's fictitious geography. In the real world, the Bay View Hotel, attached to Diekmann's, was at the bottom of the Taylor Street hill.

CONTEMPORARY VIEW LOOKING DOWN THE TAYLOR STREET HILL IN BODEGA BAY

The Santa Cruz Bird "Invasion"

THE TINY TOWN OF CAPITOLA, A FEW MILES SOUTH OF SANTA CRUZ, IS CALIFORNIA'S oldest seaside resort. On August 18th, 1961 a massive bird invasion occurred in Capitola and other nearby communities. *The Santa Cruz Sentinel* described the invasion this way:

"A massive flight of sooty shearwaters, fresh from a feast of anchovies, collided with shore-side structures from Pleasure Point to Rio del Mar during the night. Residents, especially in the Pleasure Point and Capitola area, were awakened about 3 A.M. today by the rain of birds, slamming into their homes. Dead and stunned seabirds littered the streets and roads in the foggy early dawn. . . . They probably became confused and lost and headed for light. . . ."

THE TRAVELING SALESMAN . . .

The birds severed power lines, broke windows, bit at least eight people, and disgorged partially-digested fish bones all over the area, leaving a foul, fishy odor. Explanations for the incident ranged from the birds being scared by artillery fire at Fort Ord to the birds eating toxic anchovies.

It is interesting to compare the actual press account of the incident as quoted above with the dialogue from *The Birds* describing the Santa Cruz incident:

> TRAVELING SALESMAN: "Say, something like this happened in Santa Cruz last year. The town was just covered with seagulls."

> MRS. BUNDY: " . . . a large flock of seagulls got lost in the fog and headed into town where the lights were . . ."

> TRAVELING SALESMAN: "and they made some mess, smashing into buildings and everything . . ."

. . . AND MRS. BUNDY COMMENT ON THE SANTA CRUZ ATTACK

The Santa Cruz Bird "Invasion"

THE SANTA CRUZ SENTINEL, AUGUST 18, 1961

Alfred Hitchcock was not in his Scotts Valley home during the attack. He heard about the incident and personally called the *Santa Cruz Sentinel*, asking them for a copy of the August 18th paper as research material for his upcoming film, *The Birds*. According to the August 20, 1961 edition of the *Sentinel*:

"Despite its obvious publicity benefits for his new picture, Hitchcock denied having anything to do with the feathery invasion of Capitola. 'Merely a coincidence,' Hitchcock purred knowingly."

The Birds was based on the Daphne du Maurier novel and the planning of the film was well underway when the Santa Cruz incident occurred. However, it does appear the screenplay writer, Evan Hunter, used the *Sentinel's* account to help write the dialogue in *The Birds*.

In addition to the Santa Cruz invasion, and the incident with the lamb mentioned in Truffaut, there was at least one other real-world bird incident of which Hitchcock was aware. According to Kyle Counts, writing in *Cinfantastique* magazine, during the filming of *The Birds* Hitchcock was quoted as saying, "Even the most extraordinary events in our story have a basis in fact." The director reportedly reviewed newspaper accounts of an earlier bird incident in Southern California near San Diego. In that case, a large number of sparrows flew down a chimney, severely damaging the house. This was reminiscent of the scene in the Brenner house when the sparrows flood the house during dinner.

In the Tides

Once Melanie reaches the bottom of the hill, she enters the Tides Restaurant, which is located in Hitchcock's "downtown" Bodega Bay near Brinkmeyer's. However, as mentioned earlier, in reality the Tides Wharf complex is located a quarter-mile south of the foot of the Taylor Street hill—on Highway 1 in Bodega Bay.

In the Tides Restaurant, Melanie is on the phone with her skeptical father, a newspaper publisher, in San Francisco. As Melanie tells him about the attack on the school, an older townswoman, Mrs. Bundy (Ethel Griffies), speaks up, adding scientific commentary about birds. Patrons and workers at the restaurant, including a traveling salesman and a mother with her children, begin to debate the reasons behind the recent bird incidents. Mitch arrives with the local sheriff and they explain that the police from Santa Rosa, the nearest city, believe that Dan Fawcett was killed by an intruder and the birds only entered after Fawcett was dead. The traveling salesman remembers a similar incident where a flock of seagulls flew through the town of Santa Cruz (100 miles south of Bodega Bay) attacking people.

As the discussion of the bird attacks continues in the Tides, Melanie hears a bird cry and sees a gull swoop down and strike a man at the nearby gas station while he is filling up his tank. When he falls over, the gas starts spilling onto the ground. At the same time, the traveling salesman, who recently left the Tides, lights a cigar and unknowingly drops his match into a pool of gas causing a massive fire and explosion. The gas station, a specially constructed set, was located on a studio lot in Southern California where live-action footage of the fire was filmed.

After the explosion, the gulls start diving down on the town and attacking the townspeople. There is a bird's-eye-view or "balloon shot" of Bodega Bay showing the red-roofed buildings of the Tides Wharf complex, the surrounding buildings, and the gas fire, as gulls swoop down toward the town. The scene was filmed using matte technology. The view of the Tides complex itself was based on the actual layout of the complex, but the other buildings shown around the Tides did not exist and were painted in. Hitchcock explained to Truffaut that one of the reasons he did the balloon-shot scene was "to show the exact topography of Bodega Bay, with the town, the sea, the coast, and the gas station on fire in one single image." Hitchcock was careful to help the audience understand the imaginary geography he had created for Bodega Bay, and to consistently depict this geography throughout the film.

VIEW OF THE GAS STATION SET IN "DOWNTOWN" BODEGA BAY

A BIRD'S-EYE VIEW OF BODEGA BAY USING MATTE TECHNOLOGY. THE BUILDINGS WERE PAINTED INTO THE SCENE, AND THE BIRDS WERE ADDED USING SPECIAL EFFECTS.

Filming in Downtown Bloomfield

HITCHCOCK FILMED A SCENE SHOWING A FRIGHTENED Mitch and Melanie walking down a bird-littered street. There are a number of old wooden buildings and one has a car crashed into it.

The footage was intended to be used during, or immediately after, the Bodega Bay fire-and-explosion scene, but was ultimately not used in the final cut of the film. In the scene it looked like civilization itself had been destroyed. It was filmed in tiny downtown Bloomfield, located 15 miles east of Bodega Bay along Bodega Avenue. This village is even smaller than Bodega, but it has the charming, near-deserted, one-block-long historic downtown shown in the scene. The old wooden buildings include Stormy's Tavern and a Masons lodge.

CONTEMPORARY VIEW OF DOWNTOWN BLOOMFIELD

MITCH AND MELANIE WALKING THROUGH DESERTED BUILDINGS IN DOWNTOWN BLOOMFIELD. THIS FOOTAGE WAS NOT USED IN THE FILM'S FINAL CUT.

In an interesting side note to the gas station explosion scene, locals in Bodega Bay who watched *The Birds* were amused by the horse and buggy shown spilling cabbages during this sequence. It had been many decades since anyone had seen this mode of transport in Bodega Bay.

Melanie gets trapped in a phone booth outside the Tides Restaurant, until she is rescued by Mitch. Several birds crash into the booth, splintering the glass; a bloody-faced man appears in front of the booth desperately seeking refuge from the birds who are pecking him to death.

During this scene, Melanie appears like a bird trapped in a cage. The phone booth used in this scene actually existed by the Tides Restaurant in 1963. It was removed when the building was rebuilt.

MITCH RESCUES MELANIE FROM A PHONE BOOTH AT THE TIDES RESTAURANT DURING THE BIRD ATTACK

The End of the World

Following the attack, Mitch and Melanie walk up Bodega Lane toward the schoolhouse and Annie's residence, looking for Cathy. There is a view of the schoolhouse and the Druid Hall across Bodega Lane.

The Druid Hall, located at 132 Bodega Lane, was used as a meeting place by the Ancient Order of Druids, a beneficent society and social organization related to the Masons. The building still exists, although it has been painted bright yellow and remodeled with outside porches added—looking nothing like the building in the movie. Today, this building houses the Wooden Duck Antique Shop specializing in 18th- and 19th-century furniture and housewares.

After arriving at Annie's cottage, Mitch and Melanie discover Annie is dead. Cathy Brenner has survived and is hiding in the cottage. She is rescued by Mitch and all three flee in Melanie's car.

VIEW OF THE BODEGA BAY SCHOOLHOUSE COVERED IN BIRDS

MITCH AND MELANIE WALK UP BODEGA LANE TOWARDS THE SCHOOLHOUSE AND DRUID HALL IN BODEGA

CONTEMPORARY VIEW OF THE WOODEN DUCK ANTIQUE SHOP
(FORMERLY THE DRUID HALL) IN BODEGA

HITCHCOCK ON LOCATION IN FRONT OF THE "BODEGA BAY SCHOOL," DIRECTING SUZANNE PLESHETTE AND ROD TAYLOR

The next scene cuts to the Brenner house, with Mitch on a ladder boarding up the windows. The phone has been knocked out by the most recent bird attack, but the power is still working. After Mitch and Melanie go inside, the first of two news updates comes in from a San Francisco radio station. The news announcer reports on the bird attack at the Bodega Bay School, mentioning that a little girl is in the hospital in Santa Rosa. The announcer continues: "We understand there was another attack on the town but the information is rather sketchy. So far, no word has come through to show if there have been further attacks."

With the loss of the phone, Bodega Bay's connections to civilization are slowly being severed. This radio broadcast is a clever way of heightening the tension and reminding the audience of Bodega Bay's geographic context. The area is isolated from the civilization of Santa Rosa and San Francisco. Bodega Bay is close enough to the metropolis of San Francisco to be connected by radio and car, but far enough to be remote and vulnerable. Bodega Bay is so small it does not even have its own radio station, hospital, or police force. Instead, it relies on the Sonoma County seat of Santa Rosa, itself a relatively small and isolated town.

After everyone else has fallen asleep, Melanie foolishly investigates a fluttering sound upstairs. She is repeatedly slashed and cut by a massive flock of various types of birds, eventually falling unconscious to the floor as the attacks continue. Finally, Mitch rescues her with Lydia's assistance.

This scene was filmed with live birds that were in extremely close proximity to the cast and crew. Crewmen with thick leather gloves hurled live birds at Tippi Hedren. At one point live birds were actually attached to the actress with loose elastic bands. To obtain less than one minute of film in the final cut of the movie, seven days of filming were needed.

Following this attack, Mitch goes out to the garage and listens to another short broadcast from San Francisco on his car radio. The newscaster intones that bird attacks have continued in Bodega Bay and some minor attacks have also occurred in nearby Sebastopol and in Santa Rosa. Apparently Bodega Bay has been cordoned off and the military is considering going in. Bodega Bay's isolation is nearly complete and the bird attacks are spilling into nearby communities.

In the final scene, the whole group walks nervously out to the car, through a mass of birds silently watching from all over the house and grounds. The Brenners and Melanie drive slowly away from the house with the area covered by birds.

There has been a considerable amount of discussion about the ambiguousness of the ending. The film's screenwriter, Evan Hunter, planned to have the Brenners and Melanie drive through a devastated, bird-strewn Bodega Bay. The group would survive one final bird attack by speeding away from town so quickly that the birds could not keep up. Hitchcock also reportedly considered ending the film with a shot of the Golden Gate Bridge. He was going to show the Brenners and Melanie Daniels approaching the bridge and driving toward San Francisco with the bridge completely covered by birds, implying that the bird attacks were spreading beyond the confines of rustic Sonoma County in a sort of doomsday scenario.

MELANIE BEING ATTACKED UPSTAIRS IN THE BRENNER HOUSE

MEMBERS OF THE CREW HURLED LIVE BIRDS AT THE ACTRESS

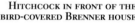

HITCHCOCK IN FRONT OF THE
BIRD-COVERED BRENNER HOUSE

VIEW OF THE BRENNER PROPERTY AND DRIVEWAY COVERED IN BIRDS.
SOME OF THE BIRDS WERE LIVE, SOME WERE DUMMIES, AND SOME WERE
ADDED USING SPECIAL EFFECTS.

Ultimately, Hitchcock decided to cut Hunter's ending down to the ambiguous version shown in the film, with the family slowly driving away from the bird-infested Brenner house. This final scene was very complicated to film and edit. It required multiple film exposures in combination with a matte painting in order to obtain the image of the Brenner house covered with birds.

Hitchcock did not want to have the words "The End" shown on the screen, preferring ambiguity. In fact, the final print and initial copies of the film did not contain "The End." However, when the film was shown at a pre-release screening in 1963, the audience was confused about whether or not that represented the real ending to the film. Based on this screening, studio executives decided to add "The End" to the film to bring a sense of finality. Because this decision was made at the last moment, it was too late to add the words to the negative, and thus the studio had to print the words on each release copy of the film.

Recently, in order to restore Hitchcock's original vision, home video and DVD releases of *The Birds* do not have the words "The End" at the conclusion of the film.

Other Films' Bay Area

Other Films

Using Bay Area Geography to Create Cinematic Suspense

"I'd concentrate on the view if I were you. That's more worthwhile. Rather reminds me of our coastline at home. Do you know Cornwall at all?"

— Maxim de Winter in *Rebecca*

Hitchcock utilized his intimate knowledge of the San Francisco Bay Area to add geographic backgrounds that accentuate the plots and moods of his movies. According to Robert Boyle, a longtime Hitchcock Production Designer (also sometimes known as Art Director or Set Designer):

"I think Northern California always reminded Hitch of England. There was something about the weather, which was very unpredictable. It was fog and rain and then sunshine. . . . It was a moody strange area both forbidding and foreboding and I believe that's what intrigued him. It had a kind of mystical quality."

In addition to *Shadow of a Doubt*, *Vertigo*, and *The Birds*, which were set primarily in the Bay Area, a number of additional Hitchcock films utilized Bay Area geography. *Rebecca*, *Suspicion*, *Psycho*, *Marnie*, *Topaz*, and *Family Plot* all had a scene or a series of scenes filmed in or inspired by Northern California locations.

Filming at Point Lobos for *Rebecca*

The dramatic seaside cliffs and rocky waters of Northern and Central California are superb settings for a Hitchcock film, and indeed the coastal areas appear in several of his films. None was more dramatic than the scenes of the Monterey County coastline in *Rebecca*.

Rebecca, based on a novel by Daphne du Maurier, was released in 1940. Although the film was the first motion picture Hitchcock directed in the U.S., David Selznick, who exercised very tight control over all his films, produced the movie. It is well documented that Selznick and Hitchcock had a tense relationship while they worked together, and struggled for control over the details of filmmaking. When analyzing *Rebecca*, it is important to recognize Selznick's powerful influence on the film. The resulting work was a haunting, Gothic romance about a woman who is ever-present, even after her own death. It was the only Hitchcock movie that won the Academy Award for Best Picture. Hitchcock also received a Best Director nomination, although he lost the Oscar to John Ford for *The Grapes of Wrath*.

Rebecca is first set in Monte Carlo, Monaco, in southern France, and then in the southern English countryside near Cornwall. However, Hitchcock mixes in background footage of tree-lined dirt roads, rocky cliffs, and scenic ocean views from the California coast at Point Lobos, which appear remarkably similar to the European settings.

THE OPENING CREDITS FOR *REBECCA*, FEATURING POINT LOBOS IN THE BACKGROUND

Point Lobos

POINT LOBOS STATE RESERVE IS A FEW MILES south of Carmel, off what is today called Highway 1. The reserve is a popular tourist destination because of its steep, rugged cliffs, sweeping views, and exotic flora. Point Lobos is such a dramatic setting that the landscape artist Francis McComas referred to it as "the greatest meeting of land and sea in the world."

Point Lobos became part of the California State Park System in 1933 when A.M. Allan donated key pieces of land, including the Monterey cypress tree grove in the northwestern part of the park, which is now named after him. In 1960, 750 acres of under-water land were added to the park, creating the first submerged reserve in the United States. In the past, the area had served as a whaling station and an abalone farm. Today, it is a protected wildlife habitat and state park. The area is home to numerous species of animals including gray whales, sea lions, harbor seals, blue herons, and cormorants.

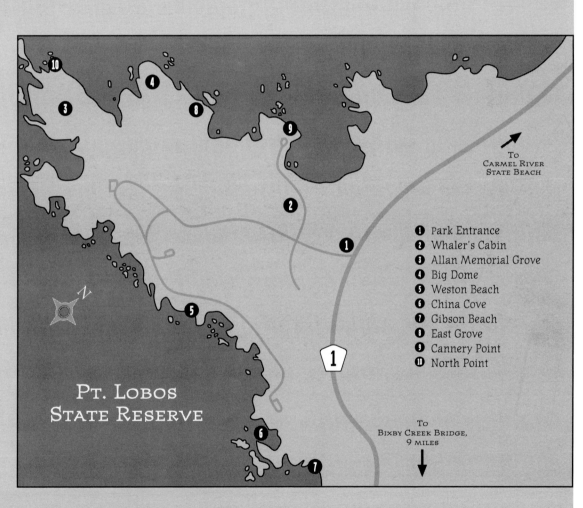

PT. LOBOS
STATE RESERVE

TO
CARMEL RIVER
STATE BEACH

❶ Park Entrance
❷ Whaler's Cabin
❸ Allan Memorial Grove
❹ Big Dome
❺ Weston Beach
❻ China Cove
❼ Gibson Beach
❽ East Grove
❾ Cannery Point
❿ North Point

TO
BIXBY CREEK BRIDGE,
9 MILES

In the early years of filmmaking, movie studios had been permitted to do full-scale location shooting at Point Lobos. Numerous films—such as *Foolish Wives* (1922), *Evangeline* (1929), and *Treasure Island* (1934)—were filmed there. The damage caused by the construction of elaborate sets and the presence of hundreds of crew and cast members led to a ban on all filming at the park, except for shooting background footage with a strictly limited presence of cast, crew, and equipment. This meant the filming for *Rebecca* had to be done without any of the principal stars actually traveling to the location. Thus, in the Point Lobos sequences in *Rebecca*, doubles are filmed on location from a distance by the "second team," led by movie director D. Ross Lederman and cinematographer Archie Stout. Additional location shots were used as background footage in process shots and later combined with the stars on the studio stage. Hitchcock was not present at Point Lobos.

Despite these restrictions on filmmaking activities at Point Lobos, while shooting the background footage for *Rebecca* the film crew moved a large amount of underbrush, scrubs, and vines; accessed environmentally sensitive areas that were off-limits; and constructed platforms and runways, altering the environment and damaging young cypress trees. This led to a firestorm of local criticism. The newspaper *The Carmel Pine Cone* ran stories such as "We Call It An Outrage" (October 6, 1939) and "State Park Rules Ignored As 'Rebecca' Scenes Shot" (October 13, 1939). The locals considered it poetic justice that the entire film crew developed severe cases of poison ivy, most requiring hospitalization, from working in the park's brush.

VIEW OF TWO TREES IN POINT LOBOS DURING THE OPENING TITLE
SEQUENCE OF *REBECCA*

During the opening credits of *Rebecca*, there is a series of shots showing a shadowy, forested area with fog floating over a dirt path, creating the impression of a mysterious or fantastic landscape. This footage was filmed a quarter of a mile from the main entrance of Point Lobos Park. The actual forested area in Point Lobos has a mysterious quality with pockets of mist regularly appearing and a range of different, exotic-looking vegetation.

The story begins with a shot of a rocky shoreline covered by foaming waves. The heroine sees a distraught Maxim de Winter (Laurence Olivier) outside of "Monte Carlo." De Winter appears to be contemplating suicide, staring down a high cliff toward the rocky waters below. As a side note, the heroine (Joan Fontaine) is unnamed in the film, referred to in the screenplay as "I," because the story begins as a first-person narrative told by the leading lady.

CONTEMPORARY VIEW OF THE WOODS NEAR THE ENTRANCE TO POINT LOBOS

Early in this clifftop scene, there is a wide shot of the background scenery. De Winter is in the foreground, the heroine is in the mid-ground with Monterey cypress trees behind her, and an arm-like outcropping of land reaching into the ocean across a small bay is in the background.

The shots in this scene, which show the actors at a distance, were live action, filmed on location with stand-ins for the stars. The close-up shots that show Olivier and Fontaine were process shots with background footage taken from Point Lobos.

The precise location at Point Lobos where this footage was shot is unknown. Kurt Loesch, a park docent and resident historian, believes the scene was filmed at North Point just off the Cypress Grove Trail, in the Allan Memorial Grove. The off-camera production photo with Olivier and Fontaine's doubles, shown on the following page, does appear to have been taken at North Point, which suggests that at a minimum, the crew considered shooting film footage at this location, even if it was not used in the final cut of the movie. However, the views from this location are not identical to the footage in *Rebecca*.

DE WINTER AND HEROINE ON A DRAMATIC CLIFF NEAR "MONTE CARLO," BUT ACTUALLY FILMED AT POINT LOBOS

CONTEMPORARY VIEW OF THE OCEAN FROM NORTH POINT ON THE CYPRESS GROVE TRAIL

PRODUCTION PHOTO OF FONTAINE'S AND OLIVIER'S DOUBLES AT NORTH POINT ON THE CYPRESS GROVE TRAIL

Monterey Cypress Trees

Other docents believe the footage was filmed off one of the other northern trails at Point Lobos, speculating it could have been shot at Big Dome, East Grove, or Canary Point. If the scene was filmed on the northern part of Point Lobos, the outcropping of land seen across a bay from the actors would have been Carmel River State Beach, which is east of the park. There does not appear to be a definitive match with the view shown in the film anywhere along the coastal trails on the north side of the Point Lobos Peninsula. Due to erosion, the route of the trails in this part of the park has changed substantially in the intervening 60-plus years since *Rebecca* was filmed. In earlier times, the trails were closer to the rocky coastal cliffs than they are today. There are, however, many similar views of cypress trees and the Carmel River State Beach.

Another reason why the actual view is not discernible is that some of the background views are partial matte drawings, modifying the actual geography. According to George E. Turner's essay *Du Maurier + Selznick + Hitchcock = Rebecca*, matte artist Al Simpson and special effects cinematographer Clarence W.D. Slifer used matte shots to modify the details of many shots in the film.

Later in the film, there is a scene set in "Monte Carlo," where the heroine is painting a seascape view from a hotel veranda by the water. De Winter approaches and remarks that the view reminds him of the coast in his home at Cornwall, England.

DISTANT VIEW OF THE VERANDA WITH HEROINE

THE PRESENCE OF MONTEREY CYPRESS TREES (*Cupressus macrocarpa*) in the background of the scene where the heroine meets De Winter is notable and helps identify the location as Point Lobos, since the trees have a very limited natural range. There are only two groves of naturally appearing Monterey cypress trees in the world: one at Point Lobos, and the other at nearby Cypress Point at Pebble Beach. The trees are part of a fragile ecosystem, living on the exposed rocky cliffs overlooking the ocean.

According to Brende and Lamb, tree care experts in Northern California:

"Before it was widely cultivated, the Monterey cypress always grew within a half mile of high tide in a small area between Monterey and Point Lobos. Sea winds twisted and thickened the trunks into fantastic, whimsical shapes, giving the wild cypress a mystical, elfin appearance."

The striking visual quality of the trees make them a perfect backdrop for filmmaking. Hitchcock used the trees again almost twenty years later in the Cypress Point scene in *Vertigo*, filmed a few miles north of Point Lobos at Pebble Beach.

The opening shot in this scene was taken in Point Lobos. This shot is a live-action distant view down to the veranda with the heroine standing by herself in the distance. A distinctive series of hill-shaped rocks appears in the background. The location where this footage was filmed can be identified as Weston Beach—named after photographer Edward Weston—by the distinctive rock outcroppings poking up through the water visible in the background of the scene. The woman shown in this shot was Joan Fontaine's stand-in.

For this shot, the film crew gave the scene a manicured, civilized feeling by dressing up the landscape of Weston Beach. The set was built on rock outcroppings on the beach, but through the use of clever camera angles, props, and matte work, the fact that the location was only a small set on a remote rocky beach, instead of a large veranda at an elegant hotel in Monaco, is disguised. Wooden baluster posts and large flower pots were set up on location to provide the façade of a veranda balcony. The wooden planks and shrubbery were also brought to the location by the filmmakers. Finally, the large mountains and buildings in the background were added in as a matte that was overlaid around the low-lying coastal hills actually present in the location.

The other images in this scene are closer views from behind and in front of the characters, with the heroine painting and de Winter standing at the balcony. The shots from behind the characters looking out at the ocean are process shots filmed on the studio stage with Olivier and Fontaine standing in front of footage taken from Point Lobos.

VIEW OF THE VERANDA SET USED IN REBECCA AT WESTON BEACH IN POINT LOBOS

CONTEMPORARY VIEW OF THE DISTINCTIVE SERIES OF ROCKS NEAR WESTON BEACH AT POINT LOBOS

CONTEMPORARY VIEW OF THE WOODEN BALUSTER POSTS USED IN THE VERANDA SET AT WESTON BEACH

VIEW UP THE STAIRS FROM THE BEACH AT MANDERLEY

The baluster posts used on the location set for the opening distant shot are still kept at Point Lobos in the Whaling Cabin as part of an exhibit on the history of filming in the park.

After de Winter and the heroine are married, the action shifts to de Winter's estate called Manderley, located in "Cornwall, England." In the film, Manderley looks both magnificent and intimidating. With its grand size, expansive grounds, and oceanside location, Manderley makes a strong visual impact.

In reality, the Manderley house consists of miniature scale models, constructed by the studio crew and filmed on a studio lot. Manderley's grounds were filmed in Southern California. The shots of ocean waves crashing on the rocks, interspersed throughout the second part of the film, are taken at Point Lobos.

In his interview with Truffaut, Hitchcock compares the remote location of Manderley with the rural isolation of the Brenner house in *The Birds*. In each film, the dramatic California coast adds suspense because the setting indicates there is no one to turn to outside the immediate household members and friends.

As the movie progresses, the heroine walks from Manderley down a steep wooden staircase to the beach in pursuit of her dog, and once on the beach she finds a mysterious stone cabin.

VIEW FROM THE TOP OF THE CLIFF LOOKING DOWN AT THE STAIRS LEADING TO THE BEACH AT MANDERLEY

VIEW OF THE STAIRCASE AT GIBSON BEACH, POINT LOBOS, TAKEN DURING
THE FILMING OF *REBECCA*

CONTEMPORARY VIEW OF THE STAIRCASE AT CHINA COVE

The location of the stairway portion of this scene was Gibson Beach at Point Lobos. The footage of the heroine descending the stairs uses the double for Joan Fontaine, and was filmed on location. The close-up shot that actually shows Fontaine and views of the stone cabin was filmed on a studio set. Footage of the beach was shot on Catalina Island in Southern California.

Today, the trail and stairs leading to Gibson Beach are closed due to storm damage. However, the wooden stairs at nearby China Cove are very similar to those at Gibson Beach and reminiscent of the stairs shown in *Rebecca*.

The rest of the footage in *Rebecca* was filmed in Europe or on studio sets. Nevertheless, the Northern California coast sets the stage for the movie and its gloomy atmosphere.

Filming the Coast Between Carmel and Big Sur for *Suspicion*

Just one year (and three films) after *Rebecca*, Hitchcock returned to the Monterey County coast. This time, the coastal highway doubles as the English coastline in sequences for *Suspicion*, released in 1941.

Partway into the film, Lina Mackinlaw (Joan Fontaine) and her husband John Aysgarth (Cary Grant) are driving back home from her father's funeral along a narrow coastal road after attending the reading of Lina's father's will. The couple stop to admire a dramatic view of an undeveloped, jagged, U-shaped cliff area high above the ocean. John gets the idea that the land would be a good location for a real estate development.

This "English coast" vista is fictitiously located at Tangmere-by-the-Sea, in West Essex, England. In reality, the scene was filmed at the picturesque cliffs near the Bixby Creek Bridge, between Carmel and Big Sur, along Highway 1.

PRODUCTION SKETCH OF TANGMERE-BY-THE-SEA

THIS WIDE SHOT WAS FILMED ON LOCATION WITH A STAND-IN FOR JOAN FONTAINE

Bixby Creek Bridge

THE BIXBY CREEK BRIDGE, BUILT IN 1932, IS ONE of the more dramatic bridges in California. The bridge, which still stands today, crosses a coastal bluff that drops almost 300 feet to the water below.

Although the highway and views around the bridge are included in *Suspicion*, the bridge itself is carefully hidden. Tangmere-by-the-Sea was supposed to be a desolate and undeveloped area, so a bridge would have spoiled the effect. Hitchcock directed the angle of the shot to keep the bridge just out of the camera's range.

Interestingly, there are several location-scouting photographs of the Bixby Creek Bridge from the movie *Rebecca*. The advance crew apparently considered the Bixby Creek Bridge site during location work for *Rebecca*, although Hitchcock did not end up using the area until *Suspicion*.

LOCATION-SCOUTING IMAGE OF BIXBY CREEK BRIDGE AND THE SURROUNDING AREA, CIRCA 1938

CONTEMPORARY VIEW OF THE BLUFFS AROUND THE BIXBY CREEK BRIDGE. THIS PHOTO WAS TAKEN FROM HURRICANE POINT, SOUTH OF THE BIXBY CREEK BRIDGE ON HIGHWAY 1, AND IS ROUGHLY THE SAME SHOT AS WAS USED WHEN LINA RACES TO TANGMERE-BY-THE-SEA FEARING THAT JOHN HAS MURDERED BEAKY.

After the initial coastal scene with Lina and John at the cliff, the film cuts to a snapshot of the same cliffside location inside John and Lina's house as John and his friend, Beaky (Nigel Bruce), discuss a proposed resort development at the location. Later, when Lina sees the photo of the coast during a Scrabble game, she has a premonition of her husband John pushing his friend Beaky off the cliff, and faints at the horror of her vision.

The next day, Lina wakes up and realizes John and Beaky have gone to see the cliffside property. Fearing the worst, she jumps into her car and drives over to the location. There are several dramatic shots of Lina looking out at the spectacular coast, and down over the cliff at the treacherous rocks and ocean below. The close-ups of Joan Fontaine were process shots filmed on the studio stage. The distant shots were filmed on location at Hurricane Point, with a double standing in for Fontaine.

In the climactic scene in *Suspicion*, Lina thinks John has killed Beaky and fears for her own life. John drives a frightened Lina to her mother's house. He speeds along a narrow twisting road high above the ocean and Lina believes he is about to kill her. She panics and practically jumps out of the car in an attempt to save herself, but it turns out that her husband, while dishonest, is not a murderer. Footage used in this scene was also filmed along Highway 1, slightly south of Carmel before the Bixby Creek Bridge.

In all of these scenes along Highway 1, Hitchcock was apparently able to get permission to stop traffic for filming. More than twenty years later, during the filming of *The Birds*, the authorities were not so accommodating and refused to grant the filmmaker similar permission.

These coastal scenes wonderfully utilize the rugged beauty of the California coast in order to heighten the level of suspense in the movie.

Psycho's Connections to Northern California

Psycho, released in 1960, is one of the most shocking and disturbing thrillers of all time. The film broke new ground in the horror genre when it was first released, and remains one of Hitchcock's most memorable and most popular films. The director himself considered it a dark comedy, but many viewers who see the film are never able to forget the horrific shower scene.

In the film, after stealing forty thousand dollars from her employer's safe, Marion Crane (Janet Leigh) drives from Arizona to California. During a heavy rainstorm, she pulls into the lonely Bates Motel for the night. While waiting to check in, she notices the Gothic Bates Mansion obscured by the darkness and rain, with its wooden watchtower and peering windows, looming ominously just up the hill.

NIGHT VIEW OF THE BATES MANSION FROM THE MOTEL

The Bates Mansion appears many more times during the film, but the full view of the house is obscured in the early scenes. As the plot unfolds, so too does the eerie appearance of the mansion. Like a monster in a classic horror film, the mansion is not shown from a direct frontal view until its final appearance. Instead, it is shown from the side, at an uncomfortable angle, looking up from below.

HITCHCOCK IN FRONT OF THE BATES MANSION

WIDE VIEW OF THE BATES MANSION AND MOTEL

CREW SETTING UP A SHOT IN FRONT OF THE BATES MOTEL WITH THE
MANSION IN THE BACKGROUND

The Bates Mansion and the attached motel are so prominently featured in *Psycho* that they almost have a co-starring role. Although the mansion was a studio set, there has been a great deal of speculation surrounding the inspiration for its design. Hitchcock himself hinted that the Bates Mansion was inspired by Northern California architecture, as he explained in an interview with French director François Truffaut:

"The mysterious atmosphere [of *Psycho*] is, to some extent, quite accidental. For instance, the actual locale of the events is in Northern California, where that type of house is very common. They're either called 'California Gothic,' or, when they're particularly awful, they're called 'California Gingerbread.' I simply wanted to be accurate, and there is no question but that both the house and the motel are authentic reproductions of the real thing."

During the early stages of screenplay writing, Hitchcock told the *New York Times* that the action in *Psycho* would take place near Sacramento, also hinting at a Northern California location.

According to Stephen Rebello in *Alfred Hitchcock and the Making of Psycho*, Joseph Hurley and Robert Clathworthy, the art direction and set design team, built the house with only a small amount of input from Hitchcock. Rebello credits Edward Hopper's painting, *House by the Railroad*, as one of several possible influences.

WIDE VIEW OF THE HOTEL McCRAY IN SANTA CRUZ, CIRCA 1970

FRONT VIEW OF THE BATES MANSION DURING THE DAY

However, according to Santa Cruz lore, the dilapidated Hotel McCray, now the refurbished Sunshine Villa, inspired the Bates Mansion. This interpretation is more consistent with Hitchcock's reference to Northern California in the Truffaut interview. This building is located on Beach Hill at 80 Front Street (between River and Pacific Avenues) in Santa Cruz.

CONTEMPORARY VIEW OF THE SUNSHINE VILLA, FORMERLY THE HOTEL MCCRAY IN SANTA CRUZ

VIEW OF THE HOTEL MCCRAY IN SANTA CRUZ, AFTER IT WAS CLOSED AND JUST BEFORE IT WAS REMODELED, 1988

VIEW UP THE STAIRCASE TO THE SECOND FLOOR OF THE BATES MANSION
INTERIOR SET

In addition, Bernheim House, once located at Broadway and Ocean Streets in Santa Cruz but now demolished, was also reputed to resemble the Bates Mansion. Given that Hitchcock was a frequent visitor to Santa Cruz while he was staying at his nearby Scotts Valley Ranch, it is possible that he was familiar with both the McCray and Bernheim buildings and could have been referring to one or both of them when he spoke to Truffaut.

The Bates Mansion shares characteristics with many of the Victorian buildings in the Bay Area. For example, despite some obvious architectural differences, Hitchcock uses it to convey the same haunted quality as he did with the Portman Mansion, an actual building in San Francisco used in *Vertigo* as the "McKittrick Hotel." The central, interior staircase on the Bates Mansion set had a similar design to the staircase in the McKittrick scene in *Vertigo*.

According to Rebello, there is one piece of the Bates Mansion set that is definitively traceable to the Bay Area: the front door. The massive door to the Bates Mansion, shown only briefly in the film, was originally built for a studio set of the Crocker House, an actual San Francisco mansion.

Today, the Bates Mansion and Motel set is part of the Universal Studios back lot tour in Los Angeles. It is one of the most popular attractions.

FRONT DOOR OF THE BATES MANSION

The final Bay Area connection to *Psycho* was the desolate swamp scenes where Norman Bates (Anthony Perkins) dumps the cars of his victims. According to Rebello, the crew considered filming on location at Grizzly Island near Fairfield, California (forty miles northeast of San Francisco), but ultimately used a studio lot set in order to save money.

HITCHCOCK INSIDE THE BATES MANSION, WITH THE STAIRWELL AND
NEWEL POST IN THE BACKGROUND

PROMOTIONAL PHOTO OF NORMAN BATES AND THE BATES MANSION

MARNIE ON THE "HARTFORD, CONNECTICUT" RAIL STATION PLATFORM

Marnie: Two Key Northern California Locations

Marnie released in 1964, stars Sean Connery as Mark Rutland and Tippi Hedren as Marnie, a mysterious woman who is a compulsive thief and has an odd fear of the color red. *Marnie* is set in Hartford, Philadelphia, Virginia, Baltimore, and other places on the East Coast where most of the location shooting was done. However, two locations used in the movie were filmed in the San Francisco area.

In the opening scene of the movie, Marnie is shown walking on a train platform. We later learn she is fleeing her employer in Hartford whom she has robbed. This scene shows a brief, nicely composed shot of her on a train platform carrying a bulky yellow handbag and a suitcase. The platform has a distinctive wing-shaped umbrella above it, with a single set of supporting poles in the middle of the wingspan. There is a water tower in the background and a train on the platform.

The train station, which is supposed to be in Hartford, Connecticut, is actually the San Jose train station, today called the Diridon Station, located at Cahill and West San Fernando Streets. Early in the scene, the letters "Southern" are briefly visible on the train, a reference to the Southern Pacific Railroad, which provided passenger service at the San Jose station.

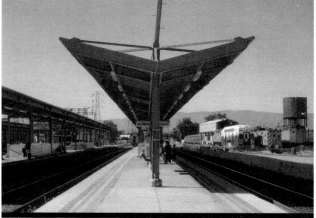

CONTEMPORARY VIEW OF THE RAIL STATION PLATFORM AT SAN JOSE'S DIRIDON STATION

Hitchcock had originally filmed this scene at the Hartford Union Station while the company was doing its location shooting on the East Coast. He apparently was not happy with the results. The director decided to shoot the scene again in San Jose—a short flight up from Los Angeles where the studio filming was taking place. According to studio records, on March 14, 1964, Tippi Hedren and six other cast and crew members flew up from Los Angeles and returned to L.A. the same day after the filming was completed. The scene was shot at dusk, adding an element of tension to Marnie's escape from her employer.

The Diridon Station passenger platform, constructed in 1935, looks very similar today to the way it did during *Marnie*. The refurbished station now accommodates long-haul Amtrak passenger trains and Caltrain commuter trains.

MARNIE AND MARK TALKING ON THE DECK OF THE SS PRESIDENT CLEVELAND

Later in the film, Marnie and Mark take their honeymoon cruise on board a ship headed for the South Seas. The location where they board the ship is never named. However, in the film, they catch a flight to get to the port of departure and it is implied that the ship is leaving from the West Coast since their destinations include Honolulu and Fiji.

Many of the exterior shots were filmed on board the SS President Cleveland of the American President Lines. At the time the scenes were filmed, the ship was docked at Pier 50 (the Mission Rock Terminal) in San Francisco, which was a frequent port-of-call and terminus for the SS President Cleveland.

All the footage on the ship was filmed on February 6, 1964, with the cast and crew flying up from Los Angeles and returning back to L.A. the same day via a chartered flight.

According to studio records, the exterior scenes on the promenade deck and stairway, boat deck and rail, ladder and pool, and sun deck were all filmed on the SS President Cleveland.

AFTER MARK RAPES HER IN THEIR CABIN, MARNIE ATTEMPTS TO COMMIT SUICIDE IN THE SHIP'S POOL

The interior scenes in the dining room and ship's cabin were filmed in a Hollywood studio, as were some close-up shots of the ship's sun deck and pool.

MARK ON THE PROMENADE DECK OF THE SS PRESIDENT CLEVELAND

The SS President Cleveland

THE SS PRESIDENT CLEVELAND, BUILT AT THE BETHLEHEM-Alameda shipyard in the East Bay, was completed in 1947. The ship was a luxury ocean liner that carried passengers and freight. At the time of its completion, along with its sister ship, the SS President Wilson, it was the largest commercial ship ever built on the West Coast. The Cleveland was 609 feet long and weighed more than 15,000 gross tons.

The ship offered a luxurious first class passage with cabins on the forward and higher decks. There were fine dining salons, large lounges and reading rooms, and rows of deck chairs. The passenger list for first-class could accommodate 379 people and the tourist class held 200 people.

In the 1950s and '60s, the ship frequently ran between California and Japan, either from San Francisco or the Port of Los Angeles at San Pedro. It was thus a realistic setting for a honeymoon cruise on the Pacific Ocean. The SS President Cleveland was used as a setting for the fictitious SS Ocean Queen in the 1956-to-1960 TV series *The Gale Storm Show*, a precursor to the *Love Boat*. It was sold to Oceanic Cruise Development, Inc. on February 9, 1973 and renamed Oriental President before being scrapped at Kaohsiung, Taiwan in 1974.

THE SS PRESIDENT CLEVELAND NEAR PIER 50 IN SAN FRANCISCO, 1950

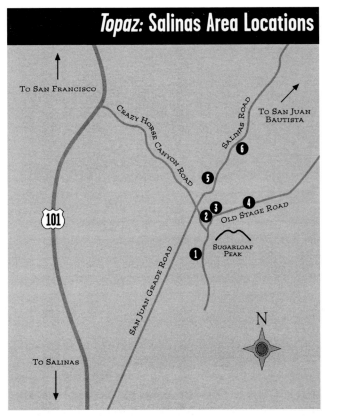

Topaz: Salinas Area Locations

TO SAN FRANCISCO

CRAZY HORSE CANYON ROAD

SALINAS ROAD

TO SAN JUAN BAUTISTA

6

5

101

3
2
4

OLD STAGE ROAD

SAN JUAN GRADE ROAD

1

SUGARLOAF PEAK

N

TO SALINAS

❶ Oak tree (military checkpoint in film)

❷ 200 Old Stage Road/Salinas Transplant Co.

❸ Gabilan Stream Bridge

❹ View of Sugarloaf Peak

❺ Road segment shown in film with matte of palm trees

❻ "Grassy knoll" shown in film

Salinas as a Stand-in for Cuba in *Topaz*

Topaz, released in 1969, is a cold war espionage thriller based on the novel by Leon Uris. The movie stars Frederick Stafford as Andre Devereaux, the French spy who assists the CIA in understanding Russian activities in Cuba during the Missile Crisis. The film features location shooting in Paris, Copenhagen, New York, and Washington D.C. For the extensive Cuban sequence in the middle of the film, some of the exteriors were filmed in Salinas, California, 106 miles south of San Francisco.

During the Cuban portion of the film, Andre visits his lover, Juanita de Cordoba, played by Karen Dior, a widow of a Cuban revolutionary hero. With the help of Juanita and a Cuban couple named the Mendozas (played by Lewis Charles and Anna Navarro), Andre obtains photographs of the Russians unloading missiles at the Cuban port of Viriel.

The Mendozas, hiding on a grassy knoll, observe and photograph the Russian missiles being unloaded at Viriel (actually filmed at the Port of Los Angeles, in San Pedro Bay). Soldiers at a nearby checkpoint notice seagulls flying with bread (which they have swiped from the Mendozas' picnic lunch). The soldiers run up the knoll to investigate and shoot at the fleeing Mendozas.

The entire sequence showing the soldiers chasing the Mendozas was filmed in a geographically discontinuous series of locations near Salinas. According to studio records, the grassy knoll location was filmed along Salinas Road (also called the San Juan Grade), which runs between Salinas and San Juan Bautista, to the east of Highway 101. The footage of the knoll was modified by painter Al Whitlock, who painted several mattes used in *Topaz*. Mr. Whitlock also painted the mattes used in Hitchcock's earlier film *The Birds*. In a side note, bird handler Ray Berwick, who trained the live birds used in *The Birds*, trained the seagulls used in this scene.

THE GRASSY KNOLL WHERE THE MENDOZAS OBSERVE THE RUSSIANS UNLOADING MISSILES IN CUBA

CONTEMPORARY VIEW OF ONE OF THE MANY GRASSY KNOLLS NEAR THE SUMMIT OF THE SAN JUAN GRADE. THE EXACT KNOLL WHERE THE ACTUAL SCENE IS SHOT IS NOT KNOWN.

The soldiers who spot the Mendozas are stationed at a checkpoint on a narrow road with a metal gate and a large shade tree to the right of the gate. According to studio records, the location of the checkpoint was on Old Stage Road about half a mile south of the intersection with Crazy Horse Road and 1.2 miles south of the Gabilan Creek bridge. The film crew constructed an 8-foot-tall swinging gate for the checkpoint and obtained permission from the County Highway Commissioner to halt traffic during filming. The large tree to the right of the checkpoint is one of the many old oak trees that dot the hills and line the roads in the inland areas of the South Bay.

THE CUBAN ARMY'S CHECKPOINT

CONTEMPORARY VIEW OF AN OAK TREE ON OLD STAGE ROAD AT THE APPROXIMATE LOCATION WHERE THE FILM CREW CONSTRUCTED THE CHECKPOINT GATES

THE SOLDIERS' JEEP DRIVING ALONG A "PALM-TREE-LINED ROAD"

CONTEMPORARY VIEW SOUTH ON SALINAS ROAD/SAN JUAN GRADE AT THE
LOCATION THE JEEP WAS LIKELY FILMED SPEEDING PAST THE PALM TREES

THE SOLDIERS' JEEP WITH A VIEW OF A LARGE MOUNTAIN PEAK IN
THE BACKGROUND

CONTEMPORARY VIEW OF SUGARLOAF PEAK. THE VIEW OF SUGARLOAF
PEAK IN *TOPAZ* IS NORTH OF THE GABILAN CREEK BRIDGE ON OLD STAGE
ROAD. THIS VIEW IS A FEW HUNDRED FEET SOUTH OF THE GABILAN CREEK
BRIDGE ON OLD STAGE ROAD.

In the same sequence, the soldiers' jeep is shown speeding along a road, chasing after the Mendozas. There are several different shots of the countryside as the soldiers drive along a curving road with many tall palm trees dotting the landscape.

Based on a driving survey of the area, the first shot in the scene is a view heading south on the Salinas Road/San Juan Grade less than a mile north of the intersection with Crazy Horse Canyon Road. Studio records confirm this shot was modified by an Al Whitlock matte. The palm trees were painted in to better reproduce the landscape in Cuba.

As the jeep speeds along the road, there is a cut to a dramatic view of a mountain peak up ahead, and a car stopped by a bridge on the upcoming length of road. The large mountain shown in this shot is Sugarloaf Peak, with an elevation of 954 feet at its summit.

A good landmark for the area is the Salinas Transplant Company at 200 Old Stage Road—a large strawberry farm that provides strawberries to Dole Foods. The farm is located a couple of hundred yards south of the bridge. This area outside Salinas is intensively farmed, providing a wide variety of fresh produce; it is also John Steinbeck country. The author fished at Gabilan Creek and camped with the boy scouts on Sugarloaf Peak.

A MAN AND HIS HORSE AT A BRIDGE GUARDRAIL IN "CUBA"

Sugarloaf Peak is north of the checkpoint on Old Stage Road, but the views of Sugarloaf Peak depicted in the film shows the jeep heading south on Old Stage Road. For the sequence to be geographically continuous, the footage on Salinas Road would have to have been omitted. To make it geographically accurate, the soldiers and the Mendozas would need to travel more than a mile north of the checkpoint and then make a U-turn and head back south towards the bridge.

The soldiers arrive at the bridge and see the Mendozas, who pretend to be innocent bystanders with a broken-down car. However, one of the soldiers notices Mrs. Mendoza is bleeding. The soldiers realize the Mendozas are the couple they are chasing and take them as prisoners. After the soldiers drive off with the Mendozas, an old man on a horse appears and removes the Mendozas' film from the hollow pipe guardrails of the bridge. Although the Mendozas have been captured, their film of the Russian missiles is safe.

This scene was filmed at the Gabilan Creek Bridge (Bridge Number 119), which is located on Old Stage Road, 1.2 miles north of the location where the soldiers' checkpoint was filmed. At the bridge, the film crew temporarily replaced the existing guardrail that was bolted to the steel uprights with a 3-inch hollow pipe railing. This allowed the pipe ends to serve as a hiding place for the Mendozas' film. After shooting the scene, the crew replaced the original guardrails. Since the filming, new uprights have been added which are shorter than those shown in the film.

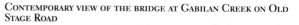

CONTEMPORARY VIEW OF THE BRIDGE AT GABILAN CREEK ON OLD STAGE ROAD

THE SOLDIERS HEAD BACK TOWARD THE CHECKPOINT WITH THE SLOPE OF THE MOUNTAIN IN THE DISTANCE

As the soldiers drive off from the bridge with the captured Mendozas, there is a view looking south down Old Stage Road. The tree-covered peak of a mountain sloping upward from right to left is obstructed by hills and brush on the side of the road before the summit is visible. The soldiers continue heading south on Old Stage Road, back toward the checkpoint. The obscured peak in the view is Sugarloaf Peak.

Later in the Cuban sequence, we learn that the Mendozas have been tortured and have revealed Juanita's role in the scheme to obtain the photos of the missiles. Juanita is killed for her efforts, but Andre escapes back to the West with the photographs of the missiles.

In all, the cast and crew spent a week in Monterey County to obtain the Salinas footage. Shooting occurred between March 22 and 29, 1969. If the filming had taken place later in the year, the lush green look of the grassy hills visible in the movie would have been a less tropical dry brown. The filmmakers set up their base of operations at the Casa Munras Hotel in the city of Monterey. For Hitchcock, the filming marked his return to Monterey and San Benito Counties. San Juan Bautista, home to the famous mission filmed in *Vertigo*, is only about 10 miles away from the locations where the Salinas footage was shot.

CONTEMPORARY VIEW OF THE SLOPE OF SUGARLOAF PEAK

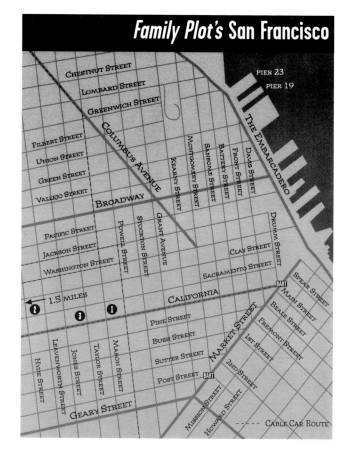

Family Plot's San Francisco

❶ Fairmont Hotel

❷ "Adamson Mansion"/2230 Sacramento Street

❸ "St. Anselm's Cathedral"/Grace Cathedral

Family Plot: Hitchcock's Finale

Family Plot (produced in 1975, released in 1976) was Hitchcock's 53rd and final film. It was made during the golden anniversary year of his career as a director, 50 years after the release of the first film he directed, the British silent picture *The Pleasure Garden* (1925).

Family Plot is a cat-and-mouse suspense film about two couples whose paths intersect in a number of odd ways. Fran (Karen Black) and Arthur Adamson (William Devane) are carrying out a series of kidnappings and diamond thefts. At the same time, George Lumley (Bruce Dern) and Blanche Tyler (Barbara Harris) are searching for the sole surviving heir of a very wealthy elderly woman. The intertwined events that follow include the attempted murders of George and Blanche. Eventually, Arthur and Fran are identified and captured, and it is revealed that Arthur is the heir, although he is unaware of this fact.

Family Plot is notable for its contemporary language and 1970's style. When the movie is compared to Hitchcock's early Northern California films, particularly *Shadow of a Doubt*, there is a strong sense of the director's incredible longevity in the film industry and the immense social changes that occurred in the United States—and the Bay Area—between the 1940s and the 1970s.

Some critics have referred to *Family Plot's* setting as "Los Angfrancisco" or "SanFrangeles," because the film was shot in both San Francisco and Los Angeles under the confusing fiction that the locations are in a single, unnamed city. Even in the script, the location is only generically referred to as "The City." The film often weaves together the two locations into a single scene or sequence. While much of the movie is actually shot in Los Angeles (such as the Rainbird Mansion, golf course, Barlow Creek cemetery, winding mountain road, jewelry store, and other scenes), there are a number of distinctive and notable San Francisco locations that were filmed in the spring and early summer of 1975.

NIGHT VIEW OF THE ADAMSON MANSION GARAGE

In the documentary, *Plotting Family Plot, Family Plot*'s assistant director, Howard Kazanjian, describes Hitchcock's instructions to deliberately and mysteriously obscure the location and setting of the film:

"One of the things he [Hitchcock] did at the very last minute, which was quite unusual for Hitchcock, was to really take away the setting it [*Family Plot*] was originally designed in or the period and location. . . . 'I want to take away anything that said Northern California. I don't want any names [of cities] on police cars. I don't want names on badges. I want you to investigate every person's name in the screenplay and make sure that that person really doesn't exist. And if he does, change it. I want it no city.' And he never gave me an explanation for that. But it was a challenge to change it. We shot in San Francisco. We shot a great deal on the stages, but it was nondescript."

One possible explanation for the use of an unnamed setting in *Family Plot* was that Hitchcock did not want to be accused of "doing the same trick twice" by setting another film explicitly in San Francisco, which he had done so successfully 20 years earlier in *Vertigo*.

CONTEMPORARY VIEW OF THE GARAGE, LOCATED ON BUCHANAN STREET NEAR THE CORNER OF SACRAMENTO STREET

One scene early in the film illustrates this creative blending of geography. After exchanging a kidnapping victim for ransom, Fran and Arthur are driving along what appears to be a low-density suburban residential neighborhood at night (notice the grass and low fence briefly visible through the rear window in the background) before they quickly turn a corner and drive into the garage of their house. Once inside, it is revealed that Fran and Arthur use a room beneath their house as a dungeon for holding their kidnapping victims.

The drive along the suburban neighborhood is in Southern California, but when they turn the corner and enter the garage of their house, the footage was filmed in the dense but upscale urban neighborhood of Pacific Heights in San Francisco. Right before they turn the corner, they are shown driving west on Sacramento Street and then making a right turn onto Buchanan Street. The front of the Adamson House, with the curving staircase and large tree that casts shadows on the house, are briefly shown.

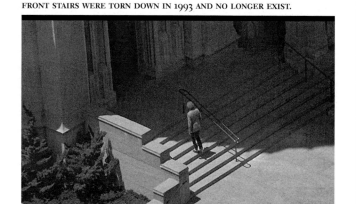

LUMLEY WALKING UP THE STEPS AT "ST. ANSELM'S CATHEDRAL." THESE FRONT STAIRS WERE TORN DOWN IN 1993 AND NO LONGER EXIST.

Later in the film, George is seen walking up the steps and into "St. Anselm's Cathedral." The scene starts with a view of the steps leading to the church, followed by a dramatic shot of the front exterior of the Cathedral with the camera zooming backwards to reveal the full size of the building.

The actual location for this scene is the marvelous Grace Cathedral, at 1051 Taylor Street, atop San Francisco's Nob Hill. The old front stairs on the Cathedral, which existed from 1964 to 1993, were used for this scene. In

EXTERIOR OF "ST. ANSELM'S CATHEDRAL."

1993, the Cathedral House, a large building which sat between the main Cathedral and Taylor Street, was demolished, and the original front stairs shown in *Family Plot* were also removed. In their place, the current, grand front stairs were built leading directly from Taylor Street to the Cathedral's ornate front doors (known as the "Doors of Paradise").

Grace Cathedral

GRACE CATHEDRAL IS LOCATED ON THE SITE OF the former mansions of Charles Crocker, one of the "big four" railroad barons who helped build the transcontinental railroad, and his son, W.H. Crocker. These homes were destroyed in the fire that followed the 1906 earthquake. After the fire, the Crocker family donated the valuable land to the church for construction of a Cathedral. Construction of the French-Gothic-inspired Cathedral began in 1927, but, due to financial constraints and construction interruptions, was not finished until 1964. The seismically sound structure is made of steel and concrete. Grace Cathedral is an Episcopal church, but also serves many interfaith functions as well. It is one of the most grand and famous churches on the West Coast. According to studio records, Universal actually donated $5,000 to Grace Cathedral for the permission to film *Family Plot* there.

GRACE CATHEDRAL, SHOWING THE CATHEDRAL HOUSE AND THE OLD FRONT STEPS, 1964

CONTEMPORARY VIEW OF THE EXTERIOR OF GRACE CATHEDRAL, FROM THE ROOF OF THE MARK HOPKINS HOTEL

INTERIOR OF "ST. ANSELM'S CATHEDRAL," WITH VIEW OF PARISHIONERS

HITCHCOCK, INSIDE GRACE CATHEDRAL, DURING THE FILMING OF FAMILY PLOT

George arrives inside the church just in time to witness Fran and Arthur—disguised as a gray-haired old lady and a man in a verger's robe—kidnap Bishop Wood during a worship service in front of a stunned congregation. The interior of the church, shown during the kidnapping sequence, was also filmed at Grace Cathedral, with church lay staff serving as extras in the scene. However, the end of the church kidnapping scene, where Fran and Arthur spirit the bishop out the back door, was filmed at Emmanuel Presbyterian Church on Wilshire Boulevard in Los Angeles. Again, the locations blend seamlessly from San Francisco to Los Angeles.

As Arthur and Fran drive away from the church, they are next shown driving along a commercial strip development. After they turn a corner, they are in a dense urban neighborhood with apartment buildings and historic houses.

Once again, Los Angeles and San Francisco are blended. As in the earlier sequence, the drive starts out in Southern California, this time in a low-rise commercial strip with palm trees visible out the window. The scene quickly cuts to their car turning left off Clay Street in San Francisco onto the 2200 block of Buchanan Street. There is a view of the California Pacific Medical Center in the left corner of the screen, and of the dramatic 10-story apartment building located at 2210 Jackson Street in the background.

Today, the view of the 2200 block of Buchanan Street is almost unchanged, except for the fact that the view of the apartment building at 2210 Jackson Street is obscured by the growth of a large tree.

Later in the film, Blanche drives by the main entrance of a large hotel. She pulls into the passenger drop-off cul-de-sac in front of the hotel and leaves a message for George with the doorman.

ARTHUR AND FRAN DRIVING IN THE 2200 BLOCK OF BUCHANAN STREET, WITH THE CALIFORNIA PACIFIC MEDICAL CENTER AND THE APARTMENT BUILDING AT 2210 JACKSON STREET IN THE BACKGROUND

CONTEMPORARY VIEW OF THE 2200 BLOCK OF BUCHANAN STREET

This hotel scene was shot on location at the Fairmont Hotel on San Francisco's Nob Hill. The Fairmont Hotel's main entrance is at 950 Mason Street, just two blocks from Grace Cathedral. Almost twenty years earlier, Hitchcock filmed several shots of this same location in *Vertigo*, and the director frequently stayed here when he was in San Francisco.

CONTEMPORARY VIEW OF THE CANOPY AT THE FAIRMONT HOTEL

BLANCHE TALKS WITH THE DOORMAN BENEATH THE CANOPY OF THE FAIRMONT HOTEL

THE INTERIOR OF THE ADAMSON MANSION WAS FILMED ON A STUDIO SET

Blanche next drives over to the Adamson Mansion, fictitiously located at 1001 Franklin Street. This address is repeated several times during the film, but it does not appear to be a deliberate allusion to an actual location. In the real world, 1001 Franklin Street in San Francisco is home to a senior citizens housing facility built in the early 1960s called the Martin Luther Towers. The Towers is located in the Western Addition neighborhood, near the corner of Ellis and Franklin Streets.

When Blanche drives from the Fairmont Hotel to the Adamson Mansion, this is one of the few San Francisco sequences in the film that is geographically reasonable. The Fairmont Hotel is less than a mile and a half away from the corner of Sacramento and Buchanan Streets where the mansion is located.

Blanche climbs the stairs to the front door of the Adamson Mansion. The curving steps and the front exterior of the house are shown for the first time in the film.

According to the building's owner, Hitchcock himself spent several days driving around Pacific Heights in his chauffeured limousine, trying to find the right location to film the Adamson Mansion. The key feature that attracted Hitchcock to this particular house was a large Hollywood juniper tree in the front, near the entry stairs. The tree provided a spooky atmosphere, adding shadows to the front of the house during the nighttime scenes.

BLANCHE AT THE ADAMSON MANSION FRONT DOOR

Once the site was selected, Hitchcock reportedly drove up to the house to see if the lunar cycle was bright enough to project the desired shadows on the front door. The director would quickly drive away if the shadows were not dramatic enough. The film crew, however, was present at the location every night for more than two weeks to get what turned out to be less than two minutes of on-screen footage.

Unfortunately, the juniper tree was removed a few years ago, as it was damaging the building's front exterior staircase.

The Adamson Mansion

CONTEMPORARY VIEW OF THE FRONT EXTERIOR OF 2230 SACRAMENTO STREET

BLANCHE IN FRONT OF THE ADAMSON MANSION

AT THE TIME OF FILMING, THE ADAMSON MANSION WAS ACTUALLY AN APARTMENT BUILDING and not a single-family home. It is located at 2230 Sacramento Street, at the corner of Buchanan Street. The fictitious address, 1001 Franklin Street, is less than a mile from the building's actual location on Sacramento Street.

The house was originally built around 1890 as a single-family Victorian mansion. During World War II, the U.S. Army converted the house into an office building. Around this time, stucco was added to the exterior of the wooden structure, covering up the original Victorian details. After the war, the building was converted to apartments.

Today, the apartment building retains the sweeping steps up from the sidewalk to the front door, the distinctive corded concrete archway, and the Buchanan Street garage around the corner from the front entrance, as shown in the film.

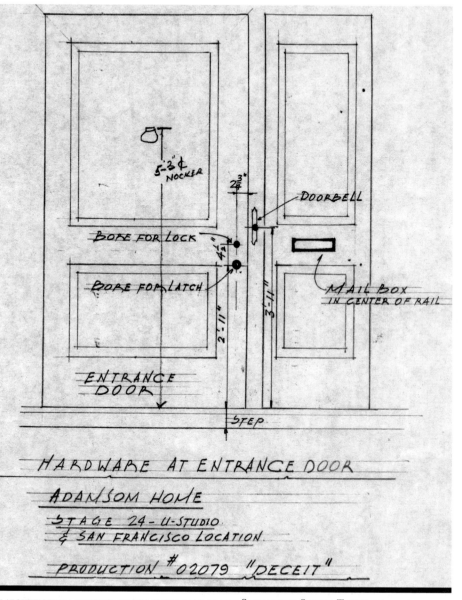

AN ARCHITECTURAL DRAWING OF THE FRONT DOOR AT 2230 SACRAMENTO STREET. THIS SKETCH WAS DONE BY THE STUDIO TO HELP BUILD AN ACCURATE SET. NOTE: AS STATED AT THE BOTTOM OF THE SKETCH, THE FILM WAS ORIGINALLY TITLED DECEIT.

In the film, only some of the exterior sequences show the actual apartment building in San Francisco. Some of the close-up exteriors and all interior views were filmed on a studio set. Hitchcock based his re-created set on the actual apartment building, including a detailed architectural drawing of the front door.

After ringing the Adamson Mansion doorbell and getting no response, Blanche walks back to her car, which is parked in front of the garage on Buchanan Street. As Blanche reaches her car, Arthur and Fran open their garage door to leave. Blanche notices the sinister couple has Bishop Wood with them. They quickly trap Blanche in the garage and lock her in the underground dungeon. Once Arthur and Fran leave, George arrives on the scene, sneaks through a window in the garage, and rescues Blanche.

VIEW OF THE ALLEY AND GARAGE AT 2230 SACRAMENTO STREET. THIS PHOTO WAS TAKEN BY THE UNIVERSAL STUDIOS ADVANCE SCOUTING TEAM. NOTE THE WINDOW ON THE GARAGE.

GEORGE IN THE ALLEY BESIDE THE ADAMSON MANSION GARAGE

CONTEMPORARY VIEW OF THE ALLEY AND GARAGE AT 2230 SACRAMENTO STREET. NOTE THAT THE GARAGE HAS BEEN REMODELED, AND THE WINDOW IS GONE.

A few of the garage shots were filmed in the actual garage, but many were done on the studio set. At the time the film was made, the garage did have the window in the alley which George uses to break in. While the movie footage of George climbing through the window was shot on a studio set, it was modeled on the garage's actual window. Today, however, the window is no longer there.

The movie ends with Fran and Arthur being trapped in their own dungeon, while Blanche and George happily escape.

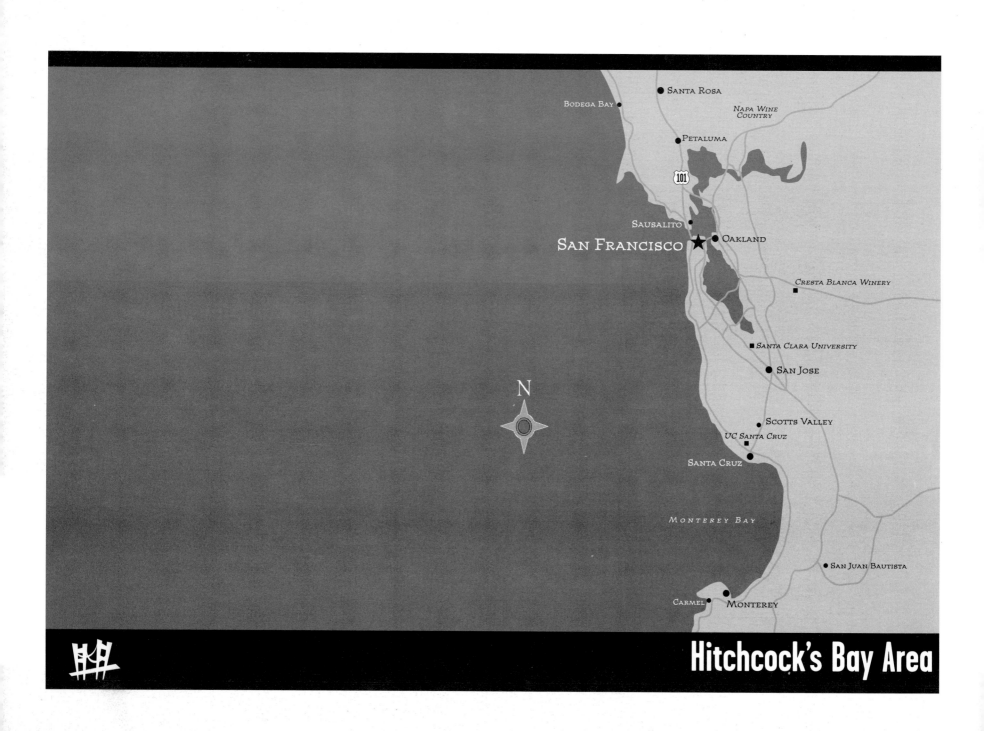

SANTA ROSA

BODEGA BAY

NAPA WINE
COUNTRY

PETALUMA

101

SAUSALITO

SAN FRANCISCO ★ OAKLAND

CRESTA BLANCA WINERY

SANTA CLARA UNIVERSITY

SAN JOSE

N

SCOTTS VALLEY

UC SANTA CRUZ

SANTA CRUZ

MONTEREY BAY

SAN JUAN BAUTISTA

CARMEL MONTEREY

Hitchcock's Bay Area

Hitchcock's Bay Area

Scotts Valley, Vineyards, Fine Cuisine, and Other Local Ties

"When the day's work is done, we go out to the vineyards and squeeze the grapes through our hair."

— ALFRED HITCHCOCK

Alfred Hitchcock had a passion for the San Francisco Bay Area. He used the region as the geographic focal point for many of his movies. But his connection to the region went deeper than his films. His Scotts Valley estate, nestled just south of San Francisco and far from Hollywood, became a home he adored. He also became an active member of the Bay Area community by making personal appearances at local universities and enjoying the culture and lifestyle of the region. In many ways, Hitchcock became a true Northern Californian. His movies present the evidence of his geographic knowledge of the Bay Area, while his active participation in the culture shows his true love for the region.

Hitchcock's Scotts Valley Estate

Soon after Hitchcock moved to the United States, he looked for land outside of Hollywood as a way to escape from the pressures of the film industry. In September of 1940, Hitchcock and his wife, Alma, purchased a 200-acre tract known as the "Heart of the Mountains," or Cornwall Ranch, at the end of Canham Road (off Glenwood Drive) near Scotts Valley. Scotts Valley is a small town between Los Gatos and Santa Cruz on Highway 17, about 67 miles south of San Francisco.

The main house was a 5,000-square-foot building in the Monterey Spanish style, with white plaster walls and a red-tiled roof. There was also a tennis court, a farmhouse, farm animals, five acres of landscaped gardens, and a vineyard. The front door was made of a wine cask and the house included a wine cellar. The house had multiple patios and at the end of the rose garden was a 12-foot mosaic by cubist artist Georges Braque. In addition to redwoods, the property had orange and grapefruit trees.

HITCHCOCK LOOKING AT THE GOLDEN GATE BRIDGE, CIRCA 1943

HITCHCOCK AT HIS SCOTTS VALLEY RANCH, DATE UNKNOWN

HITCHCOCK ON THE PORCH OF HIS HOME AT SCOTTS VALLEY RANCH, CIRCA 1960

HITCHCOCK ON THE LAWN IN FRONT OF HIS HOUSE AT
SCOTTS VALLEY RANCH, DATE UNKNOWN

John Hobart, a reporter from the *San Francisco Chronicle*, visited the house in 1950 and described the trip to the house as up a "torturous road," but thought it well worthwhile because the mountaintop house had beautiful views of redwood trees and the Monterey Bay. Even today the bumpy, winding dirt roads in this area are very rustic and pass through scenic groves of redwood trees.

The estate was a family haven for the Hitchcocks, and to this day their daughter and grandchildren have extremely fond memories of the place. Hitchcock almost always brought his two Sealyham terriers—Geoffrey and Stanley—with him from Southern California when visiting the property. He was so fond of the dogs he named one of his production companies "Geoffrey-Stanley Productions," and used the dogs in his cameo appearance in *The Birds*.

Ultimately, the Hitchcocks moved out of their Scotts Valley Ranch home in 1970 and it was sold a few years later.

HITCHCOCK WITH STANLEY AND GEOFFREY, DATE UNKNOWN

HITCHCOCK, GEOFFREY, STANLEY, AND UNKNOWN BIRDS ON THE BEACH

Grounds, Garden, and Landscaping at the Estate

The Hitchcocks had five acres of landscaped gardens with rose trestles, fruit trees, and numerous patios. Locally renowned landscape architect Roy Rydell elaborately designed the gardens for the Hitchcocks in the mid-1960s. Rydell also designed the gardens of the Pacific Garden Mall, an outdoor pedestrian area in downtown Santa Cruz, much of which was destroyed in a 1989 earthquake.

Rydell and Hitchcock maintained a regular correspondence about landscape improvements to the grounds. The following excerpt from a letter Hitchcock wrote to Rydell in 1965 suggests that Alfred and Alma took pleasure in sorting through the details of managing their gardens.

". . . Here's what she suggests we buy: a good quantity of Dahlias…but she does not want pompoms. She suggests that we put these large ones behind the new open wall to come up after the delphiniums have finished. Then she suggests a good quantity of Topmix Dahlias. . . .These can go in many of the borders. Then she would like a quantity of Lilies, possibly put in the front entrance patio. The type she likes are the Richardia. . . . And, she now wonders whether your are ordering the Delphiniums from Vetterle and Reinelt. These should be a good mixture and especially tall ones to come up behind the brick wall . . ."

ALFRED HITCHCOCK

April 1, 1965

Mr. Roy Rydell
201 Pine Flat Road
Santa Cruz, California

Dear My Rydell,

I am enclosing the catalogue you gave Mrs. Hitchcock from the de Jager people.

Here's what she suggests we buy:- a good quantity of Dahlias, as indicated on pages 13 through 16, but she does not want pompoms. She suggests that we put these large ones behind the new open wall to come up after the delphiniums have finished. Then she suggests a good quantity of Topmix Dahlias, as indicated on pages 18 and 25. These can go in many of the borders. Then she would like a quantity of Lilies, possibly put in the front entrance patio. The type she likes are the Richardia, as shown on pages 30 and 35 of the catalogue.

She told me that she thought there was a lot of room in the entrance patio where it keeps pretty damp, anyway she would like a hell of a lot of Gladioli, as shown on pages 1 through 7. These should go all over the place.

And, she now wonders whether you are ordering the Delphiniums from Vetterle and Reinelt. These should be a good mixture and especially tall ones to come up behind the brick wall.

(continued)

Incidentally, when you give the order you had better have the bulbs sent by air, either to you direct or to the house. You might discuss this with Mrs. Thomsen, as to which is the better place to have them sent. The bill should be sent to us here, however.

Kindest regards.

Yours sincerely,

Enc.

VIEW OF THE APPROACH THROUGH THE TRESTLE, WITH THE RANCH HOUSE IN THE DISTANCE, 1966

FENCED-IN GARDEN AT SCOTTS VALLEY, 1966. THE CERAMIC BIRDS WERE DESIGNED BY CUBIST ARTIST GEORGES BRAQUE.

Rydell would send photos of the landscaping progress to the Hitchcocks in Southern California for approval. Shown here are two photographs taken by Rydell and sent to the Hitchcocks in 1966.

Over time, the Hitchcocks and Rydell became friends. They invited Rydell to visit filming on the set of *Torn Curtain* (released in 1965) in Southern California.

Entertaining Film Industry Friends and Colleagues at the Estate

Hitchcock was an aficionado of fine foods, and regularly had gourmet meals at his estate. He hosted famous Hollywood guests for dinner, including Hume Cronyn, Ingrid Bergman, Jimmy Stewart, Kim Novak, and Princess Grace and Prince Rainier of Monaco, among others. These guests would often come for a mix of business and pleasure. According to Cronyn, who visited Scotts Valley to work on film scripts with Hitchcock, the director was a perfect host who "took a marvelous, malicious delight in seeing his guests fall apart with all those vintage wines and liquors." It was not uncommon for Hitchcock to fly in fresh Dover sole and steak and kidney pies from England.

LEFT TO RIGHT: ALFRED HITCHCOCK, GRACE KELLY, ALMA HITCHCOCK, AND PRINCE RAINIER OF MONACO ON THE PORCH OF HITCHCOCK'S SCOTTS VALLEY RANCH, DATE UNKNOWN

HITCHCOCK TAKING A PHOTO OF INGRID BERGMAN AT HIS SCOTTS VALLEY RANCH, DATE UNKNOWN

Mr. Hitchcock and Company's Itinerary During a Location-Scouting Trip for *Marnie*

THE FOLLOWING TRANSCRIPTION OF THE HITCHCOCKS' ITINERARY during a location-scouting trip for *Marnie* illustrates how Hitchcock used his Scotts Valley Ranch to mix business and relaxation when he was in the Bay Area.

JANUARY 8, 1963

ITINERARY

Party: Mr. And Mrs. Hitchcock, Bob Burks [Cameraman], Hilton Green [Unit Manager] & Jim Brown [First Assistant Director] and the 2 dogs [Geoffrey and Stanley].

Saturday, January 11th:

Leave Los Angeles Airport 7:00 A.M. United Fli. 788 (breakfast)

Arrive San Francisco Airport 8:02 A.M.

Ole [Hitchcock's chauffeur] will meet this flight and proceed to dock to look over S.S. President Wilson. Ole will take Mrs. Hitchcock down to Santa Cruz home and return to Jack's Restaurant (where the others will have lunch after looking over ship).

Party will then proceed to San Jose to look over railroad station and then to Santa Cruz for dinner.

Ole will take the party, excluding Mr. and Mrs. Hitchcock, to San Francisco.

Leave San Francisco Airport 11:15 P.M. T.W.A. Fli. 72

Arrive Los Angeles Airport 12:22 A.M.

Sunday, January 12th:

Ole to be at Santa Cruz at 3:00 P.M. and proceed to airport:—

Leave San Francisco Airport 5:00 P.M. United Fli. 895

Arrive Los Angeles Airport 6:04 P.M. Taxi to house.

THE ACTUAL ITINERARY DOCUMENT FOR THE *MARNIE* SCOUTING TRIP

CRESTA BLANCA WINE LABEL, CIRCA 1900

The Estate Vineyard

According to Hitchcock's family and friends, the great director was a wine connoisseur. For this reason, the vineyard on the Scotts Valley land was one of the property's most desirable features for Hitchcock. The Hitchcocks sold white Riesling grapes from their vineyard to the Cresta Blanca Winery, one of the most famous labels in the industry at that time. Hitchcock reported that in 1950 they sold 90 tons of grapes grown on the property. However, they kept some of the grapes so that the local caretakers could make a homemade red wine.

Commencement Speaker at Local Universities

As a famous local resident, Hitchcock spoke at the commencement ceremonies of two nearby schools: the University of Santa Clara and the University of California at Santa Cruz.

On June 1, 1963, Hitchcock received an honorary doctorate from the Jesuit University of Santa Clara in the South Bay. Hitchcock grew up in a Catholic family and was educated at the Jesuit St. Ignatius College in England, so he had a personal understanding of the principles of a Catholic education. Several of Hitchcock's films dealt with Catholic themes, including *I Confess* (released in 1953), a story about a priest who is torn by a moral dilemma surrounding a confession by one of his parishioners. Hitchcock was the commencement speaker at the graduation and gave a self-deprecating, humorous, and witty speech. He also could not resist giving his recently released film *The Birds* some free publicity:

HITCHCOCK IN CAP AND GOWN NEXT TO UNIVERSITY OFFICIALS PRIOR TO HIS SPEECH AT THE UNIVERSITY OF SANTA CLARA COMMENCEMENT CEREMONY IN 1963

"The thought of my being an honorary doctor of humane letters is an awesome one. I must only assume that this is the same degree that was conferred on Dr. Jekyll. And yet there is logic to my being here today. Santa Clara University was founded one hundred and twelve years ago to produce well-rounded men. If I do not qualify as well-rounded, I would like to see the man who does. . . .

"It is also open to question as to whether a doctor of letters, humane or otherwise, would ever say, 'The Birds IS Coming.' Fortunately there is no serious evidence that my appearance here is being protested. Not by the National Association of Teachers of English or even the National Association for the Prevention of Cruelty to Animals . . .

"All of you will not be fortunate enough to spend your lives committing murder, on film or otherwise, but I do hope you can keep your work flavored with the saving salt of humor."

A few years later, on June 9, 1968, Hitchcock received an honorary degree from the University of California Santa Cruz, located just a few miles from his house in Scotts Valley. In his remarks to the graduating class, Hitchcock humorously summed up his career as a filmmaker:

"In my years in the film business, I have survived the silent films, talkies, the narrow screen, the wide screen, 3-D, the drive-in movie, the in-flight movie, television, and so on. I began as a writer, then became, successively, art director, director/producer, and now, the climax of my career, after-luncheon speaker."

Hitchcock also playfully attempted to debunk the myth that he hated working with actors:

"Then there is that dreadful story that I hate actors. Imagine anyone hating, say, a nice man like Jimmy Stewart. I can't think how such a rumor began. Of course, it may be possibly because I was once quoted as saying that actors are cattle. My actor friends know I would never be capable of such a thoughtless, rude, and unfeeling remark, that I would never call them cattle. What I probably said was actors should be treated like cattle."

HITCHCOCK RECEIVING AN HONORARY DEGREE AT U.C. SANTA CRUZ. LEFT TO RIGHT: VICE PRESIDENT WELLMAN, ALFRED HITCHCOCK, DEAN MCHENRY, JUNE 9, 1968

Hitchcock's Personal Connections to Downtown San Francisco

CHESTNUT STREET
LOMBARD STREET
GREENWICH STREET
FILBERT STREET
UNION STREET
GREEN STREET
VALLEJO STREET
BROADWAY
PACIFIC STREET
JACKSON STREET
WASHINGTON STREET
COLUMBUS AVENUE
KEARNY STREET
MONTGOMERY STREET
SANSOME STREET
BATTERY STREET
FRONT STREET
DAVIS STREET
THE EMBARCADERO
PIER 23
PIER 19
CLAY STREET
SACRAMENTO STREET
DRUMM STREET
SPEAR STREET
❹ CALIFORNIA
BART
MAIN STREET
PINE STREET
BUSH STREET
SUTTER STREET
POWELL STREET
STOCKTON STREET
GRANT AVENUE
MARKET STREET
BEALE STREET
FREMONT STREET
1ST STREET
2ND STREET
POST STREET ❼
BART
❻
GEARY STREET
HYDE STREET
LEAVENWORTH STREET
JONES STREET
TAYLOR STREET
MASON STREET
❺
MISSION STREET
HOWARD STREET
---- CABLE CAR ROUTE
❶
❸
❷

❶ Former location of Ernie's Restaurant
❷ Mark Hopkins Hotel and Top of the Mark
❸ The Fairmont Hotel
❹ Jack's Restaurant (currently called "Jeanty at Jack's")
❺ St. Francis Hotel
❻ Bercut Brothers Grant Market
❼ Former location of Gump's

Hitchcock's Love of Bay Area Cuisine

The Scotts Valley–Santa Cruz area was a pleasant place to spend weekends and vacations. While there, the Hitchcock family patronized local business. They bought fresh seafood from Stagnaro's on the Santa Cruz wharf, and would eat at local restaurants. Ann Gamba, whose family served as caretakers of the Scotts Valley property and became friendly with the Hitchcocks, remembers her father driving the family to lunch at the Palomar Inn (1334 Pacific Ave.) in Santa Cruz. They took an old truck with Hitchcock riding in front and an elegantly dressed Alma, along with their daughter Patricia, and Ann, riding in the open-air back cab.

The Stagnaro family still operates Gilda's restaurant on the Santa Cruz wharf; the Palomar restaurant, which the Hitchcocks visited, has since changed to the El Palomar, a Mexican restaurant.

CONTEMPORARY VIEW OF GILDA'S RESTAURANT ON THE SANTA CRUZ WHARF

Hitchcock, however, craved the sophistication and gourmet pleasures of big city life. He was inevitably drawn out to San Francisco. Hitchcock was a regular patron of the classic, old-school San Francisco restaurants such as Jack's and Ernie's, the latter extensively featured in *Vertigo*.

Ann Gamba remembers dining at Ernie's with the Hitchcocks one evening during the spring of 1962, after a long day of location shooting for *The Birds* in Bodega Bay. As dinner was nearing completion, Alfred fell asleep while smoking a cigar. Not wanting to wake him, Alma carefully removed the cigar from his mouth and placed it in an ashtray. The group quietly finished their wine before waking Hitchcock to leave.

Jack's Restaurant, located at 615 Sacramento Street between Montgomery and Kearny Streets, was a favorite for financial district power-lunchers, political bigwigs, real estate moguls, and entertainment celebrities. This landmark dated back to 1864 and was patronized by towering figures from California's history, such as the "Big Four" railroad barons Charles Crocker, Collis Huntington, Mark Hopkins, and Leland Stanford. Celebrities such as Mark Twain, Cary Grant, Clark Gable, Ingrid Bergman, Frank Sinatra, and Ernest Hemingway were also frequent customers.

EXTERIOR OF JACK'S RESTAURANT ON CALIFORNIA STREET IN SAN FRANCISCO, 1952

The Invention of the Mimosa Cocktail

HITCHCOCK WAS A REGULAR DINER AT JACK'S WITH local luminaries such as columnist Herb Caen. He was also frequently seen with his lawyer and good friend Samuel Taylor. One of the private upstairs dining rooms, which in the rowdy old days of San Francisco had served as a bordello, was later named the Alfred Hitchcock Room. According to San Francisco lore, Hitchcock, along with wealthy San Francisco financier and real estate mogul Louis Lurie (who held court every day at Jack's for decades), invented the Mimosa cocktail—a mix of champagne and orange juice—at the restaurant one Sunday as a cure for a hangover. The Mimosa, along with the martini and highball, were favorite cocktails of Hitchcock.

LOUIS LURIE (MIDDLE) WITH FRANCIS SITEK (LEFT) AND BERNARD AVERBUCH (RIGHT) IN FRONT OF JACK'S RESTAURANT, DATE UNKNOWN

CONTEMPORARY VIEW OF THE EXTERIOR OF JACK'S RESTAURANT, BEFORE IT WAS RENAMED "JEANTY AT JACK'S"

Although Jack's closed for about a year in December of 2000, it has since re-opened as "Jeanty at Jack's," with a hearty French menu. It is the oldest restaurant in San Francisco still operating in its original location. The restaurant was originally named after the jack rabbits which used to populate nearby undeveloped fields in pre-metropolitan San Francisco. The interior was refurbished in 1998 and again in 2001. Jack's décor had a posh, old-time San Francisco feel with cream-colored walls, a painted grapevine bas-relief, and tables with fine white linen. The restaurant only started accepting credit cards very late in its history because most regular patrons maintained personal accounts.

The traditional Jack's menu consisted of American and Continental fare such as sautéed sweetbreads and charcoal-broiled mutton chops, complemented by stiff martinis. Hitchcock's favorite lunches at Jack's consisted of sourdough bread with salty butter, with either filet of trout *meuniere* or Rex sole.

Hitchcock, who liked fish, enjoyed the fresh seafood available in San Francisco, visiting places like Fisherman's Wharf and fine restaurants around the area such as Ondine.

Ondine is located at 558 Bridgeway in Sausalito, across the Golden Gate Bridge from San Francisco. From the late 1950s through 1989, the restaurant served classic French food and had spectacular bay views. Ondine was known as the most opulent restaurant in Marin County. In addition to Hitchcock, it was patronized by Marilyn Monroe, Audrey Hepburn, and political leaders such as Richard Nixon. After being closed for 10 years, the restaurant reopened in 1999 with new ownership, new décor, and a Pan-Asian theme. The name Ondine was retained and the views were enhanced with floor-to-ceiling windows.

When the Hitchcocks flew up to San Francisco International Airport, they would frequently be picked up by a driver from Gray Line Limousines. According to one of Hitchcock's regular San Francisco drivers during the 1960s, before heading to Scotts Valley they would often make detours to San Francisco where Hitchcock would patronize businesses such as the Bercut Brothers Grant Market, another one of Hitchcock's favorite food stops in San Francisco.

HITCHCOCK AT FISHERMAN'S WHARF, CIRCA 1943

CONTEMPORARY VIEW OF ONDINE RESTAURANT

The Bercut Brothers Grant Market

ONE OF HITCHCOCK'S REGULAR STOPS IN SAN FRANCISCO WAS THE BERCUT BROTHERS Grant Market at 743 Market Street. The locally famous market dated from the early days of the 20th century (circa 1910) and sold meat, fish, produce, cheese, and other food items. In his columns, Herb Caen frequently mentioned the store's lunchroom—an invitation-only gourmet haven, where Hitchcock occasionally ate.

For almost four decades, the late Bryan Flannery, who ran the meat department at the Grant Market, was the butcher of choice for San Francisco's most discriminating gourmet shoppers—including Hitchcock. The market closed in the 1960s when the building it occupied was demolished in favor of a parking garage. The Flannery family still runs a highly regarded butchery in San Francisco called Bryan's Quality Meats. Bryan's sons, Peter and Terrence Flannery, run Bryan's today. Peter remembers driving special orders (such as rack of lamb and various cuts of steaks) down to the Hitchcocks at Scotts Valley, and being greeted at the door by Geoffrey and Stanley. Hitchcock liked the market's meat so much that he had them ship supplies via San Francisco International Airport to Southern California for his dinner parties. The director even invited Bryan Flannery to the opening-night party for *Vertigo* in San Francisco.

CROWD SHOPPING AT THE BERCUT BROTHERS GRANT MARKET, 1943

EXTERIOR OF THE BERCUT BROTHERS GRANT MARKET, CIRCA 1940

Hitchcock's Favorite San Francisco Hotels

Whether he was filming on location in or around San Francisco, or visiting town on business, Hitchcock would frequently stay in one of San Francisco's world-class hotels. As noted earlier, the Fairmont Hotel was shown in both *Vertigo* and *Family Plot* and hosted Hitchcock, his casts, and crews, on various occasions. The Fairmont is a five-star landmark that is synonymous with luxury and grandeur. It regularly accommodates presidents, royalty, celebrities, and captains of industry.

HITCHCOCK HOLDING A PRESS CONFERENCE AT THE FAIRMONT HOTEL TO PROMOTE *THE BIRDS*, APRIL 1, 1963

CONTEMPORARY VIEW OF THE FAIRMONT HOTEL

HITCHCOCK AT THE TOP OF THE MARK, WITH THE RUSS BUILDING IN THE BACKGROUND, DATE UNKNOWN

Hitchcock also visited the Mark Hopkins Hotel, located across California Street from the Fairmont on top of Nob Hill at 999 California Street. The hotel opened in 1926 on the site of the former mansion of Mark Hopkins, a founder of the Central Pacific Railroad. The Hotel can be seen briefly in the Nob Hill scenes in *Vertigo*. It is home to the historic "Top of the Mark" lounge, which dates from 1939 when the hotel's penthouse was converted to a bar. The Top of the Mark sits on the 19th and top floor of the building, and offers dramatic 360-degree views of The City.

There is a great deal of lore surrounding the bar. According to their website, during World War II, Pacific-bound servicemen and their friends would come to the bar to enjoy a final toast before heading off to war. According to myth, as these military men sailed below the Golden Gate, wives and girlfriends gathered in the northwest corner of the bar and watched the ships sail out to sea. That corner became known as the "Weepers' Corner."

Each squadron of servicemen reportedly had its own bottle of liquor kept at the bar. When squadron members returned to the Top of the Mark, they could have a free drink from their squadron bottle. The only requirement was they had to sign their name on the label and the man who had the last drink was required to pay for a new bottle.

The bar is mentioned by Scottie in *Vertigo* when he describes his fear of heights to Gavin Elster. Hitchcock even shot the foggy view of downtown San Francisco—which is shown right before Scottie's nightmare sequence—from the Mark Hopkins.

When Hitchcock returned to San Francisco in 1962 to film *The Birds*, he stayed at the St. Francis Hotel, located at 335 Powell Street on Union Square. The original wing of this landmark was built in 1904 and was refurbished following the earthquake and fire of 1906. The hotel is one of the most elegant and famous in the city. The stores attached to the hotel are shown briefly in *The Birds* during the opening Union Square scene, and the hotel is shown in the background in *Vertigo* when Scottie buys Judy a rose in front of Gump's.

VIEW DOWN POST STREET WITH THE ST. FRANCIS HOTEL IN THE BACKGROUND FROM *VERTIGO*

CONTEMPORARY VIEW OF THE ST. FRANCIS HOTEL

Hitchcock's Continuing Connections to the Bay Area

To this day, the Hitchcock family retains connections to Northern California. One of Alfred and Alma's granddaughters, Tere Carrubba, lives near Santa Cruz and hosts the *Alfred Hitchcock Memorial Golf Tournament*, benefiting the Cystic Fibrosis Foundation, each summer at the Seascape Golf Club. The San Francisco law firm of Samuel Taylor and Leland Faust, long-time Hitchcock family friends, represent the Alfred Hitchcock Trust today.

Alfred Hitchcock's legacy continues to capture the hearts of all who love the San Francisco Bay Area. His life and films are intimately connected to the people and places of Northern California. Even though the Master of Suspense is gone, his footsteps remain.

HITCHCOCK WATCHING THE SUN SET AT HIS SCOTTS VALLEY RANCH

REBECCA

Produced in 1939; Released in 1940; The Selznick Studio (black & white)

Produced by David O. Selznick
Screenplay by Robert Sherwood and Joan Harrison,
  based on the novel by Daphne du Maurier
Music by Franz Waxman
Cinematography by George Barnes
Art Direction by Lyle Wheeler
Sets by Joseph Platt
Special Effects supervised by Jack Cosgrove

CAST

Maxim de Winter	Laurence Olivier
His second wife	Joan Fontaine
Jack Favell	George Sanders
Mrs. Danvers	Judith Anderson
Major Giles Lacey	Nigel Bruce
Beatrice Lacey	Gladys Cooper
Mrs. Van Hopper	Florence Bates
Frank Crawley	Reginald Denny
Colonel Julyan	C. Aubrey Smith

with Melville Cooper, Leonard Carey, Leo Carroll, Edward Fielding, Lumsden Hare, Forrester Harvey, and Philip Winter

SUSPICION

Produced in 1940; Released in 1941; RKO (black & white)

Produced by Harry Edington
Screenplay by Samson Raphaelson, Joan Harrison, and Alma Reville,
  based on the novel *Before the Facts* by Francis Iles
Music by Franz Waxman
Cinematography by Harry Stradling Sr.
Art Direction by Van Nest Polglase
Sets by Darrell Silvera
Special Effects supervised by Vernon Walker

CAST

John Aysgarth	Cary Grant
Lina MacKinlaw	Joan Fontaine
General MacKinlaw	Sir Cedric Hardwiche
Mrs. MacKinlaw	Dame May Whitty
Beaky Thwaite	Nigel Bruce
Mrs. Newsham	Isabel Jeans

with Heather Angel, Auriol Lee, Reginald Sheffield and Leo Carroll

SHADOW OF A DOUBT

Produced in 1942; Released in 1943; Universal (black & white)

Produced by Jack Skirball
Screenplay by Thornton Wilder, Sally Benson, and Alma Reville,
  based on an original story by Gordon McDonnell

CAST

Uncle Charlie Oakley	Joseph Cotton
Charlie Newton	Teresa Wright
Detective Jack Graham	MacDonald Carey
Emma Newton	Patricia Collinge
Joe Newton	Henry Travers

Shadow of a Doubt, con't.

Cinematography by Joseph Valentine
Art Direction by John Goodman and assisted by Robert Boyle
Sets by R.A. Gausman and assisted by L. R. Robinson
Music by Dimitri Tiomkin

Cast, con't.

Herbie Hawkins	Hume Cronyn
Detective Fred Saunders	Wallace Ford
Ann Newton	Edna May Wonacott
Roger Newton	Charles Bates

with Irving Bacon, Clarence Muse, Janet Shaw, Ethel Griffies

Vertigo

Produced in 1957; Released in 1958; Paramount (color)

Produced by Alfred Hitchcock
Screenplay by Alec Coppel and Samuel Taylor, based on the novel
  D'Entre Les Morts by Pierre Boileau and Thomas Narcejac
Cinematography by Robert Burks
Art Direction by Hal Pereira and Henry Bumstead
Sets by Sam Comer and Frank McKelvey
Special Effects supervised by John Fulton and assisted by Daniel McCauley
Costumes by Edith Head
Music by Bernard Herrmann

Cast

John "Scottie" Ferguson	James Stewart
"Madeleine Elster"	Kim Novak
Judy Barton	Kim Novak
Midge Wood	Barbara Bel Geddes
Gavin Elster	Tom Helmore
Pop Leibel	Konstantin Shayne

with Henry Jones, Raymond Bailey, Ellen Corby, and Lee Patrick

Psycho

Produced in 1959-1960; Released in 1960; Paramount (black & white)

Produced by Alfred Hitchcock
Screenplay by Joseph Stefano, based on the novel by Robert Bloch
Cinematography by John Russell
Art Direction by Joseph Hurley and Robert Clatworthy
Sets by George Milo
Special Effects supervised by Clarence Champagne
Music by Bernard Herrmann

Cast

Norman Bates	Anthony Perkins
Marion Crane	Janet Leigh
Lila Crane	Vera Miles
Sam Loomis	John Gavin
Detective Arbogast	Martin Balsam
Sheriff Al Chambers	John McIntire
Psychiatrist	Simon Oakland
George Lowery	Vaughn Taylor
Tom Cassidy	Frank Albertson

with Lurene Tuttle, Patricia Hitchcock, John Anderson, & Mort Mills

THE BIRDS

Produced in 1962; Released in 1963; Universal (color)

Produced by Alfred Hitchcock
Screenplay by Evan Hunter, based on the short story by Daphne du Maurier
Cinematography by Robert Burks
Art Direction by Robert Boyle and George Milo
Special Effects supervised by Lawrence Hampton, including mattes by Albert Whitlock
Bird Trainer Ray Berwick
Special Photographic Adviser Ub Iwerks
Sound Consultant Bernard Herrmann

CAST

Melanie Daniels	Tippi Hedren
Mitch Brenner	Rod Taylor
Lydia Brenner	Jessica Tandy
Annie Hayworth	Suzanne Pleshette
Cathy Brenner	Veronica Cartwright
Mrs. Bundy	Ethel Griffies
Sebastian Sholes	Charles McGraw
Mrs. MacGruder	Ruth McDevitt
Deputy Al Malone	Malcolm Atterbury
Deke Carter	Lonny Chapman
Helen Carter	Elizabeth Wilson
Traveling Salesman	Joe Mantell
Fisherman	Doodles Weaver
Mr. Brinkmeyer	John McGovern

with Karl Swenson, Richard Deacon, Bill Quinn, and Doreen Lang

---

MARNIE

Produced in 1963; Released in 1964; Universal (color)

Produced by Alfred Hitchcock
Screenplay by Jay Presson Allen, based on the novel by Winston Graham
Cinematography by Robert Burks
Art and Production Design by Robert Boyle and George Milo
Music by Bernard Herrmann

CAST

Marnie Edgar	Tippi Hedren
Mark Rutland	Sean Connery
Lil Mainwaring	Diane Baker
Sidney Strutt	Martin Gabel
Bernice Edgar	Louise Latham
Cousin Bob	Bob Sweeney
Susan Clabon	Mariette Hartley
Mr. Rutland	Alan Napier
Rita	Edith Evanson
Sam Ward	S. John Launer
Mrs. Turpin	Meg Wyllie

with Mariette Hartley, Milton Selzer, Henry Beckman, and Bruce Dern

TOPAZ

Produced in 1968-1969; Released in 1969; Universal (color)

Produced by Alfred Hitchcock
Associate Production by Herbert Coleman
Screenplay by Samuel Taylor, based on the novel by Leon Uris
Cinematography by Jack Hildyard
Art Direction by Henry Bumstead with mattes by Albert Whitlock
Sets by John Austin
Music by Maurice Jarre
Costumes by Edith Head

CAST

André Devereaux	Frederick Stafford
Michael Nordstrom	John Forsythe
Nicole Devereaux	Dany Robin
Rico Parra	John Vernon
Juanita de Cordoba	Karin Dor
Jacques Granville	Michel Piccoli
Henri Jarre	Philippe Noiret
Michéle Picard	Claude Jade
Philippe Dubois	Roscoe Lee Browne
Boris Kusenov	Per-Axel Arosenius
François Picard	Michel Subor

with Sonja Kolthoff, Tina Hedstrom, Donald Randolph, John Van Dreelen, George Skaff, Roger Til, Såndor Szabo, Edmon Ryan, Anna Navarro, Lewis Charles, Carlos Riva, Roberto Contreras, John Roper, and Lew Brown

FAMILY PLOT

Produced in 1975; Released in 1976; Universal (color)

Produced by Alfred Hitchcock
Screenplay by Ernest Lehman, based on the novel *The Rainbird Pattern* by Victor Canning
Cinematography by Leonard South
Art Direction by Henry Bumstead
Sets by James Payne
Special Effects supervised by Albert Whitlock and assisted by Howard Kazanjian
Music by John Williams

CAST

Fran	Karen Black
George Lumley	Bruce Dern
Blanche Taylor	Barbara Harris
Arthur Adamson	William Devane
Joe Maloney	Ed Lauter
Julia Rainbird	Cathleen Nesbitt
Mrs. Maloney	Katherine Helmond

with Warren Kemmerling, Edith Atwater, William Prince, Nicholas Colasanto, Marge Redmond, John Lehne, Charles Tyner, Alexander Lockwood, and Martin West

Photo Credits

All photographs for this book were sized, cropped, and, in some cases, touched-up, digitally. Any image originally shot in color was converted to grayscale for the purposes of this book. No photograph, however, was digitally altered in a manner that would falsely represent the actual location or image portrayed.

The Studios

Front Cover: middle right.

Introduction: p. 16 left.

Chapter One—*Shadow of a Doubt*: p. 24, p. 25 upper, p. 27, p. 29 lower left, p. 30 upper right, p. 33 upper right, p. 34 lower left, p. 35 upper right, lower right, and middle, p. 36 lower right, p. 39 upper left, p. 40 upper right and upper left, p. 41 upper right and upper left, p. 44 upper right, p. 45 upper left, p. 46 upper right and lower right, p. 48 right, p. 49 left, p. 50 left, p. 52 upper right and lower right, p. 53, p. 54 upper right, p. 55 left, p. 58 right, p. 59 upper left and lower left, p. 60 upper right, p. 61, p. 63 upper left and lower left, p. 64 upper, p. 65 left, p. 66 right, p. 67 left, p. 68 right, p. 70 left.

Chapter Two—*Vertigo*: p. 78, p. 80 middle left and upper right, p. 82 left, p. 85 top, p. 86 upper right, middle right, and lower right, p. 89 upper left and upper right, p. 90 upper, p. 91 upper left and lower left, p. 92 lower middle, p. 93 upper, p. 94 left, p. 95 lower left, p. 98 right, p. 101 upper left, lower left, and upper right, p. 102 upper right and lower right, p. 103 upper left and lower left, p. 104 upper middle and lower middle, p. 105 left, p. 106 upper right and lower right, p. 108 upper right, p. 111, p. 113 left, p. 114 right, p. 116, p. 117 upper left, p. 118 right, p. 119 upper left and lower left, p. 120 upper middle and lower left, p. 121 upper left, p. 122, p. 123 upper right, p. 124 upper left and lower left, p. 125 upper left and lower left, p. 126 right, p. 127 upper left and lower left, p. 128 middle left and upper right, p. 129 upper left, upper right and lower right, p. 131, p. 132 left and right, p. 133 upper, p. 135 upper left and lower left, p. 136 upper right, p. 137 upper left and middle, p. 138 upper right, p. 139 right, p. 140 upper middle and upper right, p. 141 left, p. 142 upper right and lower right, p. 143 upper left and lower left, p. 144 upper, p. 145 left, p. 148 upper right, p. 149 left, p. 150 upper left and upper right, p. 151 upper left and upper right, p. 152 upper middle, p. 153 upper left, p. 154 lower left and upper right, p. 155 left, p. 157 left, p. 159 upper right, p. 160 upper right, p. 161 upper left, p. 162 right, p. 164, p. 165.

Chapter Three—*The Birds*: p. 170 upper, p. 171 upper right, p. 172, p. 177 upper right, p. 178 upper right and lower right, p. 183 upper left and lower left, p. 184 upper right and lower right, p. 185 left, p. 188, p. 189 upper left, p. 191 middle left and lower left, p. 192 right, p. 193 upper right, p. 194 upper right, p. 195 lower left and upper right, p. 196 upper left and lower left, p. 197 upper left, p. 198 lower right, p. 199, p. 200, p. 202 upper right, p. 203, p. 204 upper right and lower right, p. 206, p. 207, p. 208 lower middle and upper right, p. 209 upper left and lower middle, p. 210 upper right and lower right, p. 212 upper right, p. 214, p. 216, p. 218, p. 220, p. 221 left.

Chapter Four—*Other Bay Area Films*: p. 223, p. 236, p. 237, p. 238 right, p. 240, p. 241, p. 242 upper, p. 243, p. 246 upper left and lower left, p. 247 upper left and lower left, p. 248 upper left, p. 249 upper, p. 251 upper, p. 252 upper left and lower left, p. 253 upper middle and lower middle, p. 254 right, p. 255 left, p. 256, p. 257 right, p. 259 upper left.

Chapter Five—*Hitchcock's Bay Area*: p. 278 upper right.

Introduction: p. 19 lower left.

Chapter One—*Shadow of a Doubt*: p. 37 upper right, p. 69.

Chapter Two—*Vertigo*: p. 73, p. 94 right, p. 97 right, p. 130 right.

Chapter Three—*The Birds*: p. 167, p. 169, p. 173, p. 179, p. 185 right, p. 186, p. 187 left, p. 191 right, p. 194 lower right, p. 198 left, p. 212 left, p. 219 upper, p. 217 right, p. 219 right, p. 221 right.

Chapter Four—*Other Bay Area Films*: p. 258, p. 259 right.

Chapter Five—*Hitchcock's Bay Area*: p. 268.

Back Cover— left, middle right

Chapter Four—*Other Bay Area Films*: p. 224, p. 227 left, p. 228 right, p. 230 lower middle, p. 232 upper right and lower right.

Chapter Four—*Other Films*: p. 234 lower middle.

Chapter Four—*Other Bay Area Films*: p. 234 upper middle.

Chapter Four—*Other Bay Area Films*: p. 229, p. 231 left, p. 233 right, p. 234 lower right.

Contemporary Photographs

The majority of the contemporary photographs in this book were taken with a Nikon FE2 using Kodak T-Max 400, Kodak Porta NC 160, and Fuji Velvia 50 35mm slide and print films.

Chapter One—*Shadow of a Doubt*: p. 26 right, p. 32, p. 33 lower left, p. 34 middle, p. 35 lower right, p. 36 upper, p. 38 right, p. 39 lower left, p. 40 lower left and lower right, p. 41 lower left and lower right, p. 42, p. 44 lower right, p. 45 upper and lower right, p. 51, lower right, 54 lower right, p. 57, p. 62 lower left, p. 65 right, p. 66 left, p. 67 right, p. 68 left.

Chapter Two—*Vertigo*: p. 80 lower right, p. 81, p. 83 upper left, p. 88, p. 89 lower left and lower middle,

p. 90 lower, p. 91 upper right and lower right, p. 92 lower right, p. 93 lower, p. 95 upper left and lower right, p. 96 lower, p. 97 left, p. 98 left, p. 101 lower middle, p. 102 upper left and lower left, p. 103 middle right, p. 104 lower left, p. 106 lower left, p. 108 lower right, p. 109, p. 111 right, p. 113 left, p. 115 left, p. 117 lower left and upper right, p. 118 left, p. 119 middle left and lower right, p. 120 upper right and lower right, p. 121 right, p. 124 upper right and lower right, p. 125 upper right and lower right, p. 126 left, p. 127 upper right and lower right, p. 128 lower left and lower left, p. 129 lower left, p. 133 lower right, p. 136 lower right, p. 137 middle left and lower right, p. 138 lower left and lower right, p. 140 lower middle and lower right, p. 141 right, p. 142 left, p. 143 upper right, p. 144 lower, p. 145 right, p. 148 lower right, p. 149 right, p. 150 lower right and lower left, p. 151 lower right and lower left, p. 152 right, p. 153 middle, p. 154 lower middle and lower right, p. 157 right, p. 158 left, p. 159 lower middle, p. 160 lower right, p. 163.

Chapter Three—*The Birds*: p. 171 lower left, p. 174 lower right, p. 176 right, p. 177 left, p. 189 lower left and right, p. 190 lower right, p. 192 left, p. 193 left, p. 195 lower middle and lower right, p. 196 left, p. 197 upper middle, p. 202 lower, p. 204 lower left, p. 205, p. 208 lower right, p. 209 middle left and lower right, p. 212 lower right, p. 213 lower, p. 217 lower left.

Chapter Four—*Other Bay Area Films*: p. 239 left, p. 251 lower, p. 253 left, p. 254 left, p. 255 right, p. 259 lower left.

Chapter Five—*Hitchcock's Bay Area*: p. 271, p. 273 middle, p. 276 right, p. 278 left.

© **Jeff Kraft, 2001-2002. All rights reserved:**

Chapter Two—*Vertigo*: p. 79 lower right, p. 135 right, p. 153 lower left, p. 155 right.

Chapter Three—*The Birds*: p. 178 lower left, p. 219 left.

Chapter Four—*Other Bay Area Films*: p. 227 right, p. 228 left, p. 230 right, p. 231 lower right, p. 232 upper middle, p. 233 left, p. 235, p. 242 lower, p. 246 upper right and lower right, p. 247 upper right and lower right, p. 248 right, p. 249 lower.

© **Laura Ackerman, 1988-2002. All rights reserved:**

Chapter Two—*Vertigo*: p. 229 middle.

Chapter Four—*Other Bay Area Films*: p. 239 right, p. 257 left.

Historical Photographs

Courtesy the Sonoma County Public Library:

Front Cover: left.

Chapter One—*Shadow of A Doubt*: p. 21, p. 23, p. 25 lower, p. 26 left, p. 29 upper left and upper right, p. 31, p. 37 lower right, p. 38 upper left, p. 39 lower right, p. 44 lower left, p. 45 lower left, p. 46 lower left, p. 47, p. 48 left, p. 50 lower right, p. 51 upper left and lower left, p. 52 lower left, p. 54 upper left, p. 55 right, p. 58 left, p. 59 right, p. 60 left and lower right, p. 62 right, p. 70 right.

Chapter Three—*The Birds*: p. 183 lower right, p. 184 lower left, p. 197 lower right, p. 211.

Courtesy San Francisco History Center, San Francisco Public Library:

Introduction: p. 18.

Chapter Two—*Vertigo*: p. 75, p. 83 right, p. 84, p. 100, p. 104 right, p. 108 left, p. 123 lower middle, p. 130 left, p. 134, p. 146, p. 147, p. 148 left, p. 156.

Chapter Three—*The Birds*: p. 170 lower, p. 180, p. 181.

Chapter Four—*Other Bay Area Films*: p. 252 lower right.

Chapter Five—*Hitchcock's Bay Area*: p. 261, p. 272, p. 273 left, p. 275 left.

Back Cover—middle left

Courtesy the Bancroft Library—University of California, Berkeley:

Chapter Two—*Vertigo*: p. 76, p. 77 right, p. 86 left, p. 87 left, p. 140 lower left, p. 159 upper left, p. 160 lower left.

Chapter Three—*The Birds*: p. 176 left.

Chapter Five—*Hitchcock's Bay Area*: p. 276 left.

© **Tere O'Connell Carrubba. All rights reserved:**

Title Page

Foreword: p. 12

Introduction: p. 15, p. 16 lower right.

Chapter Five—*Hitchcock's Bay Area*: p. 262, p. 263, p. 264, p. 267, p. 274 upper right, p. 277, p. 279.

Back Cover, right

Marc Wanamaker/Bison Archives:

Front Cover, right

Back Cover, far left

J.R. Eyerman/Timepix:

Introduction: p. 17.

Chapter One—*Shadow of a Doubt*: p. 34 upper right, p. 43, p. 49 right, p. 63 right, p. 71.

Gjon FMili/Timepix:

Chapter One—*Shadow of a Doubt*: p. 37 left, p. 64 lower.

Simmone Wilson:

Chapter One—*Shadow of a Doubt*: p. 57 upper right.

Photo Credits

Hallmark Hall of Fame:

Chapter One—*Shadow of a Doubt*: p. 57 lower left.

© Alan J. Canterbury. Image courtesy San Francisco History Center, San Francisco Public Library:

Chapter Two—*Vertigo*: p. 77 left, p. 85 lower, p. 92 upper right.

San Francisco Chronicle:

Chapter Two—*Vertigo*: p. 87 right, p. 162 left.

Podesta Baldocchi/Gerald Stevens:

Chapter Two—*Vertigo*: p. 96 upper.

Archdiocese of San Francisco:

Front Cover, middle left.

Chapter Two—*Vertigo*: p. 99.

© Larry Moon, photo by Larry Moon of San Francisco. Image courtesy San Francisco History Center, San Francisco Public Library:

Chapter Two—*Vertigo*: p. 105 right, p. 107.

Argonaut Book Shop, Robert D. Haines, Jr.:

Chapter Two—*Vertigo*: p. 110, p. 112.

© Phillip Fein. Image courtesy San Francisco History Center, San Francisco Public Library:

Chapter Two—*Vertigo*: p. 115 right.

Courtesy, www.vulcanarts.com:

Chapter Two—*Vertigo*: p. 136 left, p. 139 left.

© Waters Company. Image courtesy San Francisco History Center, San Francisco Public Library:

Chapter Two—*Vertigo*: p. 160 upper left.

© J. H. Brenenstul Photo. Image courtesy San Francisco History Center, San Francisco Public Library:

Chapter Two—*Vertigo*: p. 161 lower right.

Used with permission of *The Saturday Evening Post* :

Chapter Three—*The Birds*: p. 174 left, p. 175.

Courtesy Mary-Leah Taylor:

Chapter Three—*The Birds*: p. 187 right, p. 194 left, p. 210 left.

Courtesy Anonymous Source:

Chapter Three—*The Birds*: p. 190 left.

Courtesy The Tides Wharf & Restaurant:

Chapter Three—*The Birds*: p. 197 lower left.

Courtesy Museum of Art and History, Santa Cruz California:

Chapter Four—*Other Bay Area Films*: p. 238 left.

Aerial Photo by Pacific Aerial Surveys, a division of HJW GeoSpatial, Inc.:

Chapter Four—*Other Bay Area Films*: p. 244.

Photographs and documents courtesy of Special Collections, Roy Rydell Archive, University Library, University of California, Santa Cruz:

Chapter Five—*Hitchcock's Bay Area*: p. 265, p. 266.

Courtesy of Wine Institute of California:

Chapter Five—*Hitchcock's Bay Area*: p. 269 upper left.

Courtesy Academy of Motion Picture Arts and Sciences:

Chapter Five—*Hitchcock's Bay Area*: p. 269 lower right.

Courtesy Covello & Covello:

Chapter Five—*Hitchcock's Bay Area*: p. 270.

Courtesy Bryan's Meats, San Francisco, California

Chapter Five—*Hitchcock's Bay Area*: p. 275 right.

Courtesy of the KLP, Inc. Collection:

Introduction: p. 19 right.

Chapter Two—*Vertigo*: p. 158 right.

Chapter Three—*The Birds*, p. 201.

Chapter Five—*Hitchcock's Bay Area*: p. 274 lower left.

Blues for Bird
by Martin Gray
288 pages $16.95

The Book of Good Habits
Simple and Creative Ways to Enrich Your Life
by Dirk Mathison
224 PAGES $9.95

The Butt Hello
and other ways my cats drive me crazy
by Ted Meyer
96 PAGES $9.95

Café Nation
Coffee Folklore, Magick, and Divination
by Sandra Mizumoto Posey
224 PAGES $9.95

Collecting Sins
A Novel
by Steven Sobel
288 PAGES $13

Discovering the History of Your House and Your Neighborhood
by Betsy J. Green
288 PAGES $14.95

Exploring Our Lives
A Writing Handbook for Senior Adults
by Francis E. Kazemek
312 PAGES $14.95

Footsteps in the Fog
Alfred Hitchcock's San Francisco
by Jeff Kraft and Aaron Leventhal
288 PAGES $24.95

FREE Stuff & Good Deals for Folks over 50
by Linda Bowman
240 PAGES $12.95

Helpful Household Hints
The Ultimate Guide to Housekeeping
by June King
224 PAGES $12.95

How to Find Your Family Roots and Write Your Family History
by William Latham and Cindy Higgins
288 PAGES $14.95

How to Speak Shakespeare
by Cal Pritner and Louis Colaianni
144 PAGES $16.95

How to Win Lotteries, Sweepstakes, and Contests in the 21st Century
by Steve "America's Sweepstakes King" Ledoux
224 PAGES $14.95

The Keystone Kid
Tales of Early Hollywood
by Coy Watson, Jr.
304 PAGES $24.95

Letter Writing Made Easy!
Featuring Sample Letters for Hundreds of Common Occasions
by Margaret McCarthy
224 PAGES $12.95

Letter Writing Made Easy! Volume 2
Featuring More Sample Letters for Hundreds of Common Occasions
by Margaret McCarthy
224 PAGES $12.95

Nancy Shavick's Tarot Universe
by Nancy Shavick
336 PAGES $15.95

Offbeat Food
Adventures in an Omnivorous World
by Alan Ridenour
240 PAGES $19.95

Offbeat Golf
A Swingin' Guide to a Worldwide Obsession
by Bob Loeffelbein
192 PAGES $17.95

Offbeat Marijuana
The Life and Times of the World's Grooviest Plant
by Saul Rubin
240 PAGES $19.95

Offbeat Museums
The Collections and Curators of America's Most Unusual Museums
by Saul Rubin
240 PAGES $19.95

Quack!
Tales of Medical Fraud from the Museum of Questionable Medical Devices
by Bob McCoy
240 PAGES $19.95

The Seven Sacred Rites of Menarche
The Spiritual Journey of the Adolescent Girl
by Kristi Meisenbach Boylan
160 PAGES $11.95

The Seven Sacred Rites of Menopause
The Spiritual Journey to the Wise-Woman Years
by Kristi Meisenbach Boylan
144 PAGES $11.95

Silent Echoes
Discovering Early Hollywood Through the Films of Buster Keaton
by John Bengtson
240 PAGES $24.95

What's Buggin' You?
Michael Bohdan's Guide to Home Pest Control
by Michael Bohdan
256 PAGES $12.95

TITLE	QUANTITY	AMOUNT
Blues for Bird ($16.95)	___	___
The Book of Good Habits ($9.95)	___	___
The Butt Hello ($9.95)	___	___
Café Nation ($9.95)	___	___
Collecting Sins ($13)	___	___
Discovering the History of Your House ($14.95)	___	___
Exploring Our Lives ($14.95)	___	___
Footsteps in the Fog ($24.95)	___	___
Free Stuff & Good Deals for Folks . . . ($12.95)	___	___
Helpful Household Hints ($12.95)	___	___
How to Find Your Family Roots . . . ($14.95)	___	___
How to Speak Shakespeare ($16.95)	___	___
How to Win Lotteries, Sweepstakes . . . ($14.95)	___	___
The Keystone Kid ($24.95)	___	___
Letter Writing Made Easy! ($12.95)	___	___
Letter Writing Made Easy! Volume 2 ($12.95)	___	___
Nancy Shavick's Tarot Universe ($15.95)	___	___
Offbeat Food ($19.95)	___	___
Offbeat Golf ($17.95)	___	___
Offbeat Marijuana ($19.95)	___	___
Offbeat Museums ($19.95)	___	___

TITLE	QUANTITY	AMOUNT
Quack! ($19.95)	___	___
The Seven Sacred Rites of Menarche ($11.95)	___	___
The Seven Sacred Rites of Menopause ($11.95)	___	___
Silent Echoes ($24.95)	___	___
What's Buggin' You? ($12.95)	___	___

Shipping + Handling:
1 Book — $3.00
Each additional book
is $ .50

Subtotal ___
CA residents add 8.25% sales tax ___
Shipping and handling (see left) ___
TOTAL ___

Name _____

Address _____

City _____ State ___ ZIP _____

☐Visa ☐Master Card   Card Number _____

Exp. Date _____ Signature _____

Enclosed is my check or money order made payable to:

Santa Monica Press LLC
P.O. Box 1076
Santa Monica CA 90406

1-800-784-9553